MW00452510

1/24
STRAND PRICE
$5.00

Open Strategy

Management on the Cutting Edge series

Paul Michelman, series editor

Published in cooperation with *MIT Sloan Management Review*

The AI Advantage: How to Put the Artificial Intelligence Revolution to Work
Thomas H. Davenport

The Technology Fallacy: How People Are the Real Key to Digital Transformation
Gerald C. Kane, Anh Nguyen Phillips, Jonathan Copulsky, and Garth Andrus

Designed for Digital: How to Architect Your Business for Sustained Success
Jeanne W. Ross, Cynthia Beath, and Martin Mocker

See Sooner, Act Faster: How Vigilant Leaders Thrive in an Era of Digital Turbulance
George S. Day and Paul J. H. Schoemaker

The Leader in a Digital World: From Productivity and Process to Creativity and Collaboration
Amit S. Mukherjee

The Ends Game: How Smart Companies Stop Selling Products and Start Delivering Value
Marco Bertini and Oded Koenigsberg

Open Strategy: Mastering Disruption from Outside the C-Suite
Christian Stadler, Julia Hautz, Kurt Matzler, and Stephan Friedrich von den Eichen

Open Strategy

Mastering Disruption from Outside the C-Suite

Christian Stadler, Julia Hautz, Kurt Matzler,
and Stephan Friedrich von den Eichen

Foreword by Gary Hamel

The MIT Press
Cambridge, Massachusetts
London, England

The MIT Press would like to thank the anonymous peer reviewers who provided comments on drafts of this book. The generous work of academic experts is essential for establishing the authority and quality of our publications. We acknowledge with gratitude the contributions of these otherwise uncredited readers.

All interior illustrations were created by Guido Schlaich.

This book was set in Stone Serif and Stone Sans by Westchester Publishing Services. Printed and bound in the United States of America.

Library of Congress Cataloging-in-Publication Data

Names: Stadler, Christian, author. | Hautz, Julia, author. | Matzler, Kurt, author. |
    Eichen, Stephan Friedrich von den, author.
Title: Open strategy : mastering disruption from outside the C-suite / Christian Stadler,
    Julia Hautz, Kurt Matzler, and Stephan Friedrich von den Eichen.
Description: Cambridge, Massachusetts : The MIT Press, [2021] | Series: Management on the
    cutting edge series | Includes bibliographical references and index.
Identifiers: LCCN 2020050155 | ISBN 9780262046114 (hardcover)
Subjects: LCSH: Strategic planning. | Business planning.
Classification: LCC HD30.28 .S666 2021 | DDC 658.4/012--dc23
LC record available at https://lccn.loc.gov/2020050155

10 9 8 7 6 5 4 3 2 1

To Florence, Benjie, and Leah.—Christian
To Benedikt, Frida, and Greta.—Julia
To Maximilian, Felix, and Ruth.—Kurt
To Brigitta and Felix.—Stephan

We also want to thank those who supported our experimentation with open strategy at a time when it was a less obvious choice. These are the pioneers we salute!

And to Seth Schulman, for helping us to tell our story.

In the ancient Chinese manual *The Art of War*, military strategist Sun Tzu advised generals to keep their plans to themselves if they wanted to defeat their adversaries. "By discovering the enemy's dispositions and remaining invisible ourselves," he wrote, "we can keep our forces concentrated, while the enemy's must be divided." Most executives and managers today take such advice to heart, zealously guarding their core strategies as well as the thinking, market data, and product information that contribute to them.

—But what if they're wrong?

Contents

Foreword by Gary Hamel   ix

Series Foreword   xvii

Introduction: Win with Open Strategy   xix

1   Traditional Strategy Come Undone   1

2   Are You Truly Ready to Open Up?   21

3   Design Your Open Strategy Process   41

4   Tweak Your Open Strategy Initiative to Allow for Secrecy   59

5   Harness the Wisdom of Crowds   75

6   Peer into the Future   97

7   Disrupt Yourself before Others Do   121

8   Develop Killer Business Models   145

9   Use the Crowd to Choose Better Strategies   163

10   Execute Better   185

Epilogue   205

Appendix A: Recommended Reading   211

Appendix B: The IMP Story   213

Notes   215

Index   251

Foreword

Gary Hamel

As I recall, it was a bitterly cold winter morning in 1993. I had flown in from London and was now walking across a car park 700 kilometers south of the Arctic Circle. The sun wouldn't be up for another two hours.

A few weeks earlier I had received a call from Pekka Ala-Pietilä, the rail-thin, sandy-haired executive who had been charged with creating a world-beating telecom strategy for Nokia. Before Pekka's call I knew nothing about the company, but now here I was in Espoo, Finland's second-largest city, walking into Nokia's spartan head office. I had brought along my longtime consulting partner, Dr. Jim Scholes, an expert in systems thinking and change management. In that first meeting, both of us were struck by the soaring ambition of the young team sitting across the table. They were determined, they said, to oust Motorola as the world's leading mobile phone company.

At the time, Nokia was already a solid number 2, having sold three million phones in 1992, versus four million for Motorola. In the 1980s, Nokia had helped deploy the Nordic Mobile Telephone network, one of the world's first mobile phone systems, and in 1984 it hand-built its first mobile device, a car phone weighing 4.7 kg (10.30 lb). Yet despite the early start, beating Motorola wouldn't be easy. In 1983 Motorola had launched the world's first handheld mobile phone. The brick-size DynaTAc proved to be an instant success with on-the-go executives and others who could justify the eye-watering $4,000 price tag. Six years later, Motorola would introduce the MicroTAc—the first phone small enough to fit in a shirt pocket. At $3,000 it was still out of reach for most consumers, but its slim design solidified Motorola's position as the world's premier phone maker.

I had been invited to Nokia in part because of an article I had written a few years earlier for the *Harvard Business Review*. In "Strategic Intent," I had extolled the virtues of setting stretch goals—of aiming high and then using innovation to close the gap between resources and aspirations. But now, looking at this group of deadly earnest Finns, I gulped. Taking on Motorola seemed less stretch and more suicide mission. I knew Motorola well. They were one of the best-managed companies in America. Bob Galvin, Motorola's visionary CEO, was an icon. Having watched Japanese competitors take over the US consumer electronics industry, he was determined to defend Motorola's lead against all comers—foreign and domestic. Yet despite my reservations, the gutsy determination of Pekka and his colleagues was infectious. By the time we broke for lunch, Jim and I had signed on to help in whatever way we could.

I told my new clients that beating Motorola would require a highly differentiated strategy. The starting point was to set a bold goal that would encourage breakout thinking. Standing in front of the team, I wrote the number "1,000,000,000" on a flipchart. That's what they should be aiming for, I argued—to sell one billion phones. That was a big reach, since at the time there were only 35 million mobile subscribers in the entire world. There was a long silence, but no one objected, or even furrowed a brow. They got it. They knew the human desire to communicate with anyone from anywhere was universal. Of course a billion people would want a mobile phone. The question was whether Nokia could take the lead in slaking that demand.

To answer in the affirmative, the company would need a game-changing strategy for radically expanding the size of the market and leapfrogging the industry leader. Like most companies, Nokia had a well-disciplined process for hammering out budget priorities. But building a breakthrough strategy would require something quite different—a process that focused less on numbers and more on new thinking.

As keen students of entrepreneurship, Jim and I knew that creating a breakout strategy, such as venture investing, is a numbers game. A venture capitalist looking for the "next big thing" will review hundreds of business plans before investing in a handful of promising startups. Whether in Silicon Valley or in an established company, game-changing ideas are rare. To find one, Nokia would need to generate hundreds, even thousands, of wacky ideas, and then evaluate them for novelty, impact, and do-ability. This meant opening up the company's strategy process to a wide cross-section of employees. Nokia's leadership team was impressive, but as clever as they were, they didn't have enough creativity and bandwidth, on their own, to generate an expansive portfolio of breakout ideas. To invent the future, they'd need a lot more brains.

Over the next few weeks, dozens of employees were recruited to help build a large cache of new insights—the raw material for strategic innovation. We divided roughly a hundred employees into four teams. One team was assigned the task of identifying industry orthodoxies. What assumptions was Motorola making about consumers, technology, products, pricing, and market size, and how could this conventional thinking be challenged? A second team was charged with identifying discontinuities. What were the emerging trends in business, lifestyle, technology, and regulation that weren't yet on Motorola's radar, and how could these be leveraged to Nokia's advantage? A third team reviewed Nokia's core competencies. What unique technologies or skills did the firm possess, and what new ones would it need to build to leapfrog Motorola? The most critical task of all, uncovering unmet needs and unserved customers, fell to the fourth team.

As the teams fanned out on their study missions, they were particularly eager to connect with the "Walkman generation." The year before, Sony had sold 100 million of its portable music players, mostly to young people. Soon, Nokia engineers and marketers were hanging out in Tokyo clubs and walking along L.A. beaches, noting the behaviors and preferences of the teens and twenty-somethings who would one day become their customers.

Back in Espoo, the insights generated by the four discovery teams were used as fodder in marathon brainstorming sessions. Hundreds of employees were given the chance to mull over what had been learned.

Each insight was printed on a card, and employees were invited to shuffle them around to see what opportunities popped into their minds. This effort spawned more than two thousand "baby" strategies—nascent, semiformed ideas about how Nokia could reimagine the mobile phone business.

Finally, it was time to converge. We invited Nokia's now sizable band of strategists to scan the vast universe of options they had generated. Were there clusters of related ideas that suggested bigger, "meta" strategies? Were there themes that could give focus and consistency to Nokia's strategy? Fortunately, the answer to both questions was yes.

A slew of ideas focused on adding new functions to the mobile phone—on using the phone to take photos, make payments, send messages, and keep track of appointments. A second set of ideas focused on turning mobile phones into lifestyle products—indispensable devices that would be affordable and appealing. This bucket contained ideas for radically reducing manufacturing costs, making the phone in multiple colors, letting users customize their phones, and targeting marketing budgets on young consumers. A third set of ideas focused on the needs of network operators. Getting the big telcos on board was critical to growing the market. Operators needed turnkey solutions—network equipment and software, billing systems, and financing solutions—that would make it easy for them to build infrastructure and roll out new services.

There were other themes, but these three—going beyond voice, creating lifestyle products, and building network solutions—seemed the most potent, and would become the pillars of Nokia's strategy. Over the next decade, that strategy would propel Nokia to industry leadership and generate billions of dollars in market value.

At the outset, some questioned the wisdom of inviting so many people into the strategy conversation. It took time and effort to train hundreds of people to think like game-changers, and freeing up people to work on strategy meant downgrading other priorities. There was also a worry that the teams might come up with the "wrong" answers. What if their ideas were pedestrian or, worse, flights of fancy? Then there was the matter of privacy. How do you keep strategy a secret when hundreds of people have a hand in creating it?

Despite the doubters, Nokia's bet on open strategy paid off—big. First, it produced a strategy that was novel. In many companies the planning process is dominated by a small, incestuous group of senior leaders who, after a few years, are finishing each other's sentences. Nokia's leaders knew that if they wanted new ideas, they'd need to engage new voices. It wasn't an accident that the discovery teams were overweighted with individuals who were relatively young, had worked in other industries, and weren't based in the head office.

Second, the highly participatory process produced a strategy that was well grounded. Before asking employees to generate ideas, we trained them in creative thinking and sent them out into the field to gather data. A strategy needs to be based on facts. The trick is to search for facts that have gone unnoticed by competitors or are too discomforting for them to acknowledge.

Third, the open approach produced a strategy that was credible and widely understood. By the end of the project, employees knew exactly where the business was headed. Everyone was committed to making the mobile phone "the remote control for life." When, by contrast, strategy-making is invisible to most employees, leaders end up with a nearly insurmountable communication problem. It's hard for employees to have faith in a strategy that emerged from a black box. In such cases, many are left wondering why other, seemingly better strategies didn't make the cut. And even when a strategy seems credible, PowerPoint slides and executive blogs offer thin gruel to employees who are hungry to understand the implications of a new strategy for their own work. An open process avoids those pitfalls.

Finally, Nokia's all-hands process produced a strategy that was granular, and therefore immediately actionable. Strategies created at the top often lack specificity; they're more about the "what" than the "how." This lack of detail creates long lags between strategy formulation and implementation. Nokia's strategy, by contrast, was built from the bottom up. Each of the three major imperatives incorporated dozens of shovel-ready ideas that could be quickly operationalized. By the time the strategy gelled, employees were ready to act.

A decade later, Nokia would represent over half the value of the Helsinki Stock Exchange, and in 2005, it would sell more than a billion phones in a single year. Hailed by industry pundits as the world's best-managed technology company, Nokia seemed unbeatable. But you, dear reader, know how the story ends. At Nokia, as in so many other companies, success turned out to be a self-correcting phenomenon.

The dynamics are familiar to anyone who has studied business life cycles. As a company grows and prospers, leaders shift from playing offense to defense. Billion-dollar R&D and marketing budgets start to substitute for creativity. Once novel strategies fossilize into unthinking habits, and the spirit of dissent withers. Yesterday's pirates become today's aristocrats. Those thirty-something rebels I had worked with in the early 1990s were now, a dozen years later, celebrated, wealthy titans of tech. Sitting atop the pinnacle of success, they had little incentive to mess with a winning formula.

Never again would the executive team crowdsource the company's future to its eager, ambitious workforce. Having succeeded spectacularly in challenging Motorola, Nokia failed to challenge itself—leaving that job to a new crop of renegades. On January 9, 2007, Steve Jobs stepped onto a stage in San Francisco and unveiled the iPhone. Eleven months later, Google announced that it would license its newly hatched mobile operating system, Android, to any manufacturer across the world. As I write this, 99 percent of all smartphones run on iOS or Android, and more of those phones are made by Samsung than by any other company.

Today, the world is far more volatile and complex than it was in 1993, when I stepped off a British Airways flight into the cold, dark Finnish winter. Open strategy is more vital than ever—but, thanks to executive hubris, still all too rare. The average CEO still sees herself, or himself, as the strategist in chief. After all, how do you justify a multimillion-dollar pay package if you're not boldly plotting the future, if you're not seen as a strategy savant? Isn't that what shareholders, journalists, and employees expect? Who's going to argue when a corporate chieftain like A. G. Lafley, who served twice as head of Procter & Gamble, says, "The CEO can see opportunities others can't . . . and make the tough calls others are unable to make"? Who's going to say "rubbish" when the former managing partner of one of the world's premier consulting companies declares that it's up to a handful of top executives to "shape the destiny of the business . . . while others have their heads buried in operations"? But push back we must. Foresight and creativity don't correlate with rank, and any organization that vests the power to create strategy in a small cadre of senior leaders will soon find itself on the back foot.

In the typical organization, senior leaders are insulated from reality by layers of kowtowing subordinates who have learned that there is little profit in challenging the higher-ups. Long-tenured executives feel compelled to defend legacy strategies and are reluctant to write off their own depreciating intellectual capital. That's the problem with a top-down strategy process: it ties the organization's capacity to adapt and change to the willingness of a few senior leaders to adapt and change. When they fail at that task, as they often do, the organization falters.

For open strategy to flourish, we have to abandon the belief that a handful of people at the top are capable of creating robust, future-focused strategies. Like "Scottish cuisine" and "virtual presence," "executive humility" is a bit of an oxymoron. Nonetheless, it's an essential prerequisite for harnessing the power of open strategy.

OK, that's enough from me. You need to get busy with this book—which, I assure you, is one of the most important new business books of the new decade. In these pages, Christian, Julia, Kurt, and Stephan will give you an invaluable guide to building robust, future-focused strategies. So if you're eager to build an organization that can outrun change, outmaneuver the competition, and outperform expectations, read on!

Silicon Valley, California
December 2020

Series Foreword

The world does not lack for management ideas. Thousands of researchers, practitioners, and other experts produce tens of thousands of articles, books, papers, posts, and podcasts each year. But only a scant few promise to truly move the needle on practice, and fewer still dare to reach into the future of what management will become. It is this rare breed of idea—meaningful to practice, grounded in evidence, and *built for the future*—that we seek to present in this series.

Paul Michelman
Editor in chief
MIT Sloan Management Review

Introduction: Win with Open Strategy

Why do some of the world's most successful companies manage to stay ahead of disruption, adopting and executing on innovative strategies, while their lesser competitors don't? Do these companies have smarter leaders? Do they hire better consultants? Do they apply better intellectual frameworks for analyzing their businesses? Do they have better resources and capabilities? Do they have better processes?

None of the above.

These leading-edge companies are winning because they've quietly adopted a new way of *doing* strategy, one tailor-made to fit today's faster, more volatile business environment. Rather than limiting strategic deliberations to small executive teams, they are involving a wider group of people—front-line employees, experts, suppliers, customers, entrepreneurs, and even competitors. They are "opening up" strategy just as companies have opened up other areas of the business, such as innovation and marketing. And the results have been spectacular.

In 2012, when Ashok Vaswani took over the UK retail business at Barclays, he knew the banking giant had to make some changes—and fast. Newspapers, record labels, and telecoms had all suffered at the hands of digital disruption. With dozens of fintech (financial technology) startups taking aim, soon the big banks would feel the pain. And yet Vaswani's was a sprawling legacy organization with 30,000 employees. Any new strategy he and his team adopted not only had to address looming threats to the business, it also had to galvanize the workforce and foster a sense of ownership. Somehow the bank had to wean itself from conventional ways of operating and get ahead of change.

Historically, leaders at Barclays had devised strategies the traditional way. The executive team and their consultants would gather behind closed doors and craft the strategic plan. They would communicate the plan to employees and set budgets so teams throughout the organization could execute.

Vaswani believed there was a better way. If rank-and-file employees had a hand in crafting strategy from the very beginning, they'd feel more invested in it, they'd understand it better, and they'd do their very best to execute it. Meanwhile, leaders would be able to craft more nuanced plans if they had exposure to front-line concerns, and they'd be able to communicate the strategy better. "Strategy is not a complicated thing," he told us. "It answers three basic questions: Where are you now? Where are you going? How will you get there? Those are the *only* three questions, and answers to them exist at every level of the organization. It seems unwise to say that only leaders at the top should deal with it."[1]

Rather than monopolize the strategy-making process, Vaswani and his team would have to involve everyone. They'd have to open up.[2] And that's exactly what they did. Barclays created a series of "councils" comprising twenty to twenty-five senior product people, as well as colleagues from functional units across the business, including marketing, compliance, legal, and HR. Their job was to define the business's current state, bringing to bear deep factual knowledge of products, trends, and operational capacity. In parallel, the company created working groups of several dozen front-line employees, asking them, "What should Barclays look like in 2020?" The question was open-ended, pointing participants to think not just about the digital universe but about everything that concerned Barclays' future offerings and operations.

Front-line employees were close to the bank's customers—they understood their needs and concerns. They knew Barclays' customers wanted more speed, accessibility, and transparency from the bank. Why did it take so long to get approved for a mortgage? And why couldn't the process be more transparent, so that at any given time you knew how close you were to closing on a loan? To help improve the bank's performance in these areas, front-line workers argued that the bank should enthusiastically embrace digital platforms, making use as well of the big data that such platforms engender.

Taking these broad ideas, the work councils merged them with their own deep operational knowledge and presented a provisional strategic plan to the executive team. To fine-tune and finalize this plan, Barclays widened the conversation to include much larger numbers of front-line employees—in fact, everyone. Leaders wanted to ensure that the final strategy would be simple enough for everyone to comprehend. "A simple strategy understood by all is far better than a complex strategy understood by a few," Vaswani remarked.[3]

Over a two-month period, the bank held more than seventy town hall–style meetings throughout the UK, renting movie theaters to accommodate the entire workforce.[4] Presenting the plan as it evolved, they led lively conversations during which front-line employees explored what the plan might mean for real-life customers buying specific products and for employees selling and servicing those products. Because executives had already received input from front-line employees, they could speak in a language their people understood, making the emerging strategy seem relevant and credible—not just another initiative foisted by "corporate."

To further engage employees, Barclays held a one-week "strategy jam," using an IBM digital tool to bring all 30,000 employees into the conversation, along with senior leaders. A moderated online discussion around several main themes identified by the work groups, the strategy jam helped senior leaders understand which ideas were truly worth pursuing and which needed more work. Just as important, it increased awareness about the strategy inside the company, getting employees everywhere talking about it in much more detail than they previously had.

At one point, for instance, Domino's Pizza became part of the discussion on what speed and transparency mean for customers. Observing that Domino's had started giving people trackers for pizzas, Barclays employees wondered why Domino's could tell you that they've put the salami on the top of the pizza and whether it's gone in the oven, but Barclays couldn't tell its mortgage customers whether it had appraised the property in question, approved them for a certain loan amount, finalized the loan, or sent out checks. Conversations like this brought the bank's strategy to life in a way that a typical speech or letter from the CEO never could.

A month after the strategy jam, the bank began executing. The Consumer Lending department pioneered a new app that allowed customers to apply for loans with just a few clicks. Consumer Banking allowed consumers to customize their accounts, incorporating their preferred features. And the entire bank adopted a mobile banking platform, taking it live shortly after the jam. The strategy was a success. The number of users quickly surpassed one million, and today over 9 million customers use the app, making it one of the UK's most popular fintech products.[5] "We took a 320-year-old analogue bank and made it digital," Vaswani said.

As a result of this effort, the bank is more relevant, "younger," and more successful than ever. Some 17 percent of customers at Barclays' UK retail operation are millennials, and over 70 percent are digitally active. Barclays also claims the greatest market share among millennials.[6] In a highly competitive market that is disrupted by fintech, Barclays UK's retail business has boosted return on equity from 15 to 17 percent.[7] As for Vaswani, he's been promoted three times and today serves as a member of the Barclays Executive Committee and CEO of Consumer Banking and Payments, overseeing the execution of plans for the Group's consumer banking, private banking and payments businesses across Asia, UK, Europe, and the United States.

Instead of falling prey to disruption, Barclays proactively embraced it with the blessing and participation of its workforce. Executives didn't have to spend much time communicating and implementing strategy because implementation had already begun while executives were fine-tuning their plans, via the town halls and strategy jam. Afterward, front-line colleagues naturally adopted behaviors consistent with the strategy, driving speed and transparency, promoting access, and leveraging consumer data to improve service. As one executive reflected, "There probably wasn't a single one of our 30,000 colleagues who would not have known what [our strategy] was and would not have known what we were trying to get done and how we're trying to drive it forward."[8] By opening up, the bank had moved its strategic deliberation and execution along much more quickly and effectively than it otherwise would have.

At a glance, taking strategy deliberations out of the boardroom and engaging employees might sound like a perfectly reasonable and even unremarkable thing to do. "Transparency" and "openness" have become corporate buzzwords in recent years, applied to numerous areas from research and development to supply chain operations, marketing, and human resources. Meanwhile, traditional strategy-making clearly doesn't work. Companies spend over $30 billion each year on strategy consulting, yet, according to some studies, between half and 90 percent of all strategies fail.[9] Why wouldn't companies make strategic planning more collaborative and open?

And yet the vast majority of senior leaders have declined to do so, for any number of reasons. Many leaders think of strategy as "their" role, as opposed to execution, which managers and employees are supposed to handle—a belief that helps justify leaders' high salaries. Many leaders also harbor serious concerns about privacy. How can they possibly open up strategy to thousands of people without divulging trade secrets or alerting competitors to their plans? Finally, and most important, many leaders don't know how to engage thousands of employees as Barclays did, and fear that the whole process will devolve into chaos.

Barclays didn't lose its competitive edge by engaging staff from all levels of the corporate hierarchy in strategy deliberations. Unlike many of its peers, it saved itself from disruption and put itself on track to thrive going forward. While superficially the bank's move toward digital might seem to have been inevitable, actually executing on the strategy required that leaders make numerous small decisions, gain the support of its legacy network of retail bank branches, and maintain the legacy business while aggressively pursuing digital—none of which was preordained. Only because the bank's strategic planning process was so carefully conceived did the digital strategy unfold smoothly.

Barclays is by no means alone in adopting an open strategy approach. In recent years, the Canadian mining company Goldcorp and the Swedish telecommunications company Ericsson have engaged not merely nonexecutive employees but also outsiders to solve a range of strategic puzzles. So has adidas, the European steel producer voestalpine, the hearing aid manufacturer WS Audiology, Telefónica and, perhaps most unexpected on this list, the US Navy and the US intelligence community as well as NATO.

Smaller companies that have experimented with open strategy include Gallus (a business unit of Heidelberger Druckmaschinen and one of the world's leading producer of printing presses for label manufacturers), SSM (a leading producer of textile machinery), and BPW (Europe's leading axle and suspension manufacturer). Even very small companies such as Saxonia Systems (software development), EGT (energy services), Ottakringer (a family-owned brewery), and Buffer (a startup providing software applications services to manage social media accounts more effectively) have opened up their strategic deliberations.

As these companies and a number of others have found, taking a more collaborative approach to strategy helps executives and owners move the organization in new directions that would have been impossible otherwise. Quite profitable directions, we might add. A survey of 201 senior leaders we conducted found that the majority of them opened up less than one-third of their strategic initiatives. And yet these initiatives accounted for 50 percent of their revenues and profits. Companies in which leaders collaborated on strategy with people outside the executive team—both employees and external stakeholders—assessed their business options more fully, formulated more realistic strategies, and implemented their strategies more quickly and effectively. In some cases, companies created entirely new businesses they wouldn't have thought of had they not invited people from outside their management teams to participate. Clearly, open strategy is an approach whose time has come. Imagine if most large and small firms forged their strategies the way Barclays did! We'd see smarter, more responsive planning, far better execution, and better performance across the board.

We first discovered the possibilities of open strategy ten years ago. Two of us, Julia Hautz and Kurt Matzler, were conducting academic research on open innovation, while Kurt Matzler and Stephan Friedrich von den Eichen were working with companies to apply open innovation tools through Stephan Friedrich von den Eichen's consulting firm, Innovative Management Partner (IMP). They had an idea: What if we applied similar tools to help companies not merely develop new products but also to forge their strategic plans and help them design and implement new business logics?

Kurt and one of his graduate students set up a pilot case, using digital technologies to open up strategy discussions in a midsized company. That led to published articles and presentations, which in turn generated great enthusiasm from managers.[10] IMP began to offer open strategy as a service for clients, moving beyond digital crowdsourcing to develop tools for offline, workshop-based processes as well as digital formats. Since then, IMP has helped many of the companies mentioned above and dozens of others deploy open strategy in over two hundred initiatives. For its efforts, IMP has been recognized as Germany's leading consulting firm in the fields of strategy, disruption, business model innovation, and growth and has won prestigious industry and consulting awards.

To document the efficacy of open strategy, in 2014 we embarked on rigorous, wide-ranging academic research into the approach, funded by the Austrian Science Foundation. Reviewing the relevant academic literature, we worked with IMP to analyze its open strategy projects and fine-tune its tools. Through interviews with more than a hundred involved clients, managers, employees, and consultant teams, we sought to understand their experiences with the process—what worked and what didn't. We also collected data on open strategy initiatives other than those developed by IMP, connecting with other academics and reaching out to entities such as IBM, Ericsson, Telefónica, Barclays, Red Hat, Steelcase, the US Navy, and other organizations that had developed helpful tools. Finally, we conducted two surveys, one that collected input about open strategy from more than two hundred senior leaders and a second that surveyed 347 managers and executives about their individual mental takes on openness. All this work has given us a unique understanding of open strategy tools, how they work, and how companies can best deploy them to obtain exceptional results.[11]

How to Use This Book

Open Strategy is the first general business book dedicated to helping leaders and senior managers implement an open approach in their own businesses. Offering case studies from leading-edge companies large and small from many different industries, we present open strategy not as a mere tweak to the traditional strategy process but as a new business philosophy, a fundamental shift in thinking that, involving people outside the executive team, will better position you to meet change and build radically new business models. Traditional, "closed" approaches can certainly help leaders fine-tune their core businesses. Making important assumptions about predictability and stability, they allow leaders to guide and constrain activities within the organization. But those very assumptions render traditional strategy-making inadequate for leaders seeking not to incrementally adjust existing businesses but to create entirely new ones that will help the enterprise survive in rapidly evolving markets.

In 1987, Warren Bennis and Burt Nanus first used the term VUCA to describe how the world has become more vulnerable, uncertain, complex, and ambiguous after the end of the Cold War.[12] That era seems like a period of stability and calm compared with what leaders today must face. On average, companies take half as long today to scale up to Fortune 500 status as they did a generation ago, but these companies also stall faster once they become large. In 1994 the fifty largest companies posted a compounded annual growth rate of –4 percent. In 2014 it was –10 percent.[13] Few industries seem stable today. The highly regulated taxi industry is dominated by Uber, which owns no taxis and has drivers who no longer need to know the city in which they're driving. Major car manufacturers worry that Google and other software giants will outplay them as we move toward self-driving cars. Retailers like Walmart are hardly in a better position as Amazon draws ever more customers online.

We could go on, but the general picture is obvious: the pace of change has increased dramatically in most industries, and the boundaries between industries have become foggier.[14] In this context, organizations feel immense pressure to consider disruptive trends, act before they are disrupted, and enter new businesses. With so little time to make decisions, leaders fall back on their own experience—and they fall prey to their own cognitive biases.

Gary Hamel, one of the world's most influential management thinkers, observed more than two decades ago the need for companies to rethink their traditional, elitist way of creating strategy. "You can either surrender the future to revolutionary challengers," he wrote, "or revolutionize the way your company creates strategy."[15] Open strategy helps, giving leadership teams access to external, diverse knowledge they wouldn't otherwise have while also making individual leaders aware of their biases so that they can overcome them. Open strategy can certainly enable leaders fine-tune their core businesses, but the approach becomes most valuable in companies facing fundamental changes. In these situations, open strategy provides leaders with a way to reach beyond their industry boundaries and grasp powerful new business opportunities.

Of course, *how* leaders open up strategic discussions matters. Doing so haphazardly or unthinkingly might only create new problems.[16] Involving wider audiences might reduce the speed and flexibility of strategy-making while also yielding unpredictable ideas, discussions, and contributions.[17] A broad set of participants might arrive at conflicting interpretations because of their different frames of reference and vocabulary.[18] Sharing information with larger audiences can create competitive concerns and subject participants to information overload. Participants' diverging expectations could create tensions, leading to dissatisfaction and frustration.[19]

As Gary Hamel and his coauthor Michele Zanini put it in their new book, "an open strategy process is messier and more time consuming than the top-down alternative, but the benefits are worth the efforts."[20] To reap open strategy's considerable benefits, companies must deploy specific tools and techniques that allow them to handle the complexity of internal and external views, generate specific kinds of strategic insights, and mobilize employees in desirable ways—without compromising secrecy unduly. Our book describes these tools in detail and provides corporate executives, entrepreneurs, small-business owners, board members, consultants, business school students, and others with the step-by-step advice that has helped IMP's clients outmaneuver the competition, master disruption, and lay the foundation for sustained growth. In the chapters that follow, we address the key challenges that open strategy can present and show you how to avoid and overcome them.

We've organized the book to make open strategy clear, accessible, and as easy to implement as possible (see figure 0.1). In chapter 1, we cover the limitations of traditional strategy-making in more detail. Chapters 2, 3, and 4 help you to prepare yourself and your organization for this new business philosophy. Chapter 2 helps you to understand whether you are personally ready to open up strategy, and to what extent. Chapter 3 provides a framework for pinning down what exactly you hope to achieve through an open process, how to open up and whom it makes the most sense to involve. Chapter 4 shows you how you can to manage open strategy deliberations without revealing sensitive information.

We then present tools relating to the three phases of strategy-making: idea generation, plan formulation, and implementation. In chapters 5, 6, and 7, we introduce proven tools that help you generate the foundation of a successful strategy, a breakthrough vision of the organization's future direction, or what we call a "strategic idea." These tools include two purely digital tools, strategy contests and strategy communities, that allow you to engage a very broad set of participants, and two hybrid digital plus in-person tools that enable you to identify specific trends affecting your business (the IMP Trend Radar exercise) and to confront an imaginary competitor (the IMP Nightmare Competitor Challenge).

The next set of tools, described in chapters 8 and 9, focuses on how to turn strategic ideas into detailed plans. We present a workshop tool—the IMP Business Logic Contest—that gamifies the business model development process, and explore how to use prediction markets to pinpoint the most promising strategic focus among many. In chapter 10, we discuss how tools such as strategy jams and employee social networks can help you implement your strategic plans, sustain open strategy efforts over time, and build a culture that embraces openness.

PREPARING FOR OPEN STRATEGY

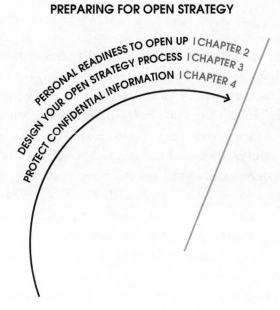

PERSONAL READINESS TO OPEN UP | CHAPTER 2
DESIGN YOUR OPEN STRATEGY PROCESS | CHAPTER 3
PROTECT CONFIDENTIAL INFORMATION | CHAPTER 4

OPEN STRATEGY TOOLBOX

TREND RADAR
CHAPTER 6

COMPETITION/COMMUNITIES
CHAPTER 5

NIGHTMARE COMPETITOR
CHAPTER 7

STRATEGIC IDEAS

SOCIAL MEDIA
CHAPTER 10

OPEN STRATEGY

STRATEGY EXECUTION

STRATEGY FORMULATION

CHAPTER 8
BUSINESS MODEL LOGIC

STRATEGY JAMS
CHAPTER 10

PREDICTION MARKETS
CHAPTER 9

Figure 0.1
Preparing for open strategy—the open strategy toolbox.

Although open strategy can enhance all phases of strategy-making and execution, you can also deploy it in partial ways to imagine the future and generate strategic ideas. According to our research, firms used open strategy in all phases of strategy-making and execution for about 25 percent of their open strategy initiatives. For 70 percent of their open strategy initiatives, they used the approach to imagine the future and generate strategic ideas, and for 46 percent they used it to frame a strategic plan based on those ideas. In more than 55 percent of open strategy initiatives, firms used the approach to help the organization execute on the plan.[21] Open strategy delivers on these objectives. In a survey we fielded of senior executives, 69 percent stated that openness increased the number and diversity of strategic ideas and 73 percent stated that opening up their strategy facilitated implementation substantially.[22]

Chapter 3 will help you to decide which phase of the strategy process to address using open strategy and which specific tools you should select, based on your specific goals. Our tools work in organizations of any size—from a ten-person startup to a global multinational with 100,000 employees. Some organizations deploy expensive technology when using these tools, but as you'll see, many others mobilize inexpensive platforms and offline solutions. It can be expensive to involve outside experts in open strategy conversations, but you don't need to—consulting with front-line employees can cost little, while making a big difference. We profile one struggling company with fewer than two hundred employees that embraced open strategy in a low-cost way and succeeded. Within a few years, the company's revenues had tripled. It wasn't struggling any longer.

The time has come for companies to end the secrecy around strategy and take a more collaborative approach. Relegating planning to executives and board members worked back when markets were stable and predictable, but today such secrecy hamstrings companies, preventing them from arriving at and deploying effective strategies. Leaders are too cloistered, their perspectives confined to their own industries and painfully removed from the perceptions of customers, employees, suppliers, technical experts, and others. Even when companies do manage to devise smart strategies on their own, they can't implement them well because employees feel little stake in plans they had no hand in designing. This is not to say that strategy-making should become democratic. It shouldn't. Under open strategy, senior leaders still make the final decisions about company strategy. But they can do so with the benefit of far more input than they had before, in a way that renders implementation far more inclusive and fine-grained.

You can stay ahead of change in your industry by engaging with customers, suppliers, technical experts, front-line employees, and others. Solicit their help to analyze your options and craft the strategic plan, using digital collaboration tools as well as in-person meetings. Continue to collaborate when you're implementing the plan, asking employees for *their* reflections on the operational tactics that will best deliver on the strategy. We're not arguing you should disavow all secrecy. You can and should decide which information to divulge. Conducted carefully and thoughtfully, an open strategy process won't compromise your business but rather enable it to spot potentially destructive market changes and adapt to them more quickly.

Barclays UK used an open strategy approach to rejuvenate its existing business. Your company can, too. Experiment with the tools in this book. Instead of fearfully erecting walls, take a risk and invite in people from outside your management team. Listen to what they have to say. You won't regret it.

1 Traditional Strategy Come Undone

For decades, General Electric was regarded one of the most successful and best-managed companies. Not anymore. Between 2001 and 2019 the company's return on capital plummeted from 29.6 percent to 3.3 percent. The company's share price declined by more than 40 percent during the period between the global financial crisis and the end of 2019. In comparison, the S&P 500 more than tripled in value during this period.[1]

What happened? A poor acquisition strategy, that's what. In 2015, GE acquired the French energy giant Alstom for $10.6 billion, GE's largest industrial acquisition ever. It has been a disaster, with profits at GE Power, the business unit that took over Alstom's operations, declining by 45 percent.[2] Nor was Alstom a lone case. During Jeff Immelt's tenure, the company made a number of deals that seemed driven by hype rather than by a respect for business fundamentals. After 9/11, when the public became obsessed with security, GE bought the explosive-detection companies First Ion Track and InVision. Although GE didn't disclose the purchase price for First Ion Track, it paid $900 million for InVision, packaging the two as GE Homeland Security. In 2009, GE sold a majority stake in that business unit at a valuation of just $760 million.[3]

GE Capital, the company's financial service arm, also joined the housing boom in 2004, acquiring the subprime mortgage company WMC for $500 million. During the housing crisis in 2008–2009, GE lost $1 billion on the business, laid off most employees, and sold WMC. In 2018, GE had to set $1.5 billion aside for a potential settlement with the

Department of Justice over WMC's conduct.[4] Risky and unprofitable deals such as this caused GE Capital's profits to evaporate. Leaders cut the company's dividend—a step not taken since the 1930s—and asked Warren Buffett to invest $3 billion to pull the company out of crisis. GE Capital never recovered, and GE has since started to dismantle it.[5]

If many (but not all) of GE's deals were lemons, the company also failed to incorporate its acquisitions operationally.[6] To some extent, this reflected complacency on Immelt's part. As a detailed analysis of GE's downfall concludes, "Executives who worked with Immelt say he appreciated the importance of execution but felt it was a self-sustaining core competency. 'Jeff assumed early on that this company is phenomenal at operational execution and will continue no matter what,' says one. 'That was a fatal mistake.'"[7]

Immelt's overarching strategy for GE—transforming the company into an industrial digital platform—also proved problematic. As a former executive at the company told us, GE failed to invest in its old-guard manufacturing facilities. The factories "had measuring equipment that was digital, but you had factories that did not have Wi-Fi. So you are getting these digital calibrators, but without Wi-Fi they did not work. You would get iPads to do your daily work that would not work. So all this money went into digital . . . but we forgot how to run industrial companies."[8] Eventually, GE ran out of money to sustain Immelt's strategy and had to sell off its core businesses, as well as many of its digital initiatives.[9]

GE is an extreme case, but many companies today struggle with strategy. According to a 2018 Bain survey, strategic planning remains the most popular tool available to managers.[10] Yet so often the results of planning fail to impress. Studies indicate that between 50 and 90 percent of strategies devised by leaders don't work.[11] Our own survey of 201 American and European executives found that 52 percent of all strategic initiatives undertaken in the previous three years had underperformed. As a glance at GE's saga bears out, all of this failure translates into value destruction on a massive scale.

Looking closer, we find that companies struggle with two specific challenges related to strategy generation. First, they have a difficult time finding new and promising business ideas and formulating strategies around them. Beate Uhse, a pioneer in the sex shop industry, was hit hard by the rise of free sex-related content on the internet. In 2007, CEO Otto Christian Lindemann came up with grand plans to transform the company into a lifestyle company, much as Puma did when it shifted from sports to fashion. It didn't work. His successor, Serge van der Hooft, took a different tack, softening the company's image to appeal to female customers. Another dud of an idea, given the company's historically male-oriented image.[12] Like many companies, Beate Uhse had a compelling brand, but it couldn't generate a strategic idea that would allow it to leverage its strategy online. In 2017, Van der Hooft's replacement led the company into bankruptcy.[13]

A second, even bigger challenge bedeviling companies concerns the implementation of strategies once they are created.[14] Although we might wish to distinguish planning from execution, in truth, managers must "be thinking about execution even as they are formulating plans."[15] And execution is hard—"more difficult than strategy making," in the opinion of the Wharton School's Lawrence G. Hrebiniak.[16] Executives at Nokia, initially a pioneer in open strategy in the 1990s, know a thing or two about that. In 1996, a decade before the appearance of the iPhone, the company launched the world's first smartphone, the Nokia 9000 Communicator. A tablet concept similar to the iPad that Apple launched years later was also presented to top executives, but according to Nokia's former head of design, Frank Nuovo, the idea didn't advance.[17] On a number of occasions, Nokia had a chance to adjust its strategy and stake its claim as a leader in smartphones. Yet, in the early 2000s, the relationship between middle managers and senior leaders had become so dysfunctional that it didn't happen.[18] With senior leaders pressuring middle managers to perform, fear and a corrosive short-termism took hold, leading to a Darwinian "jostling for resources and rank" that prevented teams from aligning behind the drive to create an iPhone competitor.[19]

Many people think of strategy as a small set of big decisions. In reality, the success or failure of any strategy hinges on thousands of executional decisions. To ensure that daily decisions align well with the company's strategic direction, leaders must translate long-term objectives into short-term ones, manipulating levers like communication, process, and incentives. Often, their efforts go awry.

NCR, a technology company, almost went under while transitioning from mechanical tabulation to electronic computing. The company had everything going for it: detailed knowledge of the new technology, a strong sales force, high profits in prior years.[20] Yet leaders failed to communicate the importance of the new technology to the workforce. The company offered paltry career opportunities to employees in electronic computing and failed to display the new initiative prominently at trade fairs. Employees got the message: the new business was second class. In addition, NCR failed to incentivize its sales force to sell electronic computing. While salespeople earned their compensation based on unit sales, the new technology was best sold on a subscription model. Thus it was no surprise that most of the sales force failed to get behind it and that some salespeople even tried to dissuade customers from moving to electronic computing.

We might expect that executives would be adept at devising and executing wise strategies. They spend more than $30 billion on consultants each year, tapping their knowledge of industries, competencies, and business models.[21] Executives also focus a great deal of their time and energy on thinking about the future of their business. As one detailed study revealed, CEOs spent more than 20 percent of their time at work, on average, focusing on strategy.[22] Most companies actively recruit leaders—MBAs in particular—who are not merely razor sharp but are trained specifically in the key analytical frameworks used to generate strategies. As far as execution goes, any number of scholarly and popular books have offered advice on how to get it right. And yet executives still come up short. Why? Is it a lack of intelligence? Flawed analytical frameworks? The wrong consultants?

Actually, it's something else: a lack of openness. Companies have little hope of charting a reliable path forward if they limit strategic deliberations to a small group of senior executives. They can't get the best ideas that way, nor can they effectively connect strategy with execution. Yet traditional strategic planning as practiced today is closely held, secretive, and bounded. Executives presume that keeping strategy to themselves keeps the company safe from competitors who would steal their ideas, and from employees or external actors who would inject unschooled or unruly thinking. But these executives are wrong. Their hoarding of strategy isn't helping their companies. It's killing them, in a number of distinct ways.

Isomorphous Strategies

Have you ever noticed that a great deal of strategic thinking in an industry sounds the same? You're not imagining it. The thinking is similar, unimaginative, and boring because of a phenomenon that organizational theorists call "isomorphism."[23]

"Isomorphic" sounds fancy, but it just means "similar in form." And we human beings are, it turns out, pretty similar in form to one another in some surprising ways. Take our behavior. As studies of eating habits have revealed, obesity is contagious.[24] If your friends are overweight, you will likely be as well.[25] When light eaters hang around heavy eaters, they tend to eat more, and the reverse also holds true. To lose weight, don't pay all that money to Weight Watchers (now WW). Just start having dinner with friends who aren't all that enamored of food!

Other behaviors are contagious, too. Teenage girls are more likely to become pregnant if they see their friends having babies. Kids earn better grades if they're surrounded by friends who are strong students. And here's an interesting one: when two people live together, they eventually start to look alike. In part that might reflect your and your roomie's similar eating habits, but it also owes to your tendency to imitate one another's facial expressions.[26] "Humans are not exactly lemmings," Richard Thaler and Cass Sunstein write in their book *Nudge*, "but they are easily influenced by the statements and deed of others. . . . If you see a movie scene in which people are smiling, you are more likely to smile yourself (whether or not the movie is funny); yawns are contagious, too."[27]

What does all of this have to do with strategy? Everything. It turns out that copycat behavior also occurs across organizations. Over time, organizations in the same environment come to "share the same appearance." They become increasingly similar.[28] Why? There are several reasons. First, companies must adapt to their environments, and only the fittest survive. Over time, the survivors will tend to look alike, as they are subject to the same environmental conditions and constraints, such as government regulations, social expectations, or other external requirements (for instance, ISO certification).[29] Second, just as human beings tend to copy others when faced with uncertain conditions, so too do companies through conventions such as "best practices" or industry benchmarks.

Finally, members of specific professions tend to undergo similar training, and as a result their values and worldviews tend to coincide (that's why sociology departments are staffed with liberals, while fiscal conservatives abound inside Wall Street firms). They tend to adopt similar practices and structures, leading their organizations to look the same.[30] Boring, unimaginative strategic thinking follows in turn—and that's a problem. Take cable TV providers. Echoing one another, the big players have doubled down on a strategy that has failed to answer the threat posed by Netflix. Year after year, they attempt to squeeze more value from consumers, boosting subscription fees and ad time. Not surprisingly, subscriptions are in free fall. In the last quarter of 2017 alone, the sector lost 500,000 subscribers.[31]

Or take the pharmaceutical industry. The world's largest drug companies are all multinationals, with operations in many countries. And yet, oddly, the product development strategies these companies pursue tend to reflect the constraints of the markets in which their headquarters are based rather than the needs of global markets. In a detailed statistical analysis of the fifty-six largest pharmaceutical firms, based in nine countries, researchers showed that product development projects tended to ignore international demand and instead reflected local dynamics such as regulation, political lobbying, and consumer demand.[32] As a result, companies based in the United States, say, were inclined to follow relatively similar product development strategies, failing to register signals from other markets.

"Competitive strategy is about being different," says Harvard professor Michael Porter. "It means deliberately choosing a different set of activities to deliver a unique mix of value. . . . A company can outperform rivals only if it can establish a difference that it can preserve."[33] It sounds convincing, but in reality, being different is extremely difficult. Companies create cohesive structure and systems with an aligned culture. They hire employees that fit their core values, socializing them to share basic principles and worldviews. These employees develop specific knowledge in narrow fields and industries on which the company focuses.[34] Under these circumstances, taking unorthodox perspectives and developing new approaches become nearly impossible. Companies need to engage with outsiders if they are to change the world. But by restricting strategic discussions to a small elite of C-suite executives, they seal themselves off from that outside input. Their strategies become unimaginative and boring—like everyone else's in the industry.

Unimaginative Strategies

We've reached a critical point in this book, the point at which we talk about jellyfish. More precisely, the story of how great glowing jellyfish won Osamu Shimomura of the Marine Biological Laboratory in Woods Hole, Massachusetts, Columbia's Martin Chelfie, and the University of California, San Diego's Roger Tsien the Nobel Prize in Chemistry. The story begins in 1960, when Osamu Shimomura, then a young researcher, was trying to answer a simple question: What makes the jellyfish *Aequorea victoria* glow bright green when agitated? It's not the sort of question you ask if you're hoping to win a Nobel Prize, but Shimomura was happy nonetheless when, after various tweaks and trials, he isolated a unique protein—dubbed green fluorescent protein (GFP)—as the source of the jellyfish's glow.[35]

Fast forward to April 25, 1989. Martin Chelfie decided to attend a lunchtime talk by neurobiologist Paul Brehm. Scientists go to many of these. Not because they expect to learn something revolutionary each time. Often, as was the case on this particular occasion, they attend simply because their department organizes them and they sort of have to go to maintain collegial relations. Recalling the seminar in an interview with *Scientific American*, Professor Chelfie noted that he had no inkling that he'd come away with anything useful for his own work, which had to do with the nervous systems of the transparent roundworm *C. elegans*.[36]

Contrary to his expectation, Chelfie did learn something new. To study the neurons of worms, his assistants had to kill them—a standard procedure in this kind of research. Now, sitting in the seminar, he heard the speaker describe how jellyfish produce light and are capable of bioluminescence. Chelfie quickly understood that this insight solved a great problem for worm scholars everywhere: if he were to insert GFP into his transparent worms, he could observe the worms while they were alive. If he were to shine ultraviolet light on the worms, he might be able to observe this protein's spread. That in turn meant he could track the cells into which the GFP was placed. "Frankly, I don't remember anything else about this seminar because I was so excited about the possibility of doing this experiment. Because I had been thinking about transparent animals for about 12 years before this. . . . I got very excited about the possibility that we could use this in *C. elegans*."[37]

Chelfie's insight revolutionized science and led to the creation of a multimillion-dollar industry. GFP today comes in various colors, can be inserted into various organisms, and can be used for many purposes. Scientists use it to watch how a virus spreads and interacts with the immune system in mice. They use it to watch breast cancer cells migrate in real time, or to capture how HIV spreads between immune cells. Thanks to this new technology, hidden biological processes now can be lit up like a firefly![38]

Chelfie's insight points us to the manner in which revolutionary ideas often emerge. A eureka moment occurs unexpectedly, triggered by the collision of ideas that occurs when specialized knowledge from different disciplines crosses boundaries. Gary Klein, the author of *Seeing What Others Don't*, suggests that seekers of creative ideas must depart from the sequential model whereby they start with a thorough and systematic analysis, discard fruitless ideas, and verify the promising ones.[39] Instead, he points to the role played by collisions, connections, coincidences, curiosities, contradictions, and creative desperation.[40]

It's tough to get ideas to cross-fertilize in corporate settings. Departments and individuals compete with one another for resources or prestige. They don't trust one another, and they clam up. Even when the powers that be mandate cooperation and silo-busting, the ideas still don't flow freely. At Sony during the 1990s, leaders unveiled their "Sony United" silo-busting initiative in hopes of boosting innovation and tapping into the freewheeling spirit of the company's founders. Yet they couldn't overcome the competitiveness of individual departments within the company. Members of these departments wouldn't share experimental ideas, nor would they brainstorm long-term strategies and investment opportunities.

The consequences of this failure were on full display some years later, at the 1999 Comdex trade show held in Las Vegas.[41] A sense of anticipation filled the majestic Venetian ballroom of the Sands Expo and Convention Center as the audience awaited Nobuyuki Idei, Sony's CEO. With the internet taking off, the industry was at a crossroads, and Sony had a reputation as a hotbed of innovation. When Idei finally appeared, he struck a dramatic tone. "What we are and will be," he told the audience, "is a broadband entertainment company." He introduced several new gadgets, including PlayStation2, bringing the console into the world of computing.

Rock star Steve Vai stepped on stage, and Idei asked him to play something on his guitar. When he was done, Vai pulled out a chewing gum-sized "memory stick Walkman," a new digital device. Howard Stringer, the British executive who succeeded Idei, stood up and took the device. "Listen!" he said. He switched on the device, playing back Vai's chord. Crystal clear! Everyone in the hall understood that Sony was trying to replicate the enormous, market-making success it had enjoyed with its Walkman product. And few doubted that Sony could.

But then something peculiar happened. Idei introduced a second pen-sized device, the Vaio MusicClip, that had also recorded the guitar solo. A competing device! That made no sense. Why would Sony introduce two devices that did the same thing? Even less sensible from a strategic standpoint was the launch of yet another similar device shortly after the convention. Although few realized it at the time, business units within the company had failed to merge their innovation efforts. They hadn't managed to exchange ideas and collaborate so as to recombine ideas into one compelling offer. Within a couple of years, Sony dropped out of digital music players, ceding the market to Apple.

Companies benefit when they combine their competencies to address unsolved problems. They lose when their competencies are sequestered in their own separate worlds. This is as true in the realms of strategy and execution as it is in innovation. A couple of years before Apple launched its iPhone, Microsoft came to understand that the device would likely change the industry. Bill Gates asked then CEO Steve Ballmer to create a similar product so that the company could compete. Ballmer turned this strategic initiative over to his senior vice presidents, who collectively had large R&D budgets and thousands of engineers at their disposal. We all know that Microsoft never produced anything close to the iPhone.

As most experts agree, this failure owed to a lack of collaboration between departments and business units inside Microsoft.[42] The company kept software developers siloed from the team making the phone operating system and incentivized the former based on user experience and innovation rather than on the success of the phone platform as a whole. Further, the company failed to collaborate well with external partners, such as third-party app developers, resulting in the absence of apps for YouTube, Instagram, and other popular services. Microsoft's takeover of Nokia exacerbated the disconnection. Nokia had its eyes on rapidly developing Asian markets, hoping to leverage its head start and brand equity, while Microsoft wanted to concentrate on a response to Apple, its old nemesis.

Such a lack of interdepartmental cross-fertilization impedes not only the formulation and execution of new strategies but also the implementation of existing strategies, sometimes with devastating results. BP generates much of its income by extracting oil in difficult terrain, such as offshore in the Gulf of Mexico. In 2010, a blowout at its Deepwater

Horizon platform caused a catastrophic oil spill in the Gulf, the largest in the history of off-shore drilling.[43] BP paid out an estimated $42 billion in damages and in 2012 agreed to submit to government monitoring of its safety practices.[44] Investigators probing the spill identified siloes within BP as one of the disaster's main causes. A technical team monitoring safety wasn't communicating with the team handling operations on Deepwater Horizon. Messages were passed on too slowly or not at all.[45]

As essential as cross-fertilization inside the organization is, research into innovation processes suggests that companies also benefit from exposing themselves to ideas from outside—even *way* outside. Lars Bo Jeppesen and Karim Lakhani studied 166 science problems pursued by the R&D labs of twenty-six firms.[46] They found that technical marginality (a person's relative lack of familiarity with the problem and its relevant technical disciplines) and social marginality (a person's marginality in his or her own professional community) enhanced problem solving. Marginal problem solvers view the problem through fresh lenses. They deploy new knowledge and problem-solving approaches, and they aren't blinded by common assumptions that others less removed bring to the problem. As a result, they can help devise novel solutions.

In the innovation realm, numerous examples exist of companies that arrived at stunning new technical solutions thanks to the involvement of outsiders. You probably know about the International Space Station. A big problem is capturing enough energy to run the satellite. The solar panels have to be precisely positioned, and the long and thin tethering beams are fragile. Highly sensitive to temperature changes, they can bend and break if the satellite spends too long in the shadow. The Space Station needs sophisticated algorithms to reposition the panels, and NASA had long struggled with the problem. Turning to crowdsourcing, NASA held a contest, offering $30,000 to the person or group who could create a working algorithm.[47]

Hundreds of participants submitted over two thousand algorithms. It turned out that more than half of the submitted solutions were better than the existing NASA-built algorithm.[48] Many of the participants implemented completely different technical approaches that NASA hadn't considered. The winner was a data scientist with no prior experience in solving problems related to space or solar capture.

What holds true for innovation also applies to strategy. Deploying traditional, closed approaches to planning, executives lock themselves into safe or familiar thinking and miss out on the seemingly outlandish ideas and approaches that, in many cases, lead to the best strategies. Companies often fail to grasp vital opportunities that at first seemed marginal, with devastating results. Think of all those magazines and newspapers whose leaders failed to recognize the threat posed by online advertising to their main revenue stream. Or think of the Swiss watch industry, which couldn't conceive that Japanese watch producers would one day dominate the market by selling cheaper quartz timepieces. If cross-fertilization and crowdsourcing work for the most challenging scientific or technical problems, why shouldn't we use these approaches to develop new strategies, explore new growth paths, or invent disruptive business models? And yet the vast majority of companies don't.

To make this situation worse, executives often lack access to paradigm-shifting ideas buried deep inside the organization. It's not siloes that are the problem here but rigid hierarchies that prevent ideas from bubbling up. As Gary Hamel observed two decades ago, the middling ranks of companies are replete with frustrated "revolutionaries" whose "voices are muffled by the layers of cautious bureaucrats who separate them from senior managers." Hamel warned that these revolutionaries wouldn't be silenced. Rather, they would leave and go work for the competition.[49] What was true then is doubly true today. Companies that seal off the strategic planning process fail to harness the intellectual ferment that might exist in their own organizations. They lose access to diverse ideas, and they don't know what they don't know. Their strategies are creatively impoverished as a result.

Biased Strategies

We've covered a lot of ground so far in this chapter, so let's take a break and have some fun. Maybe you watched the TV show *The Price Is Right* as a kid. How adept are you at estimating the value of, say, a bottle of

Australian wine? Before we start, do us a favor. Please take out a piece of paper and write down the last digit of your phone number. Have you done it? Okay, now take a look at this picture of a bottle of 2005 d'Arenberg The Dead Arm Shiraz (figure 1.1).

Look closely at the wine bottle. How much do you think the bottle costs?

We've led a group of five hundred executives through an exercise like this and have noticed a striking and somewhat bizarre pattern. Those executives whose phone numbers ended with a high number (seven, eight, or nine) offered price estimates that were *30 percent higher* than those offered by executives whose numbers ended with a low digit (one, two, or three). We double checked our calculations—yep, the pattern held. How could this be?

It's called "anchoring bias." We humans have a tendency to temper our assessments of a situation based on initial information we receive, which serves as a cognitive "anchor." In this case, the last digit of the executives' phone number served as an anchor for their cognitive processing of the task, biasing their estimates. Think about your daily life—the

Figure 1.1
How much do you think the bottle costs?

decisions you make, the information you confront, the conversations you have. Is anchoring bias affecting your judgments in big or small ways? Maybe it is.

It's affecting strategy-making, too. In fact, dozens of common biases can constrain strategic thinking, leading to some pretty awful strategic blunders. During the early 1990s, Polaroid's Electronic Imaging Division was well placed to become a big player in digital photography.[50] The division held numerous patents and was flush with new hires from digital imaging and other high-tech firms. And yet the company was slow to go to market. A prototype was ready in 1992, but it hit the shelves only in 1996. By that time, forty other companies were offering similar products. Polaroid's product won a number of awards, but it never aroused consumer excitement. What happened?

Polaroid's top management team couldn't get its act together and align behind a powerful go-to-market strategy. Some executives were married to a razor-and-blade business model. They just couldn't get beyond it. In their view, revenues had to come from film, not hardware. Obviously, that model doesn't work for digital photography. The clashes that resulted led to executional delays. It didn't help that the Electronic Imaging Division had to use the instant photography sales force, which was used to dealing with WalMart and K-Mart but not the specialist shops that were selling higher-priced digital products. In 1997, Polaroid released a second camera, but that was it. With technical staff leaving the company, the development of digital cameras stopped. The company had missed an incredible opportunity.

The underlying culprit here was what cognitive psychologists have called the "status quo trap," a strong bias to perpetuate what already exists. Leaders at Polaroid might also have been hamstrung by confirmation bias, in which they sought out or favored information that confirmed their beliefs. Other biases that commonly pop up in business contexts include the sunk-cost trap (our tendency to justify past choices by making irrational decisions), loss aversion (our tendency to perceive losses as much bigger than potential gains), and the overconfidence trap (our tendency to believe in the accuracy of our often overly optimistic forecasts).

Biases are especially dangerous to lone strategists since they don't have others around to point out their blind spots to them. But biases can also prevail in the small, cloistered groups that forge strategy under traditional approaches. In some close-knit teams, the pressure to conform can lead people to ignore negative information and disparage those who bring it up, leading to disappointing strategies.[51] The failed globalization plans of Mark & Spencer stemmed from such groupthink.[52] Once executives committed to their strategy, they prioritized facts that confirmed their thinking and discouraged dissenting viewpoints.[53] That left them vulnerable to biases and poor decision-making. Anchoring bias reared its ugly head when executives tried unsuccessfully to transfer their practices in the United States to the Canadian market, failing to account for national differences. Likewise, loss aversion led the company to take much more time than it should have to exit underperforming markets.

Had executives opened up their deliberations to include employees and others outside the company, they might have been alerted to their blind spots and adjusted for them. The lack of openness prevented the development of such mindfulness, locking executives into flawed thinking. With everyone hewing to the same perspective, the group could easily fall prey to confirmation bias, which restricts inquiry and prevents people from discussing their blind spots. In more diverse groups, such as those that include front-line staff and external actors, the presence of multiple perspectives frees people from confirmation bias, allowing them to become more self-aware.

Unpopular Strategies

It's 1985. You're an engineer working for Daimler in Untertürkheim near Stuttgart. The company pays well, offers great benefits, and is a prestigious place to work. Not infrequently, when you arrive home in your big fat Mercedes, a neighbor comes out to chat, asking if you can land him or her a job at Mercedes, too. Life is good.[54]

Then, in 1987, Edzard Reuter takes over as Daimler's new CEO.[55] He's a strange choice: he previously worked for Bertelsmann, a media company, and has been with Daimler for only a few years. Daimler is feeling pressured by competitors—BMW, Lexus, Jaguar. Reuter, cooperating with the consultancy McKinsey, has come up with a radically new strategy: to turn Daimler into an integrated technology company. The idea is to acquire companies from across multiple industries, incorporate their disparate technologies, and deploy those technologies to give Daimler a competitive advantage.

Putting this vision into practice, Daimler embarks on a buying spree, acquiring the industrial conglomerate AEG, a pair of aerospace companies, and the IT consulting firm Cap Gemini—oh, and Daimler also buys a few defense contractors. Not a big deal—except that it kind of is. Remember, this is 1985. World War II and the atrocities perpetrated by the German military still loom large, especially in Germany. All of a sudden, German newspapers are filled with negative stories about Daimler and the use of its products in war zones around the world. No longer is your neighbor so eager to talk with you about a job at Daimler. Your spouse isn't so happy either, as friends begin posing awkward questions about your job. Before long the pressure starts to eat at you, and you're not so thrilled to be working at Daimler, either. Your motivation on the job plummets.

When a small coterie of executives undertakes to chart a company's strategy, the members of the group often fail to consider whether they can mobilize employees to execute. Will employees get behind their thinking? Will they push as hard as they can? Will they feel a strong sense of ownership? Quite often the answer is no, because employees haven't had a hand in creating or debating the strategy. According to Jon L. Pierce, Tatiana Kostova, and Kurt T. Dirks, who developed a theory of psychological ownership in organizations, individuals will most likely take ownership over a strategy, process, or project if they feel some level of control, and if they develop intimate knowledge of it.[56] Without deep involvement on their part, they have a hard time feeling personally connected and engaged. It's one thing to do something because a boss tells you to, quite another because you feel like an owner.

A "closed" approach also can often lead to strategies that seem incomprehensible or misguided to employees simply because leaders failed to take their perspectives into account. If Edzard Reuter had solicited the opinions of Daimler's workforce when devising his plans (which he didn't), the employees might have articulated fears about how the company's acquisition of defense contractors would be perceived by the public (and how some of the other acquisitions did not seem like a good fit, either). He might have adjusted his grand strategy of creating an integrated conglomeration accordingly. As it stood, his strategy failed to deliver, in part because it lacked popularity among employees. In 1995, he was asked to retire, and the company announced it had lost DM 5.7 billion. It was its worst performance in fifty years, and the worst performance of any German company since World War II.

It's not that companies *never* appreciate the need to get employees on board. They do—for instance, during corporate transformations. When Munich Re, the world's second largest reinsurance company, was reorganizing itself to better serve customers, the company's leadership set up a series of task groups to discuss the plan, engaging participants from all levels of the organization. In an interview, Christian Kluge, a member of the board at the time, recounted how critical that move was to ensuring employee buy-in, especially as the company was about to abandon an organizational model it had followed for the past four decades.[57] Even employees whose jobs would be phased out under the transformation wound up supporting it as their involvement in the process raised their confidence that the company would find new jobs for them. Moreover, leaders were able to anticipate potential problems with the plan, since they had solicited the opinions of frontline workers who would have to execute it. Munich Re's plan didn't go off seamlessly, but it didn't encounter the kind of pitched resistance that transformations often engender.[58] Imagine what might happen if companies took the consultative approach they use in transformations and applied it to the high-stakes process of forging corporate strategy!

Beyond Traditional Strategy

The shortcomings of traditional strategic deliberations constitute a serious drain on a company's fortunes. Organizations fall behind in their thinking. Even when they do arrive at promising strategies, they become bogged down in execution. And as a number of examples presented above suggest, the traditional, closed strategy leaves companies utterly paralyzed in the face of that scourge of contemporary markets, disruption. As Clayton Christensen has observed, disruptive ideas usually don't emerge from incumbents, for two reasons. First, disruptive innovations are unattractive to incumbents. They occupy a small niche market and are not compatible with existing business models.[59] Although executives might understand quite well the threat disruption poses, they still have a great deal of trouble crafting a plausible strategy to preempt or react to it.

Leaders who manage to overcome this cognitive barrier face a second, even more daunting challenge: implementing their own disruptive strategy. Implementation usually means cannibalizing existing products and services and rendering existing business models obsolete. As a result, internal resistance to such strategies runs high. Kodak wanted to get into digital imaging during the 1990s, but a nightmarish bureaucracy bogged down innovation, with managers forcing teams to follow the company's existing rulebooks. Risking the cash cow business model relying on film seemed foolish to most people operating in this "old line manufacturing culture."[60]

Blockbuster is another example. In 2004, when CEO John Antioco belatedly realized that Netflix was killing his business, he decided to invest heavily in an online platform and to scrap late fees at all Blockbuster stores (customers hated them and didn't have to pay them on Netflix). Other leaders demurred, arguing that Blockbuster would lose $200 million in late fees and couldn't afford to spend another $200 million to launch its online platform. With the help of activist investor Carl Icahn, they eventually prevailed and James W. Keyes became the new CEO. His plan to stick to the old business model failed, and five years later, Blockbuster was bankrupt.[61]

All of the limitations of traditional strategy processes described in this chapter exacerbate these two challenges: they make it harder for executives to break free of convention and to plunge hardily into the unknown during implementation. Sequestered in their boardrooms, executives become locked into the "same old, same old," disconnected from the fresh thinking that might allow them to seize the future of their businesses and lead their industries. They're ignorant of insights that external actors and front-line employees might possess and unable to access the dynamic collision of ideas that yields breakthrough thinking. Worst of all, executives don't know what they don't know. They think they're acting as responsible stewards of their organizations, leading them through uncertainty to a sound future. In truth, they're not.

The solution is simple: Open up. It's much easier to master disruptions to your business when you're forging strategy in concert with others who view the world through a different lens than you do. Simply put, diversity of perspective matters—a lot. As the social scientist Scott E. Page argues, progress and innovation depend less on lone thinkers with exceptional IQs than it does on diverse groups working together and capitalizing on their individuality.[62] Think back to the phenomenon of isomorphism. If you're a heavy eater who wants to lose weight, the worst thing you can do is dine regularly with fellow food lovers. Likewise, if you are running a bank, you likely won't enhance your ability to revolutionize retail banking by benchmarking yourself against your main competitors. What you need are outside perspectives, as well as those more closely connected to the front-line employees, with the latter especially helping you to consider execution and customer-facing issues.

Recall also how Martin Chelfie's chance encounter inspired his creativity. Connecting different parts of the business through more openness can help you achieve something similar in a corporate setting. Meanwhile, the presence of diverse perspectives will allow you to more reliably and quickly identify cognitive biases when they arise and, even more important, to avoid groupthink. That way, your team can correct for these biases in its decision-making.

Overcoming biases and groupthink becomes particularly important when you want to introduce radical new ideas that many staffers might not immediately embrace. Under traditional strategy-making, the more radical an idea is, the harder it is to execute; staff become overwhelmed, unsure of what the idea means for their operational areas. By involving front-line employees and possible external partners, an open strategy increases the odds of generating radical ideas that people can actually execute. The process gives participants a chance to think about operational issues early on and build a sense of psychological ownership— both important to execution. With open strategy, radical ideas become far more executable, and hence powerful. Novelty and execution reinforce one another rather than composing a trade-off.

If traditional strategy-making yields plans that are boring, uncreative, biased, and all too frequently unsuccessful, open strategy yields plans that are fresher, more innovative, more informed, and easier to execute. Actually, as we'll see, the *only* way to make execution an integral part of strategy development is through open strategy, since this approach brings the employees who execute the strategy into the development process itself. The evidence is mounting: open approaches really work. If you haven't experimented with it yet in your organization, you're missing out.

Questions to Ponder:

- Which of your strategic initiatives seem most destined for failure, and why?

- Do you worry that a competitor will outperform you or that a newcomer will unveil an innovation that will have a negative impact on your business?

- Whom do you typically approach to discuss the future of your company and industry? Are any of these people true outsiders to your industry?

- When was the last time you brought front-line employees into the strategy process? Did it help, and if so, how?

- Does competition between business units help your company or impede it?

2   Are You Truly Ready to Open Up?

Some years ago, a midsized German specialty machine manufacturer approached us, eager to know whether an open strategy might benefit its business. The company was in great shape. It enjoyed a highly skilled and loyal workforce, happy customers, and decent margins. Probing deeper, however, we spotted looming challenges. Chinese competitors were now selling products of similar quality and at lower price. To survive in the coming years, the company would have to engineer an entirely different value proposition based on services rather than products. Since the firm lacked expertise in services, leaders would need to solicit outside perspectives when forging and executing a new strategy. An open strategy seemed a perfect approach.

The CEO seemed willing to revamp the company's strategy-making process. "We must generate fresh ideas about these services and how to deliver them," he said, "and they won't come from me alone." But when his senior team got wind of open strategy, conflict ensued. One large faction vigorously opposed introducing open strategy, seeing it as unnecessary and unwise. Since they had little experience with or knowledge of services, they felt personally uncomfortable formulating a business model based on them. The core business remained strong, they argued, and new services offerings were simply a way to bolster it. There was no burning need to bring in new insights from outside the company. Doing so might lower the quality of discourse and decision-making, since external actors would probably lack enough knowledge and expertise to meaningfully contribute. It just wasn't worth the risk.

To fathom their position, you need to understand how much Germans love producing machines. In the United States, kids get an Xbox for Christmas. In Germany, they get Lego. No other country in the world buys as many Lego sets per person. And yes, you guessed it: the most popular category is Lego Technic, which allows kids to build little toy machines.[1] All those kids grow up and want to build machines as adults. Providing services, on the other hand . . . well, let's just say it's not as cool from the perspective of the average German businessperson or engineer.

A second faction inside the company consisted of people who probably did not play with Lego much growing up and who saw services as a means of transcending the old business model and arriving at a fresh and competitive offering. Members of this second group were excited about open strategy. They understood that to shake up markets and generate bold new ideas, they would need to consult outsiders—even industry outsiders. "We can't do this ourselves," they argued. "We need ideas from people not held back by industry logic."

Swayed by the more conservative faction, the CEO had a change of heart. Opening up to new ideas seemed smart *in theory*. Reflecting on it further, he realized it would mean submitting himself to uncertainty, change, and to some extent loss of control. "Open strategy is a good idea," he said, "but we need to be careful how far we want to go. Complementing the core business is sensible, but should we really depart from our core competencies?" Ultimately, open strategy felt too daunting for him and a number of other senior leaders, and the company declined to transform its strategic deliberations.

For open strategy to work, leaders must buy in wholeheartedly to the basic concept as well as its underlying spirit of inclusiveness, innovation, creativity, and boldness. Some leaders, even those who think themselves open-minded and innovative, express initial enthusiasm about open strategy only to shrink from it subsequently. This typically owes to fears they harbor that open strategy will damage their executive authority and control. Business schools train leaders to see strategy as their exclusive purview. Executives "do strategy," they think, and it's everyone else's job to execute. After graduation, as leaders rise in the ranks, they perceive that crafting a vision and attendant strategies is what enables them to add significant value to the organization. They justify their large salaries to themselves and others by assuming that they, and only they, can set their companies on a path to future success and keep them focused on that path. Inviting others into the strategy-making process would compromise their unique role and diminish their stature.

Leaders also worry that they might disappoint bosses and colleagues if they adopt open strategy. Talk of flattened management structures and equality might be trendy, but most of us have been socialized to work amid hierarchy, division of labor, consistency, standardization, discipline, and stability. These elements have limited creativity, hampered innovation, stifled unconventional thinking, and made collaboration and quick action difficult, but they've also dramatically improved corporate efficiency. If we open up strategy, reaching across siloes, hierarchies, and even organizational boundaries, will efficiency suffer? And what if we get the strategy wrong? Will we look like fools when we expose ourselves to unfamiliar perspectives, adopting outlandish strategies that stand little chance of succeeding? Will we reveal our existing strategy to be wrongheaded and foolish? What kind of light will that shine on others in the company?

It's one thing to feel such fears and quite another to let them determine your decision-making. Before rushing to embrace open strategy, take a serious look at yourself and your leadership team to determine whether you're as ready as you think you are for the approach. Based on our experience with clients and research, we've identified seven key questions you should ask and answer to determine whether you can overcome any fears open strategy might trigger. We've also created an assessment tool you can use to evaluate more precisely whether you are ready to pursue open strategy. If you and your team are mentally and emotionally prepared to break from conventional strategy-making, a whole new transformative path is at hand. If not, don't worry: we'll suggest some tactics for developing mindsets favorable to open strategy.

Question 1: Do You Prefer Miles Davis or Sebastian Bach?

This question might have little to do with strategy, but humor us for a moment. Neither of these musical greats is any better than the other in aesthetic terms, but the two do mark a difference in temperament. Bach's compositions are tightly constructed and marked by order and predictability. Classical musicians perform them by adhering to a preplanned "script" that is the musical composition. Miles Davis's legendary jazz compositions, by contrast, are largely unscripted. During performances, they serve as the bare-bones frame for spontaneous, unpredictable improvisations. The best jazz musicians are masters at handling unanticipated musical challenges and turning them to their advantage.

Are you like a jazz artist, ready to embark on an unpredictable and even scary journey that might create excitement and could lead to almost unimaginable accomplishment? Or are you more like a classical pianist, committed to the mastery of your craft, but only permitting variation in the execution, and not the substance, of your performance? If you're more of an improviser, open strategy will strike you as a natural fit.

Question 2: Are You A "Yes, and" Kind of Leader?

When confronted with an exciting but unfamiliar idea, some of us say "YES this is a great idea, BUT it probably won't work in our company." Others say "YES this is a great idea, AND to make it work in our company we need to do X." A "yes, and" mindset entails an instinctive open-mindedness and willingness to confront the unfamiliar. It's a mindset that seeks to transcend deeply ingrained binary oppositions to arrive at new solutions. By contrast, "yes, but" projects only the *appearance* of open-mindedness. Leaders most commonly display "yes, but" thinking when they realize they cannot fit a new idea into their existing structure. A good example is the digitalization attempt of a German manufacturing firm with which we were consulting. The company started with great ambitions but, step by step, trimmed down the original plan to fit neatly into its existing business units. Instead of a fundamental repositioning, the company ended up delivering only marginal improvements to existing customers.

In most global companies today, leaders can't predict who in the organization holds vital information or will generate the next breakthrough idea. To discover new business opportunities, leaders must access discrete pieces of decentralized knowledge, understand them, and synthesize them into a workable solution. An open-minded, "yes, and" approach thus becomes a major advantage. As problematic as the culture of Silicon Valley is in many respects, its "yes, and" orientation has allowed the region and its prominent companies to lead the world in innovation. Leaders in Silicon Valley companies focus on spotting great ideas and helping them flourish instead of focusing on who or which department came up with them.

Of course, this mindset can also thrive elsewhere. Jim Whitehurst, current president of IBM and former CEO of North Carolina–based Red Hat, one of the most open organizations we've encountered, sees himself as catalyst in chief: "My job as catalyst is to stir the debate and ignite the conversation. From there, our associates, through their own conversations and debate, will drive the ultimate action."[2] Whitehurst's inclination as a leader is to remain open to new ideas wherever they originate and to discover profitable applications. It's "yes, and" on steroids. You know you're ready for open strategy when, like Whitehurst, you can approach it and other supposedly "crazy" ideas with interest and enthusiasm instead of skepticism.

Question 3: Can You Handle Serendipity?

Some of humanity's greatest discoveries—X-rays, Viagra, Teflon—were spawned from happy accidents. So have nearly 10 percent of results outlined in the most widely cited scientific papers.[3] A wonderful word captures the essence of accidental connections: *serendipity*. The English novelist Horace Walpole coined the term in a 1754 letter that alluded to the Persian fairy tale "The Three Princes of Serendip."[4] In this story, the protagonists were "always making discoveries, by accident and sagacity, of things they were not in quest of." As the novelist John Barth observes, "You don't reach Serendip by plotting a course for it. You have to set out in good faith for elsewhere and lose your bearings serendipitously." Though you can't prepare or necessarily manage it, "chance only favors the prepared mind," to quote Louis Pasteur. Unexpected, unplanned, and serendipitous discovery may occur, Pasteur intimates, because the right people are in the right place at the right time.[5]

When we create environments where information flows freely, meritocracy trumps status and rank, and informal contacts flourish, we increase the odds of serendipity coming into play. Google and Pixar might be best known for creating opportunities for innovative thinking, but the industrial powerhouse 3M discovered the benefits of serendipity some two generations earlier. In 1948 the company introduced a 15 percent rule, letting employees spend 15 percent of their paid time pursuing their own ideas. The policy produced some of the company's best-selling products, such as the Post-It note.[6] Serendipity-friendly climates like these are well suited to an open strategy. If serendipity excites you and you prefer the organizational features that feed it, open strategy might be a good fit. On the other hand, serendipity sometimes entails a loss of control and a willingness to proceed despite uncertainty about a preplanned outcome. If that prospect distresses you, open strategy might be a bridge too far.

Question 4: Do You Welcome Diverse Ideas?

As we saw in chapter 1, today's organizations must diversify previously homogeneous thought patterns if they are to adopt more innovative strategies. That means diversifying who is helping to generate the strategies by venturing outside the executive suite. Our experience has shown that if we ask people within closed clusters (for example, within top management teams or within R&D departments) or who have a similar industry background to assess and evaluate an organization's existing competencies, they'll arrive at homogeneous evaluations and results. However, if we pose such questions to people outside these clusters, unexpected ideas and hidden competences surface. As Jackie Yeaney, former executive vice president of Corporate Strategy and Marketing at Red Hat and current chief marketing officer at Tableau Software, said, "Years ago, I used to believe I was just doing [open strategy] because I needed to get people to buy-in, but I now believe you actually get a better edge on it. . . . The more people you can get thinking and engaging and providing their diverse opinion the more likely you are to pick the right direction."[7]

Embracing diverse thinking is challenging for many leaders, who, as we've seen, might doubt the knowledge of outsiders and their capacity to contribute. In general, it's difficult for people inside large, hierarchical organizations to reach across silos and collaborate. Those who don't fit inside the usual boundaries—those whose career paths are meandering and ill-defined—also seem suspect. Analysing 250 million emails from employees in a large company, Tuck Business School professor Adam Kleinbaum found that people with atypical career paths developed networks beneficial for the organization as they connected groups that didn't typically interact.[8] Such people destroyed silos, stimulated diverse ideas, and promoted innovation. This research doesn't merely suggest that the traditional corporate career path of steadily ascending the ranks now seems less beneficial for the organization than a more circuitous path. It also intimates that in today's companies, people who chart unusual paths promote organizational diversity. Unfortunately, many of our organizations ignore or marginalize these individuals, regarding them as "misfits."

Evidence is mounting that diversity enhances company performance. Analyzing venture capital professionals' gender and ethnicity, schooling, and work history, Paul Gompers and Silpa Kovvali of the Harvard Business School have found that diverse collaborations far outperform homogeneous partnerships.[9] For instance, an investment's comparative success rate was 26.4 to 32.2 percent lower when partners shared the same ethnicity. These differences didn't appear at the outset, when projects were selected, but later, when investors helped to shape strategy and recruitment. A McKinsey study of 366 public companies provides further evidence, showing that companies in "the top quartile for racial and ethnic diversity are 35 percent more likely to have financial returns above their respective national industry medians."[10] Gender diversity mattered, too, in the McKinsey study, although somewhat less so. Researchers documented a 15 percent greater likelihood of above-median financial returns among the most gender-diverse firms.

The message is clear: welcome diverse talent, including people with non-traditional careers, and make sure they have the support required to thrive in your organization. How willing are you to do that? If the answer is "not very," you'll find open strategy extremely challenging. If you tend to seek out people with unusual vantage points and invite their opinions, then open strategy will seem quite intuitive and natural.

Question 5: Do You Gravitate toward Partnerships?

If you're a fan of the hit television show *America's Got Talent*, you'd be forgiven for thinking that music, theater, and other performing arts are not exactly a team sport. Success on that show seems to reflect individual brilliance and little else. Probe deeper, though, and you'll find that collaboration is extremely important in the arts. The pop idol Madonna never had a great voice, but she did have a strong team of background singers, along with a dedicated production team that ensured all her concerts were true spectacles. More recently, the pop superstar Adele's Grammy Award–winning album *21* (six Grammys, to be precise), the fourth-bestselling album of all time, relied on over a hundred musicians, producers, arrangers, and engineers. If you count marketing, design, and so on, that number doubles.

Rosie Danvers, a classically trained cellist, was part of Adele's team. Describing how her collaboration with Adele arose, Adele's producer, Jim Abbiss, remembered that Rosie had played musical excerpts to which Adele reacted, with an atmosphere of openness reigning. "Everyone had to be quick and confident to adapt," Abbiss recalled, "and everybody was. Bear in mind, at this point, there isn't any money, which means there isn't any time. But in the space of three hours, everyone changed a lot of what they'd come in with and we got great performances from everyone. The whole mood was: the best idea wins. It's not about you or her or me. The best idea wins."[11]

Practices like employee ranking have traditionally discouraged such collaboration at large companies. At Jack Welch's GE, leaders rated people against one another, separating the best from the rest. Twenty percent of the workforce occupied the top of the hierarchy, 70 percent the middle, and 10 percent the bottom. Although this widely adopted approach spurred people to work harder, it discouraged them from sharing ideas or other resources. If you find yourself in the bottom 10 percent and fret over receiving a pink slip every day, you're fighting for survival and focused on furthering your agenda, not collaborating with others. Even if you enjoy a higher ranking, a similar logic applies: why share ideas with your colleagues when you must stay ahead of them? At Microsoft, leaders found that a ruthless ranking system did more harm than good, producing political games and turf wars within the organization. According to a former company executive cited in the *New York Times*, Microsoft developed a viable tablet computer around 2000 but failed to preempt Apple's success because competing Microsoft divisions conspired to kill the project.[12]

Hypercompetitiveness might make a soccer game more fun but it drags down our workplaces. To create an environment of creativity and innovation, leaders must adopt a collaborative mindset and reward others for cooperating rather than for promoting their own individual agendas. If you're inclined to share your knowledge and expertise with others and if you operate from a place of abundance rather than scarcity in your interactions with colleagues, then you'll thrive under open strategy. But if the prospect of collaborating leaves you feeling vulnerable, the process probably isn't for you.

Question 6: Do You Welcome the Revolution?

Before you can embrace open strategy, you must already feel comfortable with the prospect of disruption. Many leaders aren't, even if they believe themselves to be. Polaroid's failure in the digital camera market, according to some business analysts, stemmed from its top managers' traditional mindsets. Polaroid's top management team couldn't overcome established beliefs about the industry's business model and the potential of commercializing digital imaging technologies.[13] And Polaroid isn't alone. One global survey of more than eight hundred executives revealed that established industry titans are the least likely to disrupt.[14] Up to 25 percent of disruptions originate from industry outsiders, and between 25 and 50 percent of these disruptors are startups.[15]

Disruption is scary. But think of Netflix giving up DVD rental, Amazon moving beyond books to retail, Siemens selling its mobile business, or Target leaping past physical retail and into an omni-channel world. In each case, leaders who had focused on sustaining and exploiting an existing business model jettisoned the established script in favor of a new, untested one. Are you up for that challenge? If not, you'll have a hard time participating in the open strategy process and an even harder time executing the disruptive business models this process will produce.

Question 7: Do You Possess A Growth Mindset?

When Satya Nadella became Microsoft's CEO in 2014, he inherited a company on the brink of stagnation. During previous CEO Steve Ballmer's tenure (2000–2014), revenues and profits had soared, but Microsoft's core business of PCs no longer captured the industry's imagination. Smartphones and the cloud were the future, and in these areas Microsoft had little game. A culture of internal competition, risk aversion, and resistance to change prevailed, impeding innovation. Microsoft Windows occupied center-stage, and the company couldn't break free from it enough to develop new value propositions. "It was an enormously profitable company," reflected one business analyst. "They were in no danger of going out of business soon—it was just a question of whether they'd go into permanent decline."[16]

Only five years into his tenure, Nadella had succeeded in transforming the Windows-centric Microsoft, making huge bets on technologies like cloud computing and AI that are still driving growth.[17] Microsoft's success hinged on a tremendous cultural transformation influenced by Stanford professor Carol Dweck's book *Mindset: Changing The Way You Think to Fulfil Your Potential*, and in particular her concept of a "growth mindset."[18] As Dweck argues, individuals with growth mindsets believe their talents can be developed through hard work, good strategies, and collaboration. These individuals typically achieve more than their counterparts who believe their talents are innate gifts (a "fixed mindset," as Dweck calls it). Observing that Microsoft had become a company of "know-it-alls," Nadella sought to embed a growth mindset, creating a company of "learn-it-alls" dedicated to perpetual development. "I would say that whatever change we've been able to achieve is because the cultural meme we picked was inspired by Carol Dweck and her work around growth mindset," Nadella said at the 2020 World Economic Forum in Davos.[19]

To encourage this cultural shift, Microsoft abolished "precision questioning," a practice in which senior managers were grilled on their progress and plans. Such a tradition contributed to a command-and-control culture in which fear dominated and managers tried to paint the best picture and hide any mistake or failure. Instead, the company adopted a more coaching-oriented approach, and eventually eliminated the midyear review altogether.[20] Microsoft also invested in new events and tools to foster openness, the sharing of ideas, and learning. Every August, the company invites all employees to One Week, a weeklong gathering on its Redmond, Washington, campus during which employees make connections, find inspiration, and collaborate. The highlight is a three-day hackathon during which staff take on projects outside their everyday specialties, such as increasing the accessibility of computing for disabled people or improving the industrial supply chain.[21]

Nadella also makes full use of enterprise social networking service Yammer to connect and share his own ideas, solicit questions and feedback on his "CEO Connection" page, and encourage employee engagement on topics ranging from product strategy to employee benefits.[22] Further, Nadella hosts monthly live events during which he solicits questions on company priorities, progress, and culture during a town hall meeting that is broadcast around the globe.[23]

It helps that Nadella naturally gravitates toward a growth mindset. As he wrote in his first corporate letter to employees as CEO, "Many who know me say I am also defined by my curiosity and thirst for learning. I buy more books than I can finish. I sign up for more online courses than I can complete. I fundamentally believe that if you are not learning new things, you stop doing great and useful things. So family, curiosity and hunger for knowledge all define me."[24] Can you make similar claims? Do you believe that intelligence is static, or do you think that it can be nurtured and developed? Do you feel a strong desire to learn and thrive on challenge even when encountering setbacks? The whole point of open strategy is to build more learning and growth into strategy-making. Leaders who possess growth mindsets will reap the most benefit.

Test Your Openness

By now you understand some of the fears that prevent leaders from embracing open strategy, and, more positively, some of the mindsets that allow leaders to thrive with it. But as we've intimated, it can be hard to accurately evaluate our own tendencies and mental habits. To gain more self-awareness about your own inclination toward openness, spend a few minutes with the following self-assessment tool. It's easy. Read each pair of statements. If you strongly agree with the one on the left-hand side, give it a 1. If you somewhat agree, give it a 2. If you strongly agree with the corresponding statement on the right-hand side, give it a 4. If you somewhat agree, give it a 3.

After answering each question, calculate an average score for every section. The higher this average score, the more this dimension of your thinking aligns with an open strategy philosophy. Now tally up an average score across all seven sections. If your total score exceeds two, you should be able to implement open strategy as a new management approach. But only if you've scored a three or higher will you be most likely to realize open strategy's full benefits and to do so sustainably.

This, at least, is the finding that emerged from a survey we conducted of 347 managers and executives. We surveyed executives who

Letting loose mindset

	1 2 3 4	
When confronted with a problem, I think first what I have to do to solve it.	1 2 3 4	When confronted with a problem, I think first whom I have to involve to solve it.
I tend to give the answers to difficult situations myself.	1 2 3 4	I wait and collect the input of others before giving answers to difficult situations.
I feel uncomfortable sharing information as I think there is a lot to lose.	1 2 3 4	I feel comfortable sharing information as I am convinced that the benefits outweigh the risks.
I prefer to come to a quick agreement as situations of disagreements make me feel uncomfortable.	1 2 3 4	I am comfortable with disagreements as they are opportunities for learning.
Average score		

Yes, and mindset

	1 2 3 4	
When presented with a new idea, I instinctively look for arguments why it won't work in our context	1 2 3 4	When presented with a new idea, I instantly go through what we need to do to make it happen.
If my ideas are challenged. I tend to quickly get frustrated.	1 2 3 4	If my ideas are challenged, I tend to quickly engage in a discourse to further develop them.
Employees in non-management positions have valuable operational knowledge but won't be able to contribute to strategic questions.	1 2 3 4	Employees in non-management positions can provide a lot of relevant input for solving strategic questions.
Our industry requires specific expert knowledge.	1 2 3 4	New ideas do not require specific expert knowledge in our industry.
Average score		

Serendipity mindset

	1 2 3 4	
I like to feel in full control of a process or situation.	1 2 3 4	I am comfortable in ambiguous or high-uncertainty situations whose outcomes are unpredictable.
I feel comfortable in known, familiar, predictable situations.	1 2 3 4	I feel comfortable giving up full control of a situation or process.
When assessing different opportunities, I like to objectively assess their value on known metrics and compare them.	1 2 3 4	I am comfortable even if I am not objectively able to assess and compare the value of opportunities on known metrics.
Average score		

Diversity mindset

	1 2 3 4	
I tend to discuss my ideas and decisions with the same circle of close contacts who have quite similar backgrounds and expertise.	1 2 3 4	I tend to discuss my ideas with very different people outside the organization and outside the industry.

(continued)

I would trust industry experts over a crowd of individuals with different backgrounds.	1 2 3 4	I would trust a crowd of individuals with different backgrounds over industry experts.
I base my decisions mainly on my prior experience in the industry.	1 2 3 4	I base my decisions on information and input from several sources with various backgrounds.
Giving outsiders a voice will lead to irrelevant or negative contributions.	1 2 3 4	Giving outsiders a voice will lead to very relevant and valuable contributions.

Average score

Partner not enemy mindset

I am convinced that competition results in better performance than collaboration.	1 2 3 4	I am convinced that collaboration results in better performance than competition.
Involving others will slow down the decision process.	1 2 3 4	Involving others will increase speed to the market.
I like to tackle and approach difficult problems on my own because that is the fastest way to get the job done.	1 2 3 4	I like to tackle and approach difficult problems by collaborating with other people as this yields better results.

Average score

Welcome the revolution mindset

I am convinced that the future of our industry can only be fully understood based on deep experience and expertise.	1 2 3 4	I am convinced that someone who knows nothing about our industry can provide very valuable ideas for our future.
I am convinced that I am expert in our industry and know most about the future of our industry.	1 2 3 4	I am convinced that there is a lot I do not know about the future of our industry.
The future of our business depends primarily on becoming more efficient.	1 2 3 4	The future of our business depends on radical new ideas.
In my experience, radical new ideas rarely contribute to the bottom line.	1 2 3 4	In my experience, radical new ideas change the economics of our business faster than anticipated.

Average score

Growth mindset

I tend to avoid situations with complex challenges.	1 2 3 4	I feel comfortable when confronted with complex challenges.
When confronted with persistent difficulties and setbacks on a project, I tend to insist on and persist in following my way.	1 2 3 4	When confronted with persistent difficulties and setbacks. I tend to turn to alternative projects.
I don't think negative feedback and criticism are useful.	1 2 3 4	I see negative feedback and criticism as a great way to learn.
The success of others, especially competitors, is a threat.	1 2 3 4	The success of others, even competitors, is highly inspirational.

Average score

participated in Warwick Business School's executive doctor of business administration (DBA) and executive education programs, deliberately excluding IMP clients, in light of their affinity for open strategy. Respondents who scored in the top third (corresponding to a score of three or higher) were considerably more likely to undertake open strategy initiatives (see figure 2.1). Respondents who were top managers and scored above three tended to conduct 48 percent of their strategic projects as open strategy initiatives, compared with only 37 percent of those scoring in the lowest third. While this difference seems insignificant at first glance, the bottom third scored up to a 2.7, which means that coming in just a bit below three reduces the proportion of your strategic initiatives that take an open approach by more than 10 percent—quite a significant effect after all!

Performing a regression analysis that controlled for the number of open strategy projects, industry affiliation, and company size, we discovered that a higher score significantly affected the profits generated from open strategy initiatives. If our experience is any guide, you and your leadership team would probably feel tempted to abandon the open strategy approach midstream or struggle to execute the sometimes disruptive strategies generated by an open strategy process if you scored lower on our questionnaire.

Tips for Opening Up Your Mind

What if you scored lower than you expected but know open strategy could yield dividends for your business? You can still deploy this exciting approach, but you'll need to lay some groundwork. As we learned from Dweck, our individual orientations and capabilities aren't fixed. If you harbor at least some inclination toward flexibility, novelty, and collaboration (as demonstrated by higher scores in some subcategories of the self-assessment tool), you can take steps to change your mental habits to better embrace open strategy. This shift won't happen all at once, but with dedication and perseverance, it will come.

PERCENTAGE OF PROJECTS THAT ARE OPEN STRATEGY

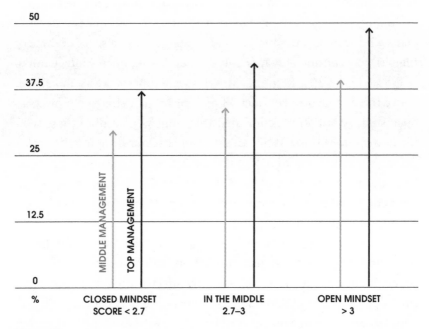

Figure 2.1
Percentage of projects that are open strategy.

Idea 1: Connect with Front-Line Employees

Begin by interacting more with your front-line employees. They'll expose you to diverse thinking you might not encounter elsewhere and will help improve your daily decision-making. Hermann Kronseder, founder of Krones AG, the world's market leader for bottling systems, kept in close personal contact with his company's service technicians, convinced they possessed invaluable knowledge and experience thanks to their daily interaction with customers. As he noted, much of this knowledge would have been lost had he not been there personally to witness service technicians report their findings to the company's design engineers. The better-educated design engineers tended to resist ideas they didn't agree with, and the service technicians weren't in a position to push back and make their ideas heard.[25] By taking time to listen to front-line employees themselves rather than rely on reports from middle managers, he could access unbiased, decentralized knowledge about his business. Although it was sometimes uncomfortable, he exposed himself to diverse perspectives and broadened his thinking. As Chris Zook and James Allen pointed out in their book *The Founder's Mentality*, leadership proximity to the front line is one of the main characteristics of high-performing companies.[26]

Idea 2: Take Part in a Good Debate

Here's another idea for how to become more open: party! No, we're not suggesting you relive your college days and throw a raging kegger. Something a little more civilized will do. As Austrians, we love to hold evening gatherings that involve good food, a few bottles of wine, and heated debates about politics, love, religion, and the human condition. Such gatherings are a historical tradition and have long been known to foster intellectual ferment. At the turn of the twentieth century, Austrian salons spurred the thinking of such brilliant innovators as the mathematician Kurt Gödel, the physicist Albert Einstein, and the philosopher Bertrand Russell. The Austrian neurologist and founder of psychoanalysis, Sigmund Freud, invited physicians, philosophers, and scientist to his weekly Wednesday evening salon at 19 Berggasse in Vienna, shaping the emerging field of psychoanalysis.[27]

Eccentricities, disagreements, and rivalries marked these salons, but the resulting insights transformed computing, astrophysics, cosmology, theory of science, and philosophy.[28] Even the godfather of business management, Peter Drucker, benefited from *Abendgesellschaften* (evening gatherings) in his parents' Viennese home, which regularly attracted state officials, lawyers, physicians, psychologists, and scientists.[29] Whom might you convene to expose yourself to new ideas and energize your thinking? Participating in these kinds of events can help you develop the seven mindsets described above.

Idea 3: Work on Your Culture

Still another strategy for cultivating more openness in yourself and your leadership team is to work on your culture. Help others adopt an open mindset by spreading specific habits and practices centered on diversity, collaboration, and transparency. Evidence-based tactics abound in each of these areas. To increase diversity in your organization, for instance, hire board members who have daughters rather than sons. As Harvard's Paul Gompers and Silpa Kovvali have found, partners at venture capital firms who have a higher proportion of daughters are more likely to hire female investors.[30] To enhance collaboration, understand what motivates various teams and divisions and ensure that every actor is incented to collaborate. It pays off! A recent study by Rob Cross from Babson College together with the Institute for Corporate Productivity found that high-performing companies are five times more likely to promote collaborative working than their peers.[31]

To foster more transparency, create forums in which others can share their thinking, and take what they say seriously. It's not easy to quantify the effects of internal transparency, but the impact that transparency to the outside world has is suggestive. Richard Whittington and Basak Yakis-Douglas of Oxford University and Kwangwon Ahn of Peking University analyzed more than nine hundred public strategy presentations by US CEOs to determine whether their decision to share the company's plans with investors affected their stock price.[32] It turns out that they did. In general, on the day of a presentation, stock prices ticked up by an average of 2 percent, or the equivalent of a $1.1 billion gain in market value. The upward trend continued over the next few days, reaching 5 percent after four days. The effect was most pronounced for new CEOs who came from outside an industry. Their presentations led to a 12 percent or $6.6 billion boost on the day of the announcement if it occurred during their first one hundred days in office. Of course, transparency didn't *always* lift stock prices—the content of the strategic presentation mattered, too. In 26 percent of the sample, strategy presentations yielded an average 4.9 percent drop in stock price the day after the announcement, reflecting investors' negative assessments of the strategies leaders had communicated.

Idea 4: Pick Up a Book

A final strategy worth trying to prepare for open strategy is to set aside time in your schedule for learning. If Bill Gates, Warren Buffett, and Oprah Winfrey can do it, why can't you? Benjamin Franklin was an early proponent of setting aside roughly an hour a day.[33] When he dropped out of school at the age of ten, he demonstrated no particular talent. However, he did have a love of books. Fifty years later, he died an influential statesman, inventor, author, and entrepreneur, his success driven, some have said, by the time he spent each week reading, reflecting, and experimenting.[34] If you watched the Netflix docuseries *Inside Bill's Brain,* you may remember that Bill Gates carries a heavy canvas bag full of books with him whenever he travels, reading about fifty each year. Elon Musk, known to go to extremes, is said to have spent ten hours a day poring through science fiction books when he was a boy (are you spotting SpaceX here?).[35]

In Sum

This chapter has presented a series of mental habits that lend themselves to open strategy. If you're a Miles Davis–style experimenter with a growth mindset who says "Yes, and," collaborates, welcomes diverse ideas, is open to serendipity, and encourages radical change, you're primed to transform and mobilize your company with open strategy. Many of us might believe we possess these mindsets and tendencies, but it's important to be brutally honest with ourselves. If you or your leadership team are more confined in your thinking than you supposed, either refrain from embracing open strategy or, as we hope, commit yourself and your team to a preparatory period in which you first cultivate more open-mindedness, both individually and organizationally. Of course, this is not the only step you must take before experimenting with open strategy. Once you're mentally and emotionally ready, you must still design important aspects of the open strategy process, most notably whom to involve. As we'll see in the next chapter, this requires that you clarify in your mind exactly what you hope to achieve by opening up.

Questions to Ponder:

- If you're honest with yourself, do you feel uncomfortable with or resistant to the idea of opening up your strategic deliberations?

- Think about the categories of questions in our assessment tool and your performance on each one. Do any of the results surprise you?
- How often do you partake of activities that might foster a greater inclination to openness? When was the last time you spoke with a front-line employee, engaged in a philosophical conversation, or read a book?
- Are other members of your leadership team ready for open strategy? Why or why not?

3   Design Your Open Strategy Process

Dozens of technology clusters around the world have adopted names inspired by Silicon Valley. There's Nairobi's Silicon Savannah, Manhattan's Silicon Alley, London's Silicon Roundabout, and, one of our favorites, Silicon Saxony, a technology cluster around Dresden, Germany. As of 2020, this hot spot boasted some three hundred software and high-tech companies employing about 40,000 people.

One of those companies was Saxonia Systems, founded by Viola Klein and Andreas Mönch. For almost two decades after the Iron Curtain came down, Saxonia Systems prospered as a privately held software consulting firm that, in addition to selling systems solutions, also handled a variety of IT tasks on an ad hoc basis. As Sylvie Löffler, the company's strategy process officer, noted, the firm was content to go wherever the market wanted to take it. If a customer had a problem, Saxonia Systems would help, especially if the request came from one of the large semiconductor firms that accounted for a large portion of Saxonia Systems' sales. "Our strategy was not to have a strategy," Löffler said.[1]

The approach had its benefits, especially when it came to serving customers. In the absence of a strategy, front-line employees enjoyed a great deal of latitude in pleasing customers without management getting in the way. At the same time, this autonomy led over time to the formation of silos inside the company. Business units were "doing their own thing" and failed to coordinate. Although this lack of cohesion didn't matter so much during good economic times, it became a serious problem during and immediately after the financial crisis of 2007–2008.

Eager to cut costs, the large semiconductor firms shifted business away from small contractors like Saxonia Systems and toward larger, lower-cost providers. Meanwhile, Saxonia Systems' most important customer at the time, a globally significant semiconductor manufacturer, went bankrupt. Within months, Saxonia Systems' revenues shrank by 40 percent. To survive, the firm had to find something unique to offer that would set it apart from other small providers. Its "jack of all trades, master of none" approach would no longer work.

Arriving at a new, more powerful value proposition wasn't easy, in large part because of Saxonia Systems' deep silos. People simply couldn't pull together to develop a unified direction for the firm and execute on it. By 2010 the company was months away from bankruptcy. Desperate, Klein and Mönch spirited away their extended management team on a retreat to figure out what, if anything, they could do. The group identified a series of measures the firm could take to avoid bankruptcy, mainly efforts to win a few new customers and retain existing contracts. These proved sufficient: within a couple of months, the business started to improve. The firm's existential crisis was over—for now.

As leaders stepped back to appraise the situation, it dawned on them: by working together, the company had managed to save itself. What more could Saxonia Systems accomplish if the entire organization broke down old fiefdoms and collaborated? Klein and Mönch agreed. As they saw it, Saxonia Systems would survive only if it pursued a clear strategy. And it would come up with the *right* strategy only if senior leaders invited a broader circle of people inside the company to participate.

Beginning in 2010, the company instituted a new strategy-making process consisting of three two-day strategy meetings per year (later called "strategy sprints"), interspersed with four-month implementation periods. This process involved both senior leaders and operational managers—about a dozen people in all. During the first of these two-day-long events, participants attended to a single question: "Where do we want to go, and how do we get there?" Over time, the sprints helped the company connect high-level thinking with tangible actions. The group formulated a strategy of specializing in the higher-value work of project management. Instead of serving merely as software developers, the company would organize and run the development and implementation process from end to end.

As helpful as the sprints were, they also led to quite a bit of discontent within the company. The problem wasn't the new strategy itself but rather the closed nature of the process by which it was generated. Now that Saxonia Systems was "doing strategy," front-line employees wanted to make their voices heard. Software development was an iterative, free-flowing process that involved everyone. Why was strategy any different? And without employees' involvement, how could leaders hope to understand the real problems they faced when working with customers? In embracing strategy, Saxonia Systems had opened up to some extent. But as leaders now realized, they hadn't opened up nearly enough. As a result, employee engagement was plummeting.

It's important not to jump unthinkingly into an open strategy process. Inviting some people to participate but not others can spur resentment, and if you're aren't careful, the very diversity you hope to tap through opening up can cause friction and impede implementation. You must take the time to thoughtfully *design* an open strategy process, paying attention to five key issues: how much to open up, whether to include internal or external participants, how many people to involve, whether to make the process digital or analog, and whether to select and invite participations or simply extend an open invitation and let people self-select. Let's examine these questions in greater detail and run through an analysis you can perform to answer them.

Question 1: How Wide Should You Open Your Strategy?

In 1999, when the popular German soft-drink brand Afri-Cola changed its recipe, a collective came together to produce, brand, and distribute the company's original recipe cola on their own, renaming it Premium Cola. According to the firm's organizing model, every one of its 1,700 members could raise and discuss strategic issues. Such radical openness led to chaos and indecision. As one member complained, "I am slightly annoyed by all the email and all the back and forth. . . . I also think you don't have to discuss everything, although I know that it is your credo to discuss and solve things collectively."[2] Perhaps as a result of all the chaos, Premium Cola never succeeded.[3]

Before starting your open strategy initiatives, you need to decide how far openness should extend. Take openness too far, and you risk losing control over your organization. You might wish to have open strategy participants focus on preformulated tasks, engaging with specific questions around preidentified issues. In other situations, leaders might find it counterproductive to restrain participants in this way.

The Swiss company Gallus, a high-tech manufacturer of printing presses and then subsidiary of Heidelberger Druckmaschinen, was once the world leader in the development, production, and sale of expensive, high-end printing presses designed for big label manufacturers. When we worked with Gallus, we identified an emerging threat: the entrance of Hewlett-Packard as a competitor. HP had long specialized in low-priced digital printing technology for the consumer market. Now it was going up-market and business-to-business. Gallus would struggle to compete with this global technology giant on price and quality.

To meet this challenge, the company would have to move beyond its traditional business of providing high-end printing presses and create a product aimed at small and midsized businesses. In opening up strategic deliberations, leaders made it very clear that their challenge was new competition from HP in their core market. Strategy discussions would extend here—but no further. Conversely, when companies like Cisco or Ericsson have crowdsourced new strategic ideas, it made sense to forgo limitations so as to help leaders generate the widest possible set of strategically relevant ideas.

Although the strategy team can provide guidance here, in the end, top leaders must decide the scope of openness based on what elements of the enterprise are in play. If a company wants to move well beyond its current businesses, structures, and capabilities, then leaders might encourage discussions that extend to these elements. IBM engaged in an open strategy process intending to bring smaller initiatives together into new business units. Since the leaders didn't know precisely which businesses it would form based on which initiatives, open strategy deliberations needed to cover these wide-ranging topics.

It's important not to restrict conversation unduly. We've seen many great ideas flounder because existing structures couldn't accommodate them and because leaders weren't prepared to allow revisions to these structures out of fear of losing influence. At the same time, open strategy isn't about turning your organization into a democracy.[4] Management must still retain traditional decision rights, maintaining tight control over experiments the organization pursues, as well as the ability to make final decisions about the company's strategic direction and implementation.[5]

Question 2: Should You Involve Internal or External Participants?

As we saw in chapter 2, it helps to include people from outside your organization and industry when attempting to chart out new opportunities that transcend your core business. Although external participants might lack knowledge and experience relevant to your current business, they can contribute valuable ideas and insights since their thinking isn't limited by prior assumptions and beliefs or shaped by the social and political pressures that might exist inside your organization.[6] Their diverse ideas and unconventional approaches, transferred from seemingly unrelated fields, have the additional benefit of catalyzing cross-fertilization, resulting in new, even radical directions and opportunities. At the same time, bringing in outsiders' perspectives can entail costs, both financial (you might have to pay them) and in terms of management time (external participants might not understand the structures, processes, and incentives in your firm or have a good grasp of how your industry works).

Bear in mind, outside perspectives need not come from beyond your company's walls. If you're an organization of any size, your employees likely are quite diverse educationally and socioeconomically. They arrive with different experiences as well. Take advantage of this rich pool of diverse knowledge. Heraldo Sales-Cavalcante, director of strategic analysis at Ericsson and founder of the online community Strategy Perspective, constantly stresses this point: "You find expertise in such magical ways that you just can't believe it!"[7] Employees from outside top management teams might inject knowledge about structures, practices, and processes in your organization that will help you evaluate and communicate strategic ideas. As we will see in chapter 4, restricting participation to employees or other internal stakeholders can also help you prevent confidential information from leaking.

In many cases, a combination of internal and external participants can prove especially beneficial. In 2012, Gallus launched a two-day IMP Nightmare Competitor Challenge (discussed in chapter 7), a tool that one of us (Stephan Friedrich von den Eichen) created to bring together internal and external participants, including engineers from Microsoft and employees from startups inside the printing industry and beyond. As the challenge had made clear, Gallus couldn't defend its current positioning going forward since competitors were attacking it both from the bottom in terms of price and from the top in terms of functionality. Addressing this problem, three mixed groups of internal and external participants generated two similar ideas related to the development of a new, entry-level digital printing machine.

Up to that point, Gallus printing machinery had cost between €600,000 and €1,5 million. These new machines would sell for as little as €100,000. But workshop participants dreamed up an even more radical idea: Don't just sell a traditional printer but create as well a digital platform on which the company could market printer services. Internal and external participants later fleshed out these concepts in a bold, two-phase business model. The company would first launch the more affordable printer, enabling a wide spectrum of businesses to easily print labels electronically. It would then build a digital platform around these entry-level machines, selling printing management and extra features, such as the ability for platform users to generate and share graphical layouts.

In June 2018, Gallus launched Smartfire, a new starter model for digital, narrow web label printing. The launch of the digital platform was originally scheduled for 2020 but was postponed because of the

COVID-19 pandemic. While leaders believe they would have managed to introduce Smartfire without opening up the strategy process and involving both internal and external participants, they acknowledge they wouldn't have done it as quickly, nor would they have come up with the digital platform–based solution. The presence of external participants allowed them to move beyond analog printing, while the inclusion of employees led to fast and smooth execution. As Klaus Bachstein, Gallus's CEO at the time, explained, "With the open approach, we were able to integrate external expertise in a structured way while simultaneously having our internal employees with us on board. This made it much easier for us to enter the implementation phase very quickly."[8]

Question 3: Should you Mobilize a Small Group or a Large Crowd?

When you decide to open up your strategy-making process, you can invite either just a few participants or an undefined, large crowd. Involving large numbers of individuals, whether they are internal or external stakeholders, will probably allow you to tap more diversity, but it will also require that you share information, creating risks that some of it might leak (a subject we consider in the next chapter).[9] Involving crowds of people also makes strategy-making more complex and slower for leaders since they must analyze and understand the contributions of hundreds, even thousands, of people. Larger groups can also struggle to reach consensus and identify solutions, and they can be harder for organizers to control—a topic we cover in chapter 5.

Tapping a larger crowd usually makes sense when you're first generating strategic ideas, and later when you're implementing a finished strategy.[10] You'll likely attract participants from domains you would have never considered and individuals you couldn't have identified because of geographic distance or other factors. Since people take the initiative and decide for themselves whether to participate (more on that below), they might feel more motivated than if they'd been invited. They participate because they have an interest in the topic or hope to forge valuable business relationships.

Once you've collected strategic ideas, when you're trying to formulate and refine a strategic plan, you'll want to involve fewer participants, since tapping the wisdom of the crowd becomes too unwieldy. Ask yourself a few questions: Are the specific issues you need to address narrow and clear or more broadly defined and opaque? Who might possess knowledge relevant for addressing your strategic issue? Where are such knowledgeable individuals located?

When you're formulating a plan based on strategic ideas you've already generated, these questions will line up quite smoothly. You'll already have a solid sense of future trends and alternative strategic directions—you'll just need others' input to help you deepen your analysis and formulate specific business models. The understanding you already possess will allow you to identify just a few relevant participants from either inside or outside your organization, especially if you are already well versed in open strategy. If you lack experience with the approach and the road ahead feels uncertain, it might make sense to relinquish control and open up just a bit beyond the usual core group.[11] This way you might inadvertently stumble across valuable knowledge, information, or solutions.

Question 4: Should You Choose a Digital or an Analog Format?

When deciding on the format of an open strategy process, companies can select from both analog options, such as workshops, world cafés, or face-to-face meetings, and digital ones, such as crowdsourcing contests or communities, prediction markets, jams, and social networks. When working with analog formats, we usually involve a carefully selected group of internal and external participants and ask them to collaborate intensively for a few days to develop or review a strategy. With digital formats, you don't have to go to the trouble of identifying and selecting participants.[12] Just broadcast an invitation to a more or less undefined group and see who shows up.

Digital formats enable much larger groups of independent individuals to share insights and knowledge regardless of time zone or location, and they also allow you to foster understanding and buy-in among crowd members.[13] The rapid communication possible through digital formats allows ideas to flow across hierarchical and functional boundaries more readily than they do with analog methods. Whereas in analog processes interactions tend to be sequential, with one individual talking or contributing at a time, digital formats enable discussions that take place in parallel and that can be more iterative and dynamic. Digital tools store and aggregate contributions, allowing participants to retrieve, revisit, and reread content at any time.[14]

Still, as powerful as digital formats are, hashing out the details of a strategy usually requires face-to-face conversation. Text alone can't capture all the nuances, and the nonverbal dimension of face-to-face communication matters. Quite often, companies benefit the most from combining analog and digital formats, much as Barclays did in the story that opened this book. IMP also developed hybrid formats for its workshops when group sizes were restricted during the COVID-19 pandemic. This worked surprisingly well, as companies rapidly developed protocols and tools to enable people in physical proximity to collaborate with those joining remotely.

Question 5: Should You Carefully Select Participants or Extend an Open Invitation?

It might seem intuitively correct to carefully select and invite participants for smaller groups and to rely on self-selection when targeting a larger unrestricted crowd by means of digital tools.[15] But some nuances arise here. When working with a large group, you need not rely *completely* on self-selection. You might invite a few people, only to find that they bring along others. As word spreads, an even wider group assembles. As one of us (Christian) can tell you, it's quite a bit like a Kenyan wedding (his wound up with an estimated six hundred guests, only a small portion of whom were invited). Likewise, if you've just begun to experiment with open strategy, it might make sense to work with a more defined group at first, familiarizing yourself with openness before taking on the challenges that very large groups entail.

In 2013 the British Dutch consumer-goods giant Unilever used the social collaboration platform Chatter to open up the company's annual conference gathering of hundreds of managers.[16] Previously the conference had been a closed-door event, after which participants cascaded down results to their departments and regions. To increase understanding of the strategy and organizational buy-in, Unilever decided to create forums for discussing strategic content after the event. Chatter invited 16,000 line managers to take part in the conference digitally. "Initially, we wanted to include all employees," explained Sarah Etherton, senior internal digital channel manager at Unilever who was responsible for the conference-related initiatives. "But we opted for a smaller audience. This was our first . . . project of this kind and we wanted to test how it would work with a smaller group of 16,000 rather than opening it up to Unilever's entire population of 95,000."[17]

The test proved successful. As Neil Atkinson, the company's head of global digital engagement, observed, the use of the social collaboration tool was great for morale. "It was a heavy resource investment to create and curate content during the event," he said, "but [it] made a very positive impression of openness and transparency, helping employees feel involved—and equipping them with the tools to comment on and share content across their own networks."[18] Of the 16,000 employees invited to participate, only 3,680 had previously used Chatter. After the event, thousands more became active users.[19] Even more important, Unilever's judicious use of restrictive selection allowed it to test the approach, gleaning important insights about potential mistakes and pitfalls when taken to a larger scale.

If you don't wish to cede control, carefully select and invite specific participants. When working with such a small selected group, you might think you'll have to sacrifice the access to cognitive diversity that a larger group affords. Not necessarily! If you pay attention to whom you invite, you can ensure cognitive diversity among participants and limit individuals with overlapping and redundant perspectives. This helps to prevent biases and the skewed dominance of specific perspectives or approaches across participants. When required to evaluate strategic ideas and projects emerging from various parts of the organization, managers, middle managers, and employees tend to evaluate these ideas unequally, favoring those emanating from their own country, site, or subunit.[20] Such in-group biases become even more persistent when ideas originate from outside the firm. A balanced and controlled composition of participants ensures that dominant groups cannot silence new, radical, or minority perspectives.

Over the years, IMP has perfected a search and identification process that enables it to build balanced workshop groups of around thirty participants. These participants hail from different knowledge domains, but they possess enough common understanding to allow them to optimize their productivity together. In constituting these groups, IMP draws from a "network of excellence" of more than 1,500 external experts from twenty-five countries, covering virtually every industry, domain, technology, and field. Since IMP has known and worked with these experts for years, it knows what each can contribute.

Linda Stifter, who together with her team is responsible for identifying, contacting, and acquiring external participants for workshops, explains that firms with little experience opening up their strategy process often find it difficult to select the right participants alone: "Firms are sometimes too focused on attracting well-known experts from big industry players or research institutions. We have had to educate them step by step, showing them that it doesn't help them if the people they select are not right for the job. . . . Their ability to contribute depends so much more on the knowledge that they bring in. It also depends on their openness and willingness to contribute and be enthusiastic."

Answering the Five Questions

Our analysis so far has suggested some key factors you should consider when designing an open strategy process. But for the best results, step back and consider your goals for open strategy. What do you ultimately hope to achieve? We posed this question to American and European executives, and their answers are listed in figure 3.1.

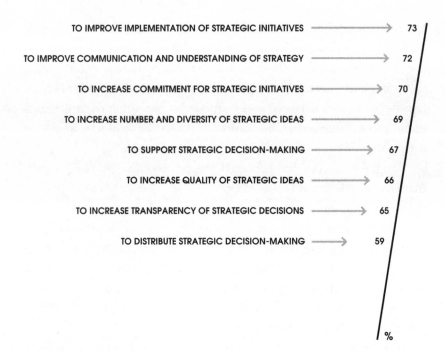

Figure 3.1
Reasons to open up the strategy process.

The greatest proportion of executives in our survey needed help with implementation and improving communication. Communication and implementation might sound relatively unsexy compared with creating new strategy, but they're more important, as strategy will most likely fail in the execution phases or when communication is poor. In a previous book, one of us (Christian) explored why some companies managed to thrive for over a century when many others died or achieved only marginal results. The ability to execute and to exploit existing knowledge proved decisive for corporate longevity. By contrast, even mediocre companies were able to generate interesting new ideas.[21]

Ultimately, open strategy can help in three core phases of strategic deliberation: *idea generation, analysis and formulation*, and *implementation*. During the idea generation phase, you consider how likely it is that your current business model will be disrupted, and identify what big opportunities lie ahead. The analysis and formulation phase is more granular: here you must determine how to transform your ideas into feasible business solutions. Implementation involves not only investment and resource allocation but also the details of execution for front-line employees.

Do you wish to glean new ideas, identify future trends affecting your industry, or seek support in transforming ideas into business models? You can unleash open strategy's full power only if you deploy the approach across all three phases. But you might want to start gradually, opening your strategy process for the idea generation phase only. Once you're clear about which phase(s) you want to focus on, you will be better able to sketch out the basic parameters of your open strategy process. As figure 3.2 shows, the best configuration of participants and specific open strategy tools will differ depending on which phase you choose.

When planning open strategy for the idea generation phase, consider how radical you'd like your new ideas to be. Are you planning to refine the core, move into areas related to the core, or aggressively pursue entirely new businesses? If the last, you might wish to allow people to "go wild," and give maximum scope to conversations. Including front-line people can help, but unless they're new hires, they've been exposed to the dominant logic of your business for a while. In very hierarchical settings, junior employees might be more aligned than senior leaders. External participants will be more likely to generate radical ideas. And you will need lots of external participants. In our experience, companies need 50 percent of participants to come from outside the organization if they want to create disruptive ideas. Any fewer than that and the external participants will become marginalized, the conversation dominated by employees.

Make use of digital tools during this phase. Crowdsourcing platforms or jams enable you to host idea contests and solicit proposals for strategic ideas, while online communities facilitate a deeper discussion of future trends and directions. These digital tools permit participant self-selection through open calls, which can prove especially valuable at this stage. Open calls might generate participants from domains you would have never considered relevant or whom you might not have previously known, thanks to their geographic distance from you. But analog tools

	STRATEGIC IDEAS	STRATEGY FORMULATION	STRATEGY EXECUTION
TIGHT VS LOOSE PROBLEM DEFINITION	LOOSE UNLESS THERE IS A CLEAR ISSUE TO TACKLE	RELATIVELY TIGHT AS STRUCTURES AND CAPABILITIES DETERMINE WHAT'S DOABLE	TIGHT IN TERMS OF THE BIG TRAJECTORIES BUT LOOSER ON THE DETAILED IMPLEMENTATION
EXTERNAL VS INTERNAL PARTICIPANTS	MOSTLY EXTERNALS TO INCREASE DIVERSITY OF IDEAS	EXTERNALS AND INTERNALS TO GET NEW APPROACH THAT IS DOABLE	INTERNALS AND OTHER STAKE-HOLDERS TO GET EVERYONE ON BOARD
DIGITAL VS ANALOG	BOTH POSSIBLE—DIFFERENT TOOLS AVAILABLE	ANALOG TO ENGAGE IN IN-DEPTH DISCUSSIONS	DIGITAL TO REACH MANY
CONTROLLED VS SELF-SELECTION	SELF-SELECTION FOR DIGITAL, MORE CONTROLLED FOR ANALOG	SELECTED EXPERTS AND STAFF	CONTROLLED—STAFF AND STAKEHOLDERS
SMALL VS LARGE GROUP	EITHER	SMALL GROUPS	LARGE GROUPS

Figure 3.2

Configuration of open strategy tools and participants.

are equally compelling at this stage. IMP has developed several workshop-based tools that help identify trends (chapter 6) and simulate a response to a "nightmare competitor" (chapter 7).

During the analysis and formulation stage, you will typically want to guide participants more closely, prompting them to consider structures, resources, and market conditions. Since this stage requires detailed knowledge of the inner workings of your company, analog, face-to-face engagement, using insiders and carefully selected external participants, works best. Schärer Schweiter Mettle AG (SSM), a three-hundred-year-old Swiss manufacturer of textile machinery, hosted a four-day workshop during which teams competed to hammer out a strategy that would allow the firm to thrive amid a decline in the high-end textile machinery market. To develop a feasible blueprint, teams didn't work on grand general ideas but instead focused on concrete value propositions and marketing plans. Externals can serve as useful reality checks early on at this stage. One large industrial company obtained exclusive rights to market the patents of a revolutionary technology. Although leaders were initially enthusiastic about the technology's potential, open strategy deliberations with outsiders left them convinced that the market wasn't ready for the technology. Leaders promptly put this high-profile strategic initiative on hold.

To mitigate fears you might have about involving external participants (discussed in chapter 4), use analog approaches and reframe the stakes by treating the process as if you were hiring a consultant. Instead of worrying about compromising secrecy, you can focus on a different question: how much money you're willing to spend. You might have to pay some participants, while others might join without receiving monetary compensation because of their interest in the topic. Getting participants to sign NDAs is a good idea if you will need to reveal confidential information in order to generate a meaningful discussion.

The final stage of implementation is a numbers game. For those working on the front lines, strategy often seems abstract and a distraction from the *real* job at hand. The best way to demystify strategy is to involve these employees in strategy-making, with the strategy itself defining the scope of the conversation. Although big, town hall–style meetings and other in-person events could prove useful, digital technologies work best with large groups of employees. As we saw in the introduction, Barclays involved 30,000 employees in a strategy jam, seeking to ensure that everyone could translate rough ideas into action. When translating corporate strategy into meaningful action, external participants can sometimes prove crucial as well. During one strategy jam, IBM involved clients and business partners from sixty-four different companies, creating new businesses that collectively generated $750 million in revenue. Not too shabby—and a story we tell in more detail in chapter 10.

For now, let's return to Saxonia Systems, the computer software consulting firm we introduced earlier. To satisfy the rank and file's desire for a voice in strategy and to help the company better integrate strategy with execution, leaders in 2014 decided to open up strategy-making to the entire company. Saxonia continued to run its four-month strategy sprints, but it now introduced a company-wide, networked strategy process that used lean management and agile methods. Facilitators installed large-format, touch-based interactive task boards in each of the company's four offices that listed all strategic initiatives in progress and action items. Leaders encouraged everyone to participate in short, biweekly strategy "standup" sessions conducted around these boards. "We wanted to include our staff in the various initiatives," Sylvia Löffler said. "Whoever felt like it and was motivated could take part."[22] At any given time, almost 20 percent of the total workforce have participated in these sessions, if you include staff working on a contractual basis. Were this Google, that would translate into over 10,000 participants; were this IBM, 50,000. To date, the majority of Saxonia Systems employees have participated in strategy development. They've done so, again, in a voluntary and flexible fashion and through short, informal, and exciting meetings.

The results have been incredible. Saxonia Systems has repositioned itself from a piecemeal consultancy hired to take on smaller chunks of work to a firm that performs higher-value, end-to-end project management. This transition was possible only because everyone got involved and understood what was happening across the organization. "The standups created true momentum," Löffler said. "Everyone knows what we are working on, which initiatives we use to achieve our goals." Since the company's near-death experience following the Great Recession, revenues almost tripled, from €12.9 million to €35.2 million in 2019, and Saxonia Systems has added over 120 permanent employees to its workforce. This exceptional performance led to the company's successful 2020 acquisition by its customer, Carl Zeiss, whose leadership has applauded the company's dynamism and approach to strategy.

Open strategy benefited Saxonia Systems because the company knew which internal stakeholders to involve and, more fundamentally, what it wanted to achieve. Its first goal was survival during a global recession. Afterward the company sought diversified growth and new business models. Notably, open strategy didn't replace traditional strategy discussions among the firm's leadership. Rather, it enhanced these discussions, making them more robust and helping leaders to socialize the strategy inside the company. In general, while transparency and inclusion are vital dimensions of open strategy, management still remains vested with final decision-making rights—as well it should be.[23]

In Sum

To do open strategy well, you can't just jump in and wing it. Just as you must evaluate whether you and other leaders are ready for the approach, so you must spend time and effort designing the process to fit your needs. What are your ultimate goals? Understand those, and you can start answering the key design questions of which and how many participants to involve, whether the process should be digital or analog, and whether or not to extend an open invitation. Even then, you're not done with the preliminaries of open strategy. As we explore next, companies must delicately balance appropriate levels of openness and control, especially when dealing with sensitive information. You might think companies like Saxonia Systems are inherently geared toward open strategy, existing as they do in an industry so open that it pioneered open source software. You might also think your secrecy requirements would make open strategy impossible. Think again. As we'll see, even the most secretive of organizations can mobilize open strategy to achieve new heights of performance within their industries.

Questions to Ponder:

- Which parts of your strategy development process would benefit the most from openness? Which are better off closed?
- If you've experimented with openness in other areas (open idea creation, for example), how might lessons learned there apply to an open strategy process?
- Is your strategy team equipped to design and manage an effective open strategy process, or would you need outside help?
- Can you access external experts in technology, market, business models, and so on who could help cross-fertilize your strategic thinking?

4 Tweak Your Open Strategy Initiative to Allow for Secrecy

Spend any time on social media, and you might have encountered some of the millions of photographs of bison taken by tourists every year in Yellowstone National Park. They're not as common as cute cat photographs, but they're up there. What if scientists tapped all this amateur bison-related photography to help them understand the migratory patterns and health of the bison population in Yellowstone? Algorithms could analyze the photographs, gleaning valuable information about individual bison and entire herds. Rather than spend thousands of human-hours physically tracking and observing these animals, scientists could have the crowd do it for them, without members of the crowd even realizing it.

In 2014, such a scheme was in the offing. A new contest opportunity popped up on topcoder.com, a platform for crowdsourcing digital talent on a project basis, asking for technical advice on how to glean useful data from bison photography. "Imagine a web dashboard," the posting said, "that could be filtered by day, season, herd size, etc. that showed on a map where each observation was made, and what it said. A tool of this kind would allow researchers to identify both a herd and individuals, its movements, health, and status."[1] Add in metadata such as a time stamp or GPS, the posting suggested, and researchers would be in scientist heaven. The posting called on participants to identify "what methods, open source tools & algorithms, and even procedures could be used to merge this structured and unstructured data and pin-point it on a map (giving date, time, and whatever else can be gleaned)."

The organization posting the contest would review the submissions, offering $2,000 to the first-place contestant and $1,000 each for the second- and third-place contestants. Others would receive $25 Amazon gift cards for their troubles.

We'd love to tell you that this contest was a success, the map was built, and the horizons of scientific knowledge were dramatically expanded. We'd love to tell you the National Park Service applied all this wonderful new knowledge to improve the health and numbers of the bison population. We'd be lying. This contest, which did in fact occur, had nothing to do with bison, the National Park Service, or animal husbandry. It was a ploy by the US Intelligence Community (IC) to tap the wisdom of the crowd to help with a very different kind of problem: tracking Russian military personnel operating in the contested territory of Crimea, and the everyday movements of hostile military vehicles across borders.

If the IC had posed a challenge to coders directly, it would have attracted unwanted attention. Russian spies might have sabotaged the contest, for instance, by filing submission after submission with smart-looking but useless algorithms. Or they might have tried to file the winning algorithm and then used their inside knowledge to adjust their movements on the ground to avoid being tracked. By framing the challenge as an exercise in nature conservation, the IC could get the knowledge it needed undetected. "The IC could get some great ideas for each subsection of the contest, do it quickly (<10 days), at a much lower price than hiring contractors to think about the problem for days, weeks and months," says Peter Van Vories, who was involved in the project. "But most importantly it was about getting the thinking of the entire world to help address the problem undetected."[2]

Our point here is not to foster paranoia, making you think every contest you happen to come across on a crowdsourcing platform is an exercise in spycraft. Rather, we seek to demonstrate that any organization can use open methods to tap the wisdom of the crowd and at the same time retain partial or even total secrecy. The IC, one of the world's most secretive organizations, used open methods to gain access to computer programming talent (with some success, our sources tell us).[3] Companies everywhere can use them to enhance their strategy-making—even yours. You might fear parting with your company's secrets by opening up the C-suite doors and inviting in people outside your management team to help you with your strategic challenges. In fact, you can take the design elements you fixed on in the last chapter and tweak or adjust them to alleviate your secrecy concerns. Even organizations that deal with highly sensitive matters can benefit from openness when they carefully design their open strategy process.

Toward a Rational Approach to Secrecy

We're not advocating that you and your company take a cavalier attitude toward your trade secrets and other competitive information. We know that keeping tight control of information matters, particularly when it comes to strategy. In the ancient Chinese manual *The Art of War*, military strategist Sun Tzu advised generals to keep their plans to themselves if they wanted to defeat their adversaries: "By discovering the enemy's dispositions and remaining invisible ourselves, we can keep our forces concentrated, while the enemy's must be divided."[4]

Businesses have long taken such advice to heart, regarding secrecy as vital for achieving and maintaining competitive advantage. During the 1950s and 1960s, candy companies engaged in pitched battles with one another, trying to steal trade secrets. To defend themselves, these companies also clamped down on the flow of information. Nestle conducted background checks on its employees. Many companies employed detectives to monitor staff.[5] And the Mars candy company, led by patriarch Forrest Mars Sr., instituted a legendary culture of secrecy. Staff were forbidden to attend industry events. The company insisted that contractors wear blindfolds if they had to walk through the factory. And after Forrest Sr. read a largely positive article based on an interview he gave in 1966, he decided he would never talk to a journalist again.[6]

These measures might sound extreme, but companies today have similar ones in place. They make employees and freelancers sign confidentiality agreements, and they file suit when those agreements are violated. They rigidly control employees' social media activity. They put password protection in place like it's going out of style. They hire an army of cybersecurity specialists to prevent hackers from breaking in and stealing valuable secrets. And, of course, they keep their strategy conversations locked down, zealously guarding core strategies and the thinking, market data, and product information that contribute to them.

A number of players in the business world have lately become aware of the benefits of more openness, in strategy-making and beyond. Many technology companies have implemented transparency, believing that the benefits of exposing themselves to ideas beyond the enterprise outweigh the potential danger of others stealing and profiting from their secrets. As PayPal cofounder Peter Thiel has said, "The greatest risk for a startup is that they are inventing something that already exists or that they haven't thought something through down to the last detail. This risk can be reduced only through openness during the phase when it is being developed. If you make a secret out of your project, you've already lost."[7]

In his book *The Silicon Valley Challenge: A Wake-up Call for Europe*, German media executive Christoph Keese describes the stupefying openness that exists in Silicon Valley; there, technology executives casually ask one another about the latest deals, financial results, new projects, plans for the future, and so on.[8] "Germans," Keese writes, "consider such questions impertinent because they are afraid that someone will steal their ideas. . . . California lives in permanent fear of losing out on intellectual exchange, or that they won't be able to absorb every possible new impulse. Nothing stokes this fear more than the idea that there might be a flaw in a product's concept, and that the mistake will only be discovered after it hits the market."[9]

Companies in a number of industries are embracing more transparency in an attempt to achieve reputational gains. In our digital era, with its ready accessibility and visibility of information, stakeholders expect more knowledge about the companies with which they do business, and they use that information to hold companies responsible for meeting environmental and ethical standards. As companies are realizing, transparent communications can increase trust, perceptions of fairness, and loyalty and engagement. Instead of hoarding knowledge, they can reap competitive benefits from communicating proactively, sharing information that it was previously unthinkable to divulge.[10]

Companies and government agencies also are turning to transparency to improve decision-making and boost innovation. Glaxo-Smith-Kline opened up the ultra-secretive world of drug development, releasing its clinical trials data on the web to aid discovery of new medicine. The Amazon subsidiary Zappos injected an unorthodox level of transparency into its supply chain, sharing sales data with every supplier to improve cooperation.[11] NASA posted images from its Kepler space telescope directly on the web so that anyone could log on and peruse actual data to locate new transiting planets. That was a good thing: two NASA interns, along with a crowd of everyday citizens, used the data to spot a rare "super Earth"—a planet twice the size of Earth whose environmental conditions could potentially support the existence of life.[12]

Bridgewater Associates, America's largest hedge fund, is well known for its culture of radical transparency. Founder Ray Dalio recognized that his own intellectual limitations had sometimes led him to make poor business decisions, so he endeavored to create an intellectual meritocracy in which everyone had equal authority to put forth ideas and in which the decision-making process was transparent to all. As Dalio remembers in his book, *Principles: Life and Work*, "I theorized that radical transparency would reduce the risk of our doing anything wrong—and of not dealing appropriately with our mistakes—and that the tapes would in fact protect us. If we were handling things well, our transparency would make that clear . . . , and if we were handling things badly, our transparency would ensure that we could get what we deserve, which in the long run, would be good for us."[13]

At Bridgewater, radical transparency hasn't entailed a perfectly free flow of knowledge. Certain information remains proprietary and highly restricted. When secret information leaks, the company suspends openness until it can determine the leak's source. Still, radical transparency entails far more openness than companies have traditionally attempted. At one point, Bridgewater reorganized its back office with an eye toward potentially spinning it off. In a town hall–style meeting, leaders informed the company about this possibility long before they came to a decision. When Bridgewater eventually decided to go through with the spin-off, morale remained high because employees had known about it all along.[14]

As Bridgewater's experience suggests, a measure of secrecy remains essential for most companies in our era of openness. Some competitive information, if released, *would* compromise a company's market position. Startups, for instance, often risk having their innovations stolen and copied by much larger incumbents in the course of pursuing partnerships with them. Although they might wish to share knowledge about their overall activities, they probably should avoid sharing details, and should also file for patents as soon as possible.

Some industries and sectors require much more secrecy than others, and indeed are compelled to maintain secrecy by law. In many emerging economies, where property rights are notoriously difficult to enforce, companies must guard their secrets closely or risk a high likelihood of theft. Some highly critical strategic actions might require an increased level of secrecy. Mergers and acquisitions can mean life or death for organizations and hence are extremely sensitive, both within organizations and beyond.[15] If information leaks before leaders announce a deal, the parties can sustain significant harm.[16] Finally, companies might sometimes wish to use secrecy strategically to help market their products. The classic example is Apple, which shrouds its product development process in secrecy, leaving many of its own employees unaware of new products in the pipeline.[17] Secrecy helps Apple build a cultish sense of anticipation around its product launches, leading to a great deal of free media coverage.

Even allowing for secrecy's importance, an absolute clampdown on information flows often won't produce the best results. Studies have shown that leaders who communicate about mergers and acquisitions beyond what the law requires can build more credibility with investors and see better reactions from the stock market.[18] And with the rise of digital technologies, strict secrecy is becoming increasingly difficult and costly to achieve, monitor, and maintain. In general, companies would do well to take a moderate approach to safeguarding information, weighing the risks and costs of divulging information and managing secrets accordingly. Companies must develop systems for sharing appropriate information—and perhaps more of it than they traditionally would have felt comfortable with—while continuing to maintain some level of secrecy. When it comes to opening-up strategy, this is precisely what leading-edge companies have done. They haven't opened up entirely but rather have carefully structured their open strategy deliberations in ways that allow them to tap into a broader community while still keeping essential information private. In fact, even the most traditionally opaque organizations have made tweaks to their open strategy process that have allowed them to conduct and benefit from this approach.

Merging Secrecy with Openness: The US Navy

In May 2011 the US Navy invited the general public to share ideas for how it might fight the Somali pirates that were then besieging international shipping, using a game platform called MMOWGLI—Massive Multiplayer Online Wargame Leveraging the Internet.[19] The game began with a brief scenario: "Three pirate ships are holding the world hostage. Chinese-U.S. relations are strained to the limit and both countries have naval ships in the area. Humanitarian aid for rig workers is blocked. The world is blaming the U.S. for plundering African resources." Next, game organizers asked participants to provide short, Twitter-like answers to two questions: "What new resources could turn the tide in the Somali pirate situation? What new risks could arise that would transform the Somali pirate situation?" During the following week, players could vote on ideas, expand on and challenge them, or ask questions of their own. Players received points depending on how many people publicly liked their ideas, and game organizers invited the best ones to participate in the next round.[20] Some 16,000 civilian and military players preregistered for the game and 800 actively engaged in the game, posting 4,000 ideas.[21] All along, the Navy refrained from divulging any of its top-secret operational details.

This game was hardly an isolated event. The Navy followed up with a number of similar contests, using the MMOWGLI platform to tackle specific challenges and issues. The Navy was taking a calculated risk since the questions posed to participants revealed the Navy's areas of interest. At the same time, most of these areas would hardly have come as a surprise to anyone following global affairs (the problem of Somali pirates, for instance, was widely reported and even became the subject of the 2013 film *Captain Philips*, starring Tom Hanks).

Buoyed by its success, the Navy took its open source strategy-making even further. In 2010 the Naval Air Warfare Center Aircraft Division (NAWCAD) had begun to develop new aviation strategies,[22] initially taking a traditional approach and convening a small group of thirty-two senior leaders. In 2014, NAWCAD launched a second phase, relying on MMOWGLI to include outsiders. The topic was more sensitive than in previous games: participants were discussing overall aviation strategy and the Navy's future programs. Still, the Navy didn't have to share much confidential information, since it merely sought to generate new ideas, not evaluate the Navy's current or planned actions. The Navy also wasn't terribly concerned that vital secrets would become compromised because it already had a culture of secrecy in place and felt reasonably certain participants from the US Navy would keep sensitive information to themselves. As Dr. Dale Moore, director of strategy at the office of the deputy assistant secretary of the navy for research, development, test and evaluation, told us, "We were very sensitive to that. I mean, we always are. That's just how we operate every day. We're very aware of what we can say and what we can't say, and we know where the lines are and that kinda thing. . . . Well, we made sure people understood that this was an open forum, and not to discuss sensitive information. That was one of the prerequisites going in to play the game."[23] In addition, organizers required all participants to share an email address, allowing them to verify the identity of participants and ensure that bad actors weren't taking part.

In addition to leaks, the Navy sought assurance that any ideas that arose during the game would remain their property. Moore's solution

was to involve closely the Navy's lawyers. "In a strong engineering organization," he said, "sometimes the legal folks are the last ones you bring
in. . . . We engaged them and we engaged them early on, and tried to
make them part of the process." While the lawyers harbored doubts, the
admiral in charge of NAWCAD decided to press ahead anyway. Moore
explained: "Our challenges are getting more and more severe in providing affordable capabilities to meet the concerns we have, and so we
wanted to challenge our assumptions, think outside of the box, gather as
many of the best ideas we can."

The game was a big success. A diverse set of 600 participants registered, generating over 5,000 ideas. Of these, organizers deemed 127 to
be "super interesting." Out of those, thirty-six action plans were created.[24] As Moore reflected, the game exposed the Navy to a much richer
set of creative ideas than it would have obtained using traditional methods. One idea called for the Navy to develop an underwater base in the
Arctic. "I mean, that never, ever would have come out" had the Navy
not opened up its strategy. "We had ideas about creating very high-in-
the-atmosphere-type nodes for communication like a deployable net in
a domain of like unmanned vehicles swarming around that were part
of an information net. Right? So stuff like that just was just outside—I
mean as soon as you saw it, you would say, 'Well, that's really wild.'"[25]

As of this writing, the Navy was working on a thirty-year research
strategy that would guide its multibillion-dollar investments in new
weapon systems. While the details of this planning remain confidential, Moore suggested that some of the ideas from the 2014 MMOW-
GLI game would influence the discussion. Mark Darrah, the admiral in
charge of NAWCAD at the time, credits the game with helping senior
leadership break free of groupthink and set up a skunkworks team that
allows engineers to "go wild" and introduce disruptive technologies.
This team now has "almost a billion dollars of work they're executing
across the five-year defense planning [cycle]," the admiral told us.[26]

As the Navy's experience suggests, companies and other organizations
can exert considerable control over the open strategy process, ensuring
that secrets don't leak. The Navy relied on four crucial elements. First, the

strategizers experimented with openness in a limited, low-risk way, help-ing them understand how open strategy worked and to build a robust, leak-proof system. Second, they relied on a culture of confidentiality—which every organization must build in the age of social media—to enforce secrecy. Third, they sought legal counsel without ceding con-trol to the lawyers. And fourth, they concentrated on idea generation, a phase of strategy-making that doesn't require much information shar-ing on the part of the organization. Subsequently the Navy published a document summarizing the ideas that emerged from the game while keeping the details, including its own intended actions, secret.

Develop a Protection Strategy

If you're nervous about sensitive information leaking at your com-pany, you too can fine-tune the open strategy process to include a sen-sible protection strategy. Paradoxically, opening up means paying *more* attention to secrecy, not less. If you clamp down too hard on informa-tion flows, you might scare off outsiders, preventing them from partici-pating and thus reducing the benefits of openness. Clamp down too little and your company's plans or knowledge might leak, including that generated by open strategy deliberations. Forging a sensible strat-egy means knowing whom to involve in strategy-making (internal or external participants), how many of them, and what to disclose.

When it comes to whom to include, the benefits that might accrue from involving internal or external participants and granting access to company-specific sensitive knowledge depend on the phase of strategy-making you're pursuing (see figure 4.1). In general, companies benefit most from including external participants in the first stages of strategy-making. External participants can prove very helpful to companies that seek to generate fresh, innovative ideas, overcome fixed mental models, challenge ingrained assumptions, and cross-fertilize ideas across domains of knowledge. Happily, during idea generation external actors usually need very little company-specific information to get the ideas flowing, making secrecy easiest to maintain during this phase. At the same time,

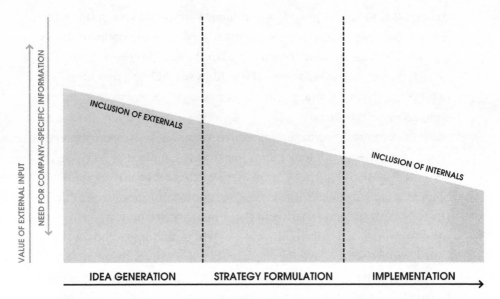

Figure 4.1
Balancing disclosure and external input.

your own people must know what they can and cannot share, just as members of the US Navy did.

During the second phase (strategy formation), open strategy works only if you release a substantial amount of information. As a result, most companies will decide to involve mostly insiders or a select group of people from outside the organization who might sign confidentiality agreements and function more like consultants.

During the third phase of strategy-making, implementation, you must share quite a bit of company-specific knowledge to realize the main benefits, understanding of the strategy and buy-in from those who must implement it.[27] This sharing makes maintaining secrecy difficult. Fortunately, the benefits of openness here far outweigh the dangers. Competitors might learn your plans, but at this stage you're already fine-tuning those plans and working with your customers to implement them, so the costs of disclosure are relatively small. Further, the main participants in this phase should be employees and business partners rather than outsiders since the former are the people who will actually implement the strategy. If competitors would have difficulty imitating your strategy or if you have a big head start, you might still consider involving outsiders, since leakage of your company's plans would not prove harmful. That, however, makes sense only if outsiders would bring new ideas on how to implement a strategy, perhaps based on experiences in other companies or industries.

To understand what to disclose when tweaking your open strategy process for secrecy, let's look more closely at NASA. Back in 2005, budget cuts forced the agency's human research and technology development program to seek out new ways to advance innovation.[28] Jeff Davis, NASA's Human Health and Performance director, learned about the crowdsourcing platform Innocentive while attending a class at Harvard Business School. Wondering whether this approach might help the agency solve some of its greatest research problems, he led NASA to launch several initiatives to harness the wisdom of the crowd both externally and internally. One of these initiatives, NASA's "tournament lab," is a platform for conducting crowdsourcing challenges. To date, close to four hundred challenges have been completed, including internal and external projects for NASA, as well as numerous projects for other federal agencies. About 25,000 unique contributors have submitted their ideas for solutions, and the agency has awarded about $6.5 million as prizes. Notable contests included the "Space Poop Challenge," in which participants attempted to devise a solution to the problem of handling human waste during long space missions, and a contest to predict solar particle events (emissions of energy from the Sun that pose a significant risk to humans and hardware). NASA has implemented 94 percent of the solutions generated by these contests, saving about $32 million in R&D costs.[29]

Another initiative, NASA@WORK, taps into the collective wisdom of the NASA community, enabling staffers to collaborate with one another in unconventional ways.[30] Employees post a challenge, and the NASA community steps in to help. As Ryon Stewart, a challenge coordinator at the Center of Excellence for Collaborative Innovation, notes, NASA@WORK has led to significant cost savings: "We have had lots of situations where folks came to us with a problem, they were ready to fund with a few million dollars and multiple years of development. And then, when they posted it on NASA@WORK, it turned out that someone at the same center or in another NASA center already had the answer, at least partially."[31]

While many of these challenges don't pose a secrecy risk, NASA has implemented strategies to deal with those that do. Organizers reflect carefully on what intellectual property they can safely share with participants. "Usually, the more IP you're willing to give, the better the solutions will be, especially for hard problems," Stewart said. Yet he notes that a trade-off exists: "If respondents are pretty much inventing something new, they might back out part way through and say, 'I don't want to win this prize. I'm going to go start my own company.' So you have to be careful on how much IP you're willing to give."[32] If some data are too sensitive to share, NASA can sometimes proceed with a contest by sharing it in disguised form. "For a data science type problem," Stewart notes, "you can change the labeling of some data or share only part of your data set, to make it unclear. For instance, if we're doing a challenge on astronaut health, we can't share health data. So we make sure that we have just columns of numbers or we scale data differently. There are lots of things you can do to prevent people from interpreting exactly what it was originally."[33]

If the very nature of a project is sensitive, you can obfuscate the problem or reframe it, as the US IC did with its Crimea crowdsourcing effort. Describing this effort, Stewart observed that "getting people help you find bison in Yellowstone National Park is the same concept and really harmless. The vendors are very good at helping folks like me reframe and restructure those problems so that we need not worry about leaking too much intellectual property or sensitive data."[34]

Our discussion of whom to involve and what to disclose gives rise to a simple decision tree you can use to tweak your open strategy process design (see figure 4.2).

First, determine whether your open strategy initiative will fall into the idea generation, formulation, or implementation stage. If you're pursuing

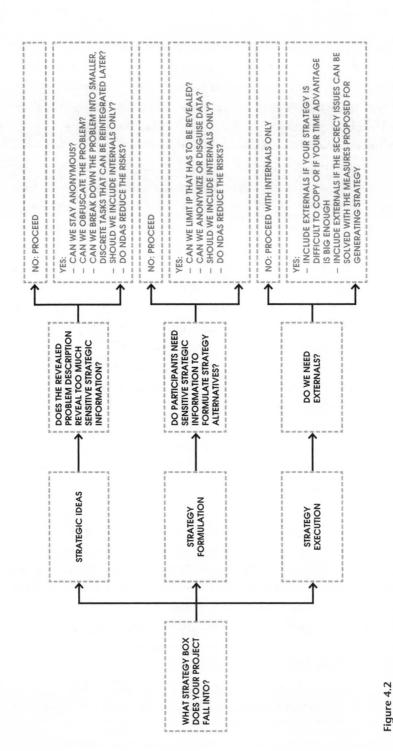

Figure 4.2
Decision tree: Open strategy and handling secrecy.

idea generation, you need not reveal any sensitive strategic information, and involving insiders or outsiders does not pose any risks. If they need strategic sensitive information to develop strategic ideas, you can ask yourself whether you might break down the problem into smaller, discrete tasks that you could integrate later. Perhaps you'll want to use only insiders or require NDAs to minimize the risk. During strategy formulation, when the sharing of company-specific information becomes necessary, ask yourself: Can you limit the IP that you must reveal? Can you anonymize or disguise data? Should you include insiders only? Would NDAs reduce the risks sufficiently? If you involve external participants during the execution phase, make sure that leakage of details about your plan wouldn't significantly harm the company.

In the story that opened this chapter, the US IC sought help with idea generation; in particular, it sought ideas to help it better track Russian movements in Crimea and the movement of enemy equipment across borders. Clearly, posting a question about Russia and Crimea or enemy equipment online would reveal too much. So the IC had to ask itself whether the agency could keep itself anonymous and formulate the question in a way that would not reveal its true objectives. The answer to both questions was yes, leading to the bison migration photo contest. But let's assume the IC wanted to open up strategy formulation. How would it proceed? It would ask whether participants needed access to sensitive information to formulate plans. The answer: absolutely. So opening up that part of the process likely wouldn't work (and to our knowledge, the IC hasn't done this).

For a retail chain considering how to open up strategy, the calculus would be different. Anonymizing information probably wouldn't work, but the chain could decide to include only internal participants, which would give it access to at least some more diverse perspectives. Have those participants sign NDAs, and this chain would likely experience no substantial secrecy issues. During the execution phase, the retail chain might well need external partners to execute its strategy. But if that strategy was, say, to pursue omnichannel (online and offline) selling, forging a partnership with a technology vendor would likely afford it a significant head start over its fellow retailers who hadn't yet pursued this strategy. By the time the competition got its act together, this first-mover retail chain would be way ahead. Thus, opening up the execution phase poses little risk even if some information leaks.

In Sum

Even the most secretive organizations have turned to open strategy. Yours can too, so long as you adjust the design of your process to address your need to control the flow of information. With strategy and most other areas of the business, companies today do well not to either clamp down entirely on disclosures or remove any boundaries whatsoever but to find a fertile middle ground. Use this chapter to find the nuanced solution that works for you.

This section of the book has prompted you to think carefully about open strategy before undertaking it. Now that you've done so, we're ready to develop the open strategy tools themselves, considering each of the three stages of strategy-making. We begin with ideation. In our survey of top executives in the United States and Europe, 69 percent agreed that openness increases the number and diversity of strategic ideas. In the next three chapters, we explain how you can engage front-line employees, experts, partners, and in some cases even competitors to arrive at breakthrough visions of the organization's future direction and to increase the odds of executional success.

Questions to Ponder:

- Have you ever analyzed the secrecy provisions you maintain relative to your strategy, honestly assessing their costs relative to the benefits they deliver?
- What unspoken anxieties and assumptions underlie the secrecy provisions you have in place? Are these anxieties and assumptions warranted?
- Do your employees demand more transparency regarding strategy and decisions than you currently allow?
- How might you reframe strategic issues in ways that allow you to involve external participants without endangering secrecy?

5 Harness the Wisdom of Crowds

On September 29, 1707, twenty-one British warships left Gibraltar bound for England.[1] As they passed the Bay of Biscay, they encountered strong winds that pushed them off course. About a month later, on finally entering the English Channel, the sailing masters (sailors on the ships responsible for navigating) breathed a bit easier, believing they had finally reached safe waters. They were wrong. These navigators had miscalculated the ships' positions, and in particular their longitude. Back then, determining latitude was easy if you knew where the sun stood at noon. But ocean navigators couldn't figure out longitude with any accuracy. Sometimes it proved fatal, as in this case. Four of the ships collided with rocks off the Isles of Scilly. Between 1,400 and 2,000 officers, sailors, and marines met their fate at the bottom of the Atlantic.

Reeling from the disaster, British leaders decided to solve this longitude problem once and for all.[2] Parliament passed legislation offering rewards for anyone who could figure out new ways of measuring longitude more accurately. "Nothing is so much wanted and desired at sea," the Longitude Act of 1714 read, "as the discovery of the longitude, for the safety and quickness of voyages, the preservation of ships, and the lives of men."[3] On one level, the challenge of determining longitude seemed straightforward: if you knew the exact time of day on the ship and the exact time at a fixed location, and if you also knew that location's longitude, you could calculate the ship's longitude. Sailors could theoretically calculate longitude by charting the movement of the Moon, but the Moon's movements were notoriously difficult to know with any precision, making longitude impossible to calculate.

Why not simply bring a clock on board? Nice idea, but as Dava Sobel explains in her book *Longitude*, "On the deck of a rolling ship such clocks would slow down, or speed up, or stop running altogether. Normal changes of temperature encountered en route from a cold country of origin to a tropical trade zone thinned or thickened a clock's lubricating oil and made its metal parts expand or contract with equally disastrous results. A rise or fall in barometer pressure, or the subtle variations in the Earth's gravity from one latitude to another, could also cause a clock to gain or lose time."[4] Confronted with these obstacles, eminent scientists were at a loss as to how to calculate longitude. No less a personage than Sir Isaac Newton, the Longitude Board's primary technical expert, declared that navigators had no choice but look to the heavens to make this calculation, imperfect and inadequate as that method was.[5]

These esteemed scientists were wrong. After some four decades of effort, John Harrison, an English carpenter and self-educated clockmaker, finally succeeded in creating a precise clock that sailors could bring on board with them. Rather than rely on astronomy, his instrument, called the H4, mustered a novel understanding of material science and mechanics.[6] Previously the motion of the ship had been the key challenge, making clocks imprecise at sea. The H4 ticks five times a second, much more rapidly than a typical watch, and with larger oscillations. This balances the instrument, providing accurate time at sea that enables the captain of a ship to identify its longitude.[7] By 1773, Harrison had received more than £23,000 from Parliament, some $2,000,000 in today's money, for his work on chronometers.[8] His device caught on. Captain Cook famously used copies of his design, and Fletcher Christian took one of these devices from Lieutenant William Bligh after the infamous mutiny on the HMS *Bounty*. Other tinkerers improved on Harrison's device, primarily to reduce its price. By the early nineteenth century it had become unthinkable to go to sea without a chronometer.[9]

You might wonder what Harrison's invention could possibly have to do with corporate strategy-making. The answer is everything. Leading-edge companies are using the same basic crowdsourcing technique the British Crown deployed to generate new strategic insights, updating it with digital technologies. They are tapping the wisdom of the crowd to turn up solutions and opportunities that experts can't see using conventional, closed ideation techniques. Quite often, they're arriving at disruptive strategies that are the envy of their peers.

In October 2007 the US-based networking hardware company Cisco Systems launched I-Prize, a global competition to help the company generate its next billion-dollar business. An early adopter of open strategy, Cisco had previously dabbled in crowdsourcing, establishing an internal wiki that allowed any of its 65,000 employees to submit business ideas, collaborate with their colleagues, and participate in the launching of a new business. Although the wiki had benefited the company, the ideas it generated weren't all that mind-blowing.[10] As Guido Jouret, Cisco's chief technology officer, related, that's because the company hadn't been able to break free of certain blind spots. In particular, leaders operated with an expert's bias and didn't know what they didn't know. "We have a highly technologically savvy view of the world but we don't always understand how to address market needs or what we might be missing," Jouret said.[11]

The company designed I-Prize to help it break free of existing assumptions and mindsets and broaden its own sense of what was possible.[12] "I-Prize is unique because it is an external competition," Jouret explaining the project said that Cisco was interested in this idea contest "as a way to find ideas from people who have unique technology and market insights but do not have the traditional connections to Cisco or venture capital."[13] Anyone in the world could participate in I-Prize, submitting new business proposals within a few key parameters: the strategic ideas submitted had to hold the potential to spawn a billion-dollar business, they had to conform to the company's strategy, and they had to leverage the company's leadership position in internet technology.

All told, 2,500 participants worldwide contributed, competing for a $250,000 prize and a commitment on the company's part to spend $10 million funding the winning idea.[14] A German team claimed the big prize, presenting a business plan that called on the company to develop a sensor-enabled smart electricity grid based on its Internet Protocol (IP) technology. Combining technology and business model innovation, the proposal was, Jouret said, "an endeavor with long-term prospects that will certainly stretch us" but that also matched the company's "strategy and competencies."[15] Participants perceived the prize as a tremendous opportunity to gain business experience. As a member of the winning team reflected, "The Cisco I-Prize contest gave us a platform to build out our idea, develop an executable business and technology plan, and receive valuable feedback from respected innovators and industry leaders. The experience has been invaluable."[16]

Many companies have turned to contests and other forms of crowdsourcing in recent years to generate new ideas.[17] One established and successful platform, Innocentive, convenes nearly 400,000 problem solvers from almost two hundred countries.[18] Another, Kaggle, hosts more than one million technical experts who have tackled problems in an array of scientific and social-scientific fields.[19] As impressive as this activity is, most of it has been confined to narrow tasks such as generating new product ideas or solving technical problems. Relatively few companies have thought to deploy crowdsourcing for that most important and highly guarded of functions, the generation of potential strategies.

This is a shame, because crowdsourcing holds immense potential in this area. As the case of Cisco suggests, crowdsourcing taps the knowledge and ideas of people who are *not* experts in the area of inquiry at hand. As discussed in chapter 2, experts, industry specialists, and professionals in a given field tend to think similarly, thanks to the education, formal training, and work experience they have in common.[20] Ask them to come up with strategic ideas and they'll deliver many good ones but few that are jaw-dropping, game-changing, or industry-making.[21] Crowdsourcing allows companies to access far more diversity in both talent and ideas (and to cross-fertilize ideas across domains), increasing the odds that they'll arrive at a highly creative solution that defies conventional wisdom. Studying hundreds of crowdsourcing contests, Lars Bo Jeppesen of the Copenhagen Business School and Harvard Business School's Karim Lakhani found that "The provision of a winning solution was positively related to increasing distance between the solv-er's field of technical expertise and the focal field of the problem."[22]

Crowdsourcing also boosts the generation of strategic ideas by gener-ating larger numbers of ideas. As Lakhani has noted, the quality of inno-vative ideas follows a bell curve.[23] A typical brainstorming exercise will yield numerous average ideas, a few really awful ones, a few decent ones, and just a couple that knock it out of the park. When it comes to strat-egy (or anything else), those positive outliers are what companies seek. The bigger the sample of ideas, the greater the odds that companies will find them. Hamel and Zanini argue: "Since game-changing busi-ness ideas are rare, the probability of coming up with a breakthrough strategy depend on the organization's capacity to generate a large num-ber of strategic options. The problem with a top-down process is that there aren't enough brains at the top to do this."[24] Crowdsourcing can yield many more ideas compared with a traditional strategy-formation exercise involving a small group of senior leaders in a boardroom. The average quality of the ideas won't be as great as it would be if you were consulting solely experts, but you'll have more diversity and a greater likelihood of getting extreme ideas, both positive and negative.[25] As one group of scholars notes, "When tackling problems where solutions lie outside normal fields of inquiry, generating a large number of diverse responses can be a powerful weapon."[26]

Early adopters such as Cisco Systems have generally turned to two basic forms of crowdsourcing for strategic ideation, online contests and communities. As the name suggests, contests are competitions in which the company poses a problem and awards a prize to those who deliver the best solutions. Communities, by contrast, are online platforms intended to host discussions on particular strategy-related issues. Both contests and communities allow companies to easily engage large numbers of people with diverse perspectives and backgrounds, helping companies to answer questions about which markets they should target, which technologies they should use to engage with customers, which disruptions loom on the horizon, and more. While senior leaders might not necessarily feel excited about debating new strategies (particularly if those strategies threaten existing businesses), crowdsourcing tends to yield highly motivated participants since they actively choose to become involved (see chapter 3). Let's examine contents and communities in some detail, unpacking how and when these open strategy tactics are useful and how you might best deploy them in your company.

Online Open Strategy Contests

Contests typically prove most productive for companies when the strategic challenges leaders seek to address are complex or novel, when established best-practice approaches don't exist, and when companies don't know which precise combinations of skills or areas of expertise are needed to succeed.[27] In such cases, companies should experiment broadly, and they benefit from tapping as much diversity as possible during the idea generation process. Contents help them access that diversity, functioning as "competitive markets" of ideas.[28]

Although contests are simple and straightforward constructs, companies should design them carefully to maximize their odds for success. Drawing on research and our work with companies, we've identified five key steps that merit attention (see figure 5.1).[29]

Frame the problem

Companies have tended to deploy crowdsourcing to solve problems that are narrow and specific. Some have argued that "crowdsourcing may only be useful when the task given to the crowd is of a modular, self-contained, closed solution type."[30] Although strategic challenges tend to be among the broadest that leaders face, companies do well to define challenges in open strategy contests as cleanly and as precisely as possible. The more specific and detailed a problem is, the more accessible it becomes to a broad audience and the more likely it will be to attract participants and generate useful solutions.

There's a balance to strike here. Humans tend to operate with a "functional fixedness" bias; they struggle to find new purposes for a tool that

Figure 5.1
Organizing an open strategy online contest.

deviate from its original intended use.[31] In a classic psychology experiment, researchers instructed participants to attach a burning candle on a wall. That sounds simple enough, but get this: participants could only use a box of matches, thumbtacks, and, of course, the candle. And the candle couldn't drip on the table below. The vast majority of participants couldn't do it—they tried to use the tacks to attach the candle directly to the wall. Only a few participants realized that they could make creative use of the box that the thumbtacks came in, not just the tacks themselves. By using the tacks to fix the box to the wall, they could create a nifty little candleholder. Problem solved.[32]

Designers of open strategy contests must take this cognitive limitation into account. The more precisely you frame a problem, the more assumptions you impose concerning the nature of the problem and the solution you expect.[33] Go too far, and participants' thinking becomes unhelpfully constrained. The solution is to define the problem precisely but give participants enough latitude to think expansively. In initiating the I-Prize, Cisco announced that it was searching for commercially viable network technology business ideas. The company did not specify further which types of ideas it sought but clearly defined what an idea should offer: "Judges will consider both the technology innovation as well as the business opportunity behind the idea. Ideas should have the potential to bring in at least $1 billion revenue to Cisco over a five- to seven-year period, and submissions must use the IP network as a platform."[34]

Establish the Prize

Rob McEwen had a problem. Goldcorp Inc., the company he led as chairman and CEO, had a fifty-year-old mine in Red Lake, Ontario, that, frankly speaking, seemed to be a bottomless pit. Nearby prospects were doing fine, but as much as they tried, Goldcorp's engineers just couldn't strike gold at Red Lake. So McEwen decided to do something his industry peers found downright crazy. He took top-secret data Goldcorp had accumulated about the Red Lake mine and put it online for the world to see. Not just a little data, mind you: all the information the company had accumulated since 1948.[35] McEwen let it be known that whoever could present the best methods for finding gold in Red Lake would receive a prize of $575,000. More than 1,400 engineers, geologists, and scientists from around the world downloaded the data. Submissions flooded in, with participants identifying 110 potential sites for drilling, 50 percent of them previously unknown to Goldcorp. Thanks to these submissions, the company found eight million ounces of gold.

In this case, it wasn't the prospect of gold, figuratively speaking, that motivated people from around the world to participate. For the winning team, a collaboration between Fractal Graphics (a company building 3D models of mines) and Taylor Wall & Associates (an accounting firm), the prize money barely covered the costs of participating. What the contest did offer was publicity, which to these companies was quite valuable indeed. As Fractal Graphics' founder Nick Archibald put it: "It would have taken us years to get the recognition in North America that this project gave us overnight."[36] The challenge had demonstrated to the mining industry that there was a new way of doing exploration.

In designing an open strategy contest, determine your prizes based on a careful assessment of participants' motivations. Money often doesn't matter so much. If you aim your contest at internal participants, you might bypass cash prizes entirely. The internal wiki that preceded Cisco's I-Prize contest didn't offer monetary compensation for winning teams since leaders feared that financial rewards would distract workers from their daily work and foster an unhelpful spirit of competitiveness.[37] Instead, the company enticed participants with the prospect of joining the internal team that would eventually develop the winning solution. For employees, the chance to escape the daily grind, claim the limelight, and see their idea come to life was tremendously exciting, and motivation enough to participate.

Develop the Platform

Companies need not expend much energy or effort actually running an open strategy contest. Providers such as Hyve, Innocentive, and Kaggle (a subsidiary of Google) specialize in designing and hosting the crowdsourcing of these events, and you would do well to draw on their expertise to make it easy for participants to register and present ideas. A key question you'll want to answer is the one Cisco faced in deciding on an incentive: How much competition do you seek to foster? As we've found, designing contests to instill a mixture of competition and collaboration usually produces the best results. We call it "communition": allowing participants to collaborate by commenting on one another's ideas and sharing knowledge, while also dangling a prize to spur competition and make life interesting.[38]

In its I-Prize contest, Cisco used a platform that allowed participants to sign up, contribute their thinking, view other submissions, and comment and vote on them.[39] After its initial experience running I-Prize, Cisco opted to grant a global pool of innovative thinkers, entrepreneurs, students, and inventors access to a wider array of digital communication and interaction tools that would let them collaborate across boundaries more effectively.[40] These tools included a video community that allowed participants to create videos and share them with others, who in turn could comment on them and rate the quality of their contents. By including functions that transcribed speech, these tools also allowed users to more easily search for and view videos. Participants could connect freely with experts and conduct web conferencing. Most intriguingly, Cisco created an idea market, allowing participants to use virtual currency to buy and sell ideas, thus allowing them and the company to peg their value[41].

In developing a contest platform, you'll also need to address important questions related to intellectual property.[42] Who owns what? Under what circumstances? What if someone submits an idea that belongs to someone else, or one that your company is already working on? In handling these and other questions, make sure not to discourage participants with too many restrictions. In running I-Prize, Cisco asked participants to pledge that ideas they submitted were their own. Only the winner would cede commercial rights to Cisco, receiving in exchange the $250,000 prize. All others were free to take their ideas elsewhere and commercialize them.

Select the Participants

We touched on this question in chapters 3 and 4, but let's revisit it specifically as it pertains to contests. In deciding whom to invite, consider your goals. Do you primarily seek access to external views and fresh perspectives? If so, then you'll want to open the contest to the largest possible group of participants, subject to any secrecy concerns you might have.[43] On the other hand, you might also choose to run a contest as a way to energize employees, give them a voice, and tap into their wisdom and creativity. In that case, there might be little need to include people from outside the organization.

Select the Winning Idea

Be fair and transparent when choosing a winner; otherwise you risk frustrating participants. Since some ideas submitted by participants might be only partially formed, you will probably want to include some kind of filtering mechanism as part of the selection process. In Cisco's case, six evaluators worked full-time for three months to select the I-Prize winner. To avoid any "expert bias" on the evaluators' part, the company also considered comments and votes of idea contributors in evaluating submissions. In appraising each submission, Cisco posed five questions: Does the idea solve a real challenge customers face? Is the market for the potential product or service large enough? Is the timing right for such an offering? Is Cisco well positioned to pursue this idea? Does the idea represent a long-term opportunity, or will the market quickly commoditize it? Applying these questions, Cisco arrived at forty semifinalists.[44] To each, the company assigned a mentor who would help the contributor refine their ideas and eliminate weaknesses.

In the next round, the company selected ten ideas, inviting contributors to present them before a judging panel that included Silicon Valley entrepreneur Geoffrey Moore. From these ten, the company selected a final winner. Cisco's Guido Jouret regarded the project as a success. Not only did the company uncover many new business opportunities, it validated certain investment decisions Cisco had already taken, and it revealed that in some respects outsiders saw much more business potential for the firm than Cisco did itself. "As a company," Jouret said, "we learned that if you ask, you can reach a worldwide audience of smart, passionate people eager to help you drive innovation."[45]

Strategy Communities

> 9 month old dd killing me by not sleeping. . . . I hate my life, soon DP and I will split up over this, god knows how I can hold on to my job. I feel sick during the day and my anxiety in the evening and at night is crippling. She has 1 nap during the day and that is it. How the fuck do people manage???? It will pass, but it will kill me first!! [Toastiemaker]

> Will she sleep in a bouncer or swing safely? Being upright might help with the reflux. Another option rather than medication is thick formula if you haven't tried it—Aptimel do it but I think it needs to be prescribed. [GrumpyHoonMain]

> I did co-sleeping with mine, would not have managed otherwise. Good luck, hope you find a solution soon x. [BrooHaHa][46]

Overstretched executives might battle sleep deprivation issues, but they have nothing on the parents of young children. Fortunately, for British parents at least, there's Mumsnet.com. If you have a question about sleep training or anything else parent-related, you can either find a discussion thread on Mumsnet to join or start one yourself. A mom named Justine Roberts started this versatile forum after suffering through a disastrous first family holiday with her year-old twins. She wasn't the only one looking for advice. Mumsnet.com today counts about ten million unique users per month.[47]

Mumsnet.com exemplifies a much broader cultural and technological phenomenon. One in five Americans use internet forums to discuss and recommend products.[48] What if we took the online forum and applied it to strategy formation? Some companies are doing it. Whereas the contests discussed above are all organized around a specific problem, task, or challenge, strategy communities are groups of people convened, usually on a voluntary basis, to work collectively and on an ongoing basis. Most people participating in online communities do so in relatively passive ways, while a small core of users do so actively.[49] Sometimes members of communities organize themselves, but companies can also initiate, sponsor, or host communities by providing spaces and platforms.[50] They can also request specific, strategy-related information. While most of these communities exist online, offline can work too.

Digital strategy communities, which primarily involve internal participants, are usually built around members who share a common deep interest in a topic.[51] Participants come together online to discuss and share knowledge and content about a topic or issue, exchanging experiences and point of views, building interpersonal relationships, and establishing norms and social structures. A true sense of membership and belonging can develop, as well as emotional attachment to the group, even though it is only convening online.[52] These communities use media-rich collaboration tools that allow knowledge sharing, evaluation, discussion, criticism, and adaptation of others' ideas. With these tools, participants don't have to convene at the same time or in the same physical location.[53]

Strategy communities are powerful because they allow companies to integrate skills and knowledge that transcend any one individual's perspective; as scholars have observed, they aggregate "a large number of diverse contributions into a value-creating whole."[54] For this reason, companies will usually choose communities over contests as an open strategy approach when the enterprise requires accumulated knowledge to solve its strategic challenge—in other words, when any solution will need to build on previous advances the company has made.[55]

But communities afford a number of other benefits beyond the ideas they generate. Because of the fellow feeling they generate, communities can give employees and other stakeholders a feeling of empowerment, energizing and emboldening them.[56] They allow companies to tap hidden, hard-to-access "reservoirs of information" that exist inside organizations.[57] They foster mutual understanding inside the organization, which can engender more commitment to the strategy. They help break down silos, allowing employees across the organization to forge helpful relationships. And they allow leaders to identify promising young talent—employees who are engaged, who understand key problems facing the company, who can produce innovative ideas, and who can influence others to adopt them.

To understand the potential communities might hold for your company, consider the experience of the Swedish multinational telecommunications company Ericsson. Like most industries, Ericsson's has undergone tremendous disruption in recent years. With software-driven and cloud-based delivery infrastructures becoming popular, traditional suppliers like Ericsson have seen their markets shrinking. Ericsson has been slower than its peers to embrace new offerings. To lead in a disruptive environment, companies need to predict and identify future trends, opportunities, and developments early in order to craft and execute a successful strategy. Here Ericsson has struggled. In 2017 the company reported a net loss of $4.4 billion and a year-over-year sales drop of 10 percent.[58]

To improve the company's ability to see the future, Heraldo Sales-Cavalcante, Ericsson's director of strategic analysis, has been seeking new ways to facilitate experimentation and learning among employees. Observing that traditional initiatives such as training courses and communities of practice didn't really spur new thinking, Sales-Cavalcante initiated an online community called Strategy Perspectives that was open to all employees regardless of rank.[59] All participants had to do was provide some explanation of why they were interested in participating and what they hoped to gain, and they were in. "We wanted to empower the employees to get more active instead of just producing more PowerPoints," Sales-Cavalcante said.[60] He also wanted to open the way for people with a variety of skills and experiences to participate in business planning, creating a stream of discourse that would influence Ericsson's formal strategy-making process.

By 2018, Strategy Perspectives counted more than two thousand registered members representing a variety of functions and backgrounds. It yielded a rich, high-quality discourse that touched not just on Ericsson's formal business strategy but on technology-related trends, culture, and management practices. "People basically write entire, comprehensive and sophisticated articles, reports, and white papers," Sales-Cavalcante related. "This way the community became very active and very engaged in the key strategic questions of the future—always a little bit ahead of the curve. . . . I think in the community we have become really good in seeing insights before anybody else." Many contributions came from lower-level employees, and some were quite provocative. "The Strategy Perspective community is unique and successful because of its grass roots," Sales-Cavalcante said, "because it is provocative, because it is really intriguing stuff, because it is not more of the same."

Sales-Cavalcante acknowledged that the company couldn't easily measure Strategy Perspectives' benefits. Still, it seemed clear that the community had served its purpose of rendering Ericsson more forward-leaning in its strategies. As early as 2014–2015, community members were speaking up about the future importance of digital services, generating papers on the subject that prompted the company to devise a plan for a digital business transformation. In 2016, Ericsson announced major strategic shifts and restructuring to capitalize on digital market opportunities, focusing primarily on network, digital support solutions/ the cloud, and the Internet of Things (IoT). The company planned to emphasize digital services and cloud-based and virtualized network infrastructure. This strategic shift from a systems integrator approach to a platform-and-solutions-led approach in IoT should enable Ericsson to exploit new market potential and capitalize on digital market opportunities. The strategy already seems to be paying off. In 2018, Ericsson swung back to a modest operating profit and sales growth for the first time since 2014.

Participants in the community also advocated early on for artificial intelligence and automation, perceiving their potential to transform the industry. As of 2020, Ericsson was pioneering an automated network infrastructure built around an array of experimental machine learning and predictive intelligence algorithms.[61] Further, the company had established itself as a leader in network functions virtualization and orchestration.[62] As the company's head of automation told Sales-Cavalcante, Ericsson never would have initiated efforts in this area without the community's input.[63] Sales-Cavalcante concurred, observing, "Three or four years ago, you can even see the moment where we were discussing automation on the community and writing papers about the need to do this and now you see the results. . . . New departments were created, new processes. . . . It was through papers, through the engagement of people."

Going forward, Ericsson would benefit even more if it integrated insights generated by the community more fully into its formal strategy process. "They are really two parallel worlds, as it is today," Sales-Cavalcante said, and the flow of insights was slower as a result than it might otherwise be. Still, the community was serving the company well as a means of overcoming the bias and groupthink that often dominate traditional, formal strategy work. As Sales-Cavalcante saw it, Ericsson discovered and exploited a major trend that it would have missed using its traditional planning process, which made the effort required to set up and run the community worthwhile.

Build a Strategy Community That Works

To succeed with strategy communities, companies should take three key steps (see figure 5.2). First, *companies should establish a common interest or focal point*, usually one that gets to the core of what a company is or does. Ericsson organized its online community around the future of its industry, with a particular eye on evolving technology. The focus engaged participants, leading them to discuss AI solutions early on and then lead the industry in adopting them. Clarity about a topic fosters a sense of connectedness, attachment, and shared meaning among participants. Communities formed around burning challenges will usually galvanize people to participate. For car manufacturers, that might be a forum on mobility; for the travel industry in 2020, that would certainly have been the COVID-19 crisis and how to navigate it. But you don't need to focus communities so narrowly. If you define a wider scope, you open the way for participants to form vibrant subcommunities. Mumsnet.com doesn't impose specific topics on its members. Still, everyone knows that this isn't the place to discuss, say, cars or video games (unless, that is, you're talking about how to regulate kids' use of them!).

Second, *companies should utilize a powerful platform to host the community*. Digital platforms for strategy communities must meet two criteria.

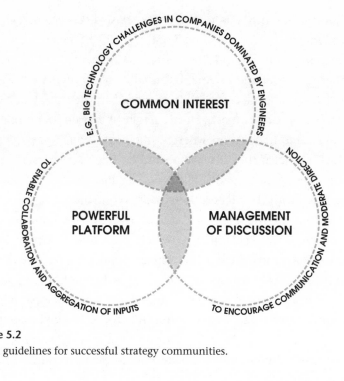

Figure 5.2
Three guidelines for successful strategy communities.

First, they must make it easy to share, evaluate, challenge, and adapt ideas. And second, they must include built-in analytical capabilities. If your community succeeds, you will potentially see thousands of contributions, most of which take the form of qualitative data. To make the most of these contributions, you need some way of tracking conversations and aggregating the knowledge that members contribute. Typical mechanisms include qualitative voting, participation scores, and formal reports based on contributions.

One mistake firms make in this area is to let participants themselves rate the quality of ideas. Reto Hofstetter and his team checked in with managers about a year after their companies ran crowdsourced idea contests online. They asked managers to rate 361 randomly ordered ideas originally evaluated by the crowd in their respective contests. For each idea, researchers wanted to know the following: Did managers find it useful to implement? Did it have an impact on the success of an innovation at their companies? As it turned out, no correlation existed between participants' votes and managers' own assessment of the quality of the ideas.[64]

Other research has found that contest participants tend to propose ideas that are novel and original but aren't necessarily very feasible.[65] For companies, of course, feasibility matters.[66] In their study of eighty-seven crowdsourcing contests, Hofstetter and his team found that participants tend to trade favors when rating ideas. If a fellow participant votes for their idea, they'll make a similar gesture. That might foster cordiality among participants, but it doesn't help moderators identify the best ideas with the highest potential.[67] While most of these studies looked at contests, the same logic applies to strategy communities.

Third, *companies should manage strategy communities actively*, implementing mechanisms to encourage ongoing participation. Active moderation is important. With larger groups of participants, conversations can easily stray beyond the designated topic. And once participants raise issues or topics, organizers often can't ignore or avoid them without losing credibility and causing frustration. If moderators aren't careful, they can lose control of a crowdsourcing effort, leading to subpar results or even failure.

In 2010 an Austrian automation supplier, a leader in wind automation, instituted "Dialogue Days," an initiative that crowdsourced strategic ideas among employees by means of an intranet forum platform.[68] During a two-week period, the company invited all of its 370 employees, as well as those based in the company's four distant subsidiaries, to submit ideas and discuss a series of strategic topics. More than two hundred employees registered on the platform, submitting over 1,300 comments.[69] Mapping these postings onto a hierarchy, moderators computed an "impact factor" that conveyed the resonance of particular discussion threads.[70] Popular threads had to do with particular technologies, the need to increase customer focus—and the quality of the food in the company's cafeteria. No, there's nothing like lunch to get people going. But how relevant was that to the company's strategy? Not very. Still, because management had engaged employees in a highly charged debate, it couldn't easily ignore this topic.

Keep conversations vibrant by posing frequent questions to the community, actively soliciting input, and monitoring for any inappropriate or unhelpful contributions. Don't wait for participants to submit ideas: jump in and post ideas yourself, inviting participants to discuss them. Not only will you alert participants to desired topics of conversation, you'll also spark their own desire to engage. You should also establish clear rules and norms from the beginning, barring certain topics or behaviors. Bear in mind, you don't want to go too far in restricting participants' contributions. When you bar the expression of unexpected views or those that might conflict with leaders' opinions, participants can become frustrated and the company might not obtain the creative contributions it desires. As one group of researchers reminds us, "Empowering creative, independent individuals implies indeterminate and uncertain reactions and creations in support of, or in opposition to, management's original thinking."[71]

We've emphasized the differences between contests and communities, but in practice, companies usually merge the two, combining the competitive nature of contests with the collaboration of a community— again, what we've termed "communitition."[72] Participants battle for prizes, but they *also* behave in ways that build community, by collaborating, agreeing to common norms, forging friendships, and so on.[73] At the German industrial conglomerate Siemens, the company's chief sustainability officer invited employees to participate in a company-wide online crowdsourcing initiative. The goal was to spawn ideas that would help the company create value in the years to come. Siemens framed the initiative as a challenge and opened it to all Siemens employees, laying out guidelines for desired ideas. At the end of two months, a pair of board members selected the winning propositions. While the company didn't award any monetary prizes, senior managers did provide funding and resources to develop the winning submissions.[74]

As competitive as the platform was, it also functioned in large part as a community. More than three thousand members registered, not merely submitting hundreds of ideas but also posting over 2,500 comments on ideas posted by others. In this way, participants could interact with others, build relationships, and develop a shared sense of community. As an academic study found, this joint sense of community led to greater commitment on the part of participants and made it easier for the company to implement its strategies later on.[75]

In Sum

The marine chronometer is still with us, and so is the crowdsourcing technique used to spur its invention. Leading-edge companies today are using online contests and communities not just to generate new inventions and ideas for marketing campaigns but to spark insights that will fuel their next brilliant business strategy. Companies are finding that although they might be able to generate these ideas themselves, opening up this part of strategy-making increases the diversity of participants, thereby boosting the odds of coming across an outlandish yet eminently promising idea that nobody else has thought of. Try fielding a contest when you're facing a complex or novel strategic challenge, when best practices don't exist, and when you don't know what kind of skills or expertise you'll need. When you need accumulated knowledge to solve a strategic challenge, convene a community and have participants churn over ideas for a period of time.

Contests and communities are powerful tools companies can use for general ideation related to strategy. Part of the work of generating strategic ideas is the more specific task of peering into the future and pondering what it might hold for a company and its industry. In the past, companies charged their executive teams with trying to predict the future. They consulted academics and gurus of one sort of another. Open strategy has a powerful tool that can give companies access to a much broader range of thinking about the future. Companies still won't be able to know exactly what the future holds, but they'll have a better sense of the next great disruption on the horizon and be able to generate far better strategies as a result.

Questions to Ponder:

- How competitive are your employees? Do you think a strategy contest would energize them, or would they more likely participate in a more cooperative setting such as a strategy community?

- Do you have hidden reservoirs of information inside your organization that strategy communities might help you tap?

- If your company has employed crowdsourcing in the past for other functions, why hasn't it applied that approach to strategy?

- If you're contemplating a contest or strategy community, do you have sufficient resources (financial and personnel) available to appropriately manage and moderate it?

6 Peer into the Future

In his book, *Sensemaking in Organizations*, the organizational theorist Karl Weick recounts a brief but striking story about a military squadron lost in the Swiss Alps. Conditions were brutal: heavy snow, frigid cold. Back at the base, the officer in charge of the men became worried—there was no sign of the men. The next day, thank goodness, the men returned. When the officer inquired what had happened, the men confirmed they'd been lost and feared for their lives. As it happened, though, one of their group had found a map in his possession. "That calmed us down," the soldiers said, per Weick's account. "We pitched camp, lasted out the snowstorm, and then with the map we discovered our bearings. And here we are." This story made sense—until the officer got his hands on the map. "He discovered to his astonishment that it was not a map of the Alps, but a map of the Pyrenees."[1]

How could this be?

As Weick relates, maps need not tell us precisely where to go in order to help us when we're lost. They can also serve a psychological function. If the soldiers hadn't had that map, they might have abandoned all hope and sheltered in place. Or conflict might have erupted, and they might have split up. By helping the soldiers stay calm and united, the map kept them in the game, putting them in a position to eventually find their way back on their own.

In business, strategic plans function much as maps do. Almost by definition, strategic plans will be wrong; humans can't know the future with perfect accuracy. But that doesn't matter. Like maps, Weick writes, strategic plans "animate and orient people. Once people begin to act, they generate tangible outcomes . . . , and this helps them discover . . . what is occurring, what needs to be explained . . . , and what should be done next."

If strategic plans are to animate and orient us, they must lay out an expansive view of the future, one that everyone can believe in and that is as realistic as possible. Traditionally an executive team at a company might have generated such a vision on their own. Leaders were expected to sit in a room, peer at reports or PowerPoint slides, and brainstorm. Or they'd expend vast budgetary sums in hiring a management consultant to do something similar. Today, leading-edge companies are taking a different approach.

Take Gallus, the Swiss high-tech manufacturing company we discussed in chapter 3. By bringing in outsiders, the company was able to respond successfully to Hewlett-Packard's entry into the B2B digital printing market, launching a new, disruptive printing offering in 2018 called Smartfire, with plans to launch a digital platform two years later on which the company could market printing services (they wound up postponing this second offering because of the COVID-19 pandemic). Easy to operate and sold at a fraction of Gallus's other printers, Smartfire targeted the lower-end customers that Hewlett-Packard sought to pick off.

Gallus's development of this strategic response, using an element of open strategy, was only part of the story. The seeds of this strategy were planted in 2013, when Gallus convened thirty-five external participants from different industries and backgrounds to help Gallus managers analyze future trends affecting their industry. Considering five topical areas (technologies and materials; customers, markets, and the competition; macroeconomic trends and geopolitics; suppliers and the value chain; and regulation and the environment), the group arrived at forty-two possible trends, analyzing them for how important and likely they were to materialize. These trends were quite technical in nature, including entries like "direct printing on bottles will make shrink sleeves obsolete" or "improvement of digital technologies, ink and print heads will substitute analog label printing." Compiling these trends cumulatively, Gallus's managers created a visualization of key strategic priorities that we call the "IMP Trend Radar" (see figure 6.1).

CHANCES TO REALIZE NOVEL STRATEGIC IDEAS

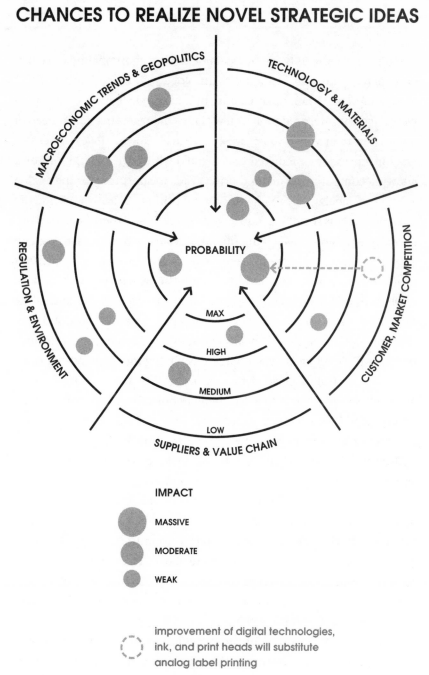

Figure 6.1
Gallus IMP Trend Radar exercise, ca. 2013–2016.

Going into the IMP Trend Radar exercise, most incumbents had downplayed the role of digital technologies and were suspicious of early adopters. Others, like Gallus, had avoided digital because they were largely unprepared for it. A few Gallus managers had taken heed of digital, but their voices went largely unheard. During the exercise, several outside experts predicted that digital technologies would improve, allowing computerized ink and print heads to substitute for the analog printing of labels. "The market for digital printers is growing, while the analog market is shrinking," observed one of these experts. Gallus managers were dubious, perceiving digital as a minor trend or passing fad. The external participants insisted, with one even furnishing pictures of the first digital print solutions during the workshop. "Others have made substantial progress. They are far ahead. Here is the proof," he said. That input was effective. The group put "improvement of digital technologies, ink and print heads will substitute analog label printing" on the IMP Trend Radar, classifying it as having moderate relevance.

Leaders at Gallus decided to repeat the IMP Trend Radar exercise annually, sensing that it afforded them an objective view of future challenges, as well as a holistic understanding of industry dynamics. They charged a Gallus manager with keeping tabs on the five topical areas, constantly reevaluating the trends and looking out for new ones. This sensitivity to trends paid off. Gallus's top managers began to pay close attention to the IMP Trend Radar. Within a few years, they spotted a greater increase in digital printing than they had originally anticipated, and by 2016 they had elevated digital printing to the highest level of relevance on their radar scan and were acting accordingly. Alerted by the IMP Trend Radar, the company accomplished what so many incumbents couldn't: they cued into weak signals, took swift and timely action, and got ahead of disruptive change.

To navigate in a volatile, uncertain, complex, and ambiguous world, companies must constantly scan the horizon, identifying and interpreting any changes and seizing opportunities. With the IMP Trend Radar exercise, they're not relying on one super-smart forecast for insight. Rather, a more precise picture of the future emerges as they compile a number of somewhat less precise forecasts. Drawing on the wisdom of the crowd, the IMP Trend Radar process allows you to derive a holistic, shared understanding of emerging developments that can lead to exciting new business models. From there you can further develop your strategy using open strategy techniques, identifying "nightmare competitors" for your company, and crafting a business logic—subjects we cover in later chapters. Even if no strategy can fully anticipate the future, inviting outsiders into the boardroom to participate in a structured discussion of potential trends and opportunities can render you far more prescient as an organization than you might think—with the innovative business plans to prove it.

Experts Aren't Clairvoyants

You might wonder why Gallus's leaders needed to bring in outsiders while performing the IMP Trend Radar exercise. Why couldn't they have brainstormed trends themselves, ranked them, and developed a vision for the future? They certainly could have, but they wouldn't have cued in nearly as early to the disruptive threat that digital technology posed. In general, insiders can't imagine the future as well as a mixed group of insiders and outsiders can—not because they have too little expertise or knowledge about their business but because they have too *much* of it.

Deep expertise in a given business, industry, or field is vital when making strategic decisions, but it can backfire when trying to conjure the future. In the summer of 1956, a group of renowned scientists gathered at Dartmouth College in Hanover, New Hampshire, to develop ideas about machines that simulated human intelligence. The conference gave birth to the discipline of artificial intelligence, spurring an initial burst of research. In 1965, Nobel laureate Herbert A. Simon bullishly predicted that "machines will be capable, within 20 years, of doing any work a man can do."[2] Marvin Minsky, a cognitive scientist and early pioneer of AI research, was equally ebullient: "In from three to eight years we will have a machine with the general intelligence of an average human being."[3]

Decades later, AI can exceed human capabilities in specific areas, but we're still awaiting a machine that is generally as intelligent as an average human. And all those highly publicized advances that have been made in machine learning have occurred only in the past decade. On balance, the dream of "superintelligent" machines that can think as well as humans can or even outdo them "has been receding at a rate of one year per year," as Nick Bostrom observes in his book *Superintelligence*.[4] Futurists forecasting the dawning of artificial general intelligence still place intelligent machines several decades into the future.[5]

History would suggest caution when predicting the future, replete as it is with false, overly optimistic prognostications on the part of experts. In a 1911 interview Thomas Alva Edison, inventor of the light bulb, painted a wondrous portrait of life in our present times: "The baby of the 21st century will be rocked in a steel cradle; his father will sit in a steel chair at a steel dining table, and his mother's boudoir will be sumptuously equipped with steel furnishings, converted by cunning varnishes to the semblance of rosewood, or mahogany, or any other wood her ladyship fancies."[6] We don't know about your kids, but ours haven't had the pleasure of rocking in steel cradles, nor does steel figure prominently in any of our homes. Or consider what Steve Ballmer, CEO of Microsoft, said about the iPhone in 2007: "There's no chance that the iPhone is going to get any significant market share. No chance." During an interview with CNBC he laughed at the iPhone: "Five hundred dollars? Fully subsidized? With a plan? I said that is the most expensive phone in the world. And it doesn't appeal to business customers because it doesn't have a keyboard. Which makes it not a very good email machine."[7]

Certainly, experts have proven prescient at times: Edison predicted that steam locomotives would go the way of the dodo bird, while in 1926 Nikola Tesla predicted the advent of wireless communication. But in general, experts have a track record that is unimpressive at best. A researcher at the International Monetary Fund, Prakash Loungani, found that professional economists have consistently failed to predict recessions. In fact, as an article in the *Guardian* noted, "The record of failure to predict recessions is virtually unblemished."[8] Another researcher invited 284 experts who earned their keep "commenting or offering advice on political and economic trends" and solicited their forecasts in their specialized fields.[9] These experts generated 82,361 forecasts, many of which were outright embarrassing. When the specialists were convinced that something was fully or almost impossible, that future event occurred 15 percent of the time. When they professed to being absolutely sure about a future event, it didn't occur in more than a quarter of cases. Overall, when given a set of three future scenarios, experts were less accurate at predicting the future than if someone had guessed randomly among these scenarios. As Louis Menand remarked in the *New Yorker,* "Human beings who spend their lives studying the state of the world, in other words, are poorer forecasters than dart-throwing monkeys, who would have distributed their picks evenly over the three choices."[10]

Bureaucrats are bad forecasters as well. Having studied hundreds of public infrastructure projects around the globe, Oxford University's Bent Flyvbjerg found that they almost uniformly failed to unfold as projected. A whopping 90 percent proved more expensive than initially estimated, with actual costs running 50 to 100 percent more than expected. These projects dramatically overestimated demand for infrastructure, typically by 20 to 70 percent.[11] The Berlin-Brandenburg Willy Brandt airport was supposed to open in 2012 at a cost of $1.9 billion. As of this writing, the project has cost over $8 billion and has been opened for commercial traffic October 31, 2020, a state of affairs that has Berlin residents joking that perhaps the entire city would be better off just moving to a functioning airport.[12] The Channel Tunnel between France and the UK overran construction costs by 80 percent, while demand was half what was anticipated. The Sydney Oopera House opened after a delay of ten years and a total cost more than ten times initial estimates.[13]

Why do bureaucrats (and, by implication, business leaders and other experts) get it so wrong? Bad luck plays a role, but Oxford's Flyvbjerg offers two other intriguing explanations. First, public managers often base their decisions or forecasts on "delusional optimisms rather than on a rational weighting of gains, losses, and probabilities. They overestimate benefit and underestimate costs and time. They involuntarily spin scenarios of success and overlook the potential for mistakes and miscalculations."[14] In business, such "optimism bias" is omnipresent. In the United States, only 35 percent of small businesses survive the first five years. Yet when asked about chances that a "business like yours" would survive, American entrepreneurs pegged it at 60 percent. Asked to estimate the likelihood that their own business would succeed, one-third of respondents reported that the risk of failing was zero.[15] As Columbia University's Rita McGrath has observed, people have a strong tendency to ignore signs of change and to pretend that all is well, or as George Day and Paul Schoemaker put it, "The more intelligent we are, the better we also are at rationalising away important signals of impending doom."[16]

A simple cure for optimism bias exists: adopt an outsider's perspective. Planners and forecasters run into trouble because they tend to focus unduly on the particularities when constructing future scenarios, assuming that everything will go according to plan and discounting "distributional information" (data about other possible outcomes from a wider set of similar projects). "The prevalent tendency to underweight or ignore distributional information is perhaps the major source of error in forecasting," Flyvbjerg said. "Planners should therefore make every effort to frame the forecasting problem so as to facilitate utilizing all the distributional information that is available."[17] Considering comparable data when making projections seems intuitive, but many planners don't when undertaking public works projects, nor do leaders in business contexts. By opening up strategy-making via the IMP Trend Radar exercise, leaders can bring in outside perspectives and glean insights from comparable experiences.

Flyvbjerg identifies a second culprit in forecasting disasters: strategic misrepresentation. As he has written, managers or project champions "deliberately and strategically overestimate benefits and underestimate costs in order to increase the likelihood that their projects, and not their competitions', gain approval and funding."[18] We constantly witness this in business settings. When it comes to strategy projects or decisions, self-interest leads many participants to artificially inflate the promise of projects or ideas beyond what the data warrant. This proves especially problematic when champions of projects possess more information than decision-makers do. Flyvbjerg aptly characterizes this dynamic as "survival of the unfittest": the more project champions underestimate costs and overestimate benefits, the more likely they are to win approval for their projects.

To protect against strategic misrepresentations in public infrastructure projects, Flyvbjerg advocates for more openness. Leaders can subject forecasts and business cases to independent peer review, organize public hearings to allow stakeholders or outsiders to voice criticisms, organize scientific and professional conferences at which forecasters can present and defend their projects and forecasts, and so on. As he suggests, leaders must create opportunities for outsiders to challenge the internal experts who typically champion projects, confronting them with a broader set of data bearing on the future. As we've seen, the IMP Trend Radar serves allows for precisely this sort of challenge.

Because of optimism bias and strategic misrepresentation, forecasting fails to register weak signals early enough to allow enterprises to respond without being forced to take sudden or drastic action.[19] But even when strategists discern these weak signals, they often fail to interpret them correctly; their biases prompt them to jump to the most convenient or plausible conclusion.[20] Leaders might seek, study, interpret, and remember information that confirms their assumptions (confirmation bias). They might lend too much credence to the first piece of information they receive (anchoring bias). They might interpret information in a given way because they fear loss, ignoring the prospect of gains from taking other courses of action (loss aversion bias). They might weight the opinion of an authority more heavily, independent of the content, or overestimate the extent to which others think of them as authorities (authority bias). They might spend more time discussing information all group members possess and less energy discussing information only some group members possess (shared information bias). In groups, the desire for harmony and conformity might lead to dysfunctional consensus decisions (groupthink).

These and other individual and social biases require special attention if leaders are to properly interpret signals and identify trends. As George

Day and Paul Schoemaker have argued, leaders must develop and test competing hypotheses to reveal and correct for hidden biases. Opening up the strategy-making process to multiple perspectives, including external ones, is essential. If we take "outside views" and tap into the collective wisdom of larger crowds, we can dramatically improve our ability to detect the right signals of change early enough, and we can improve our ability to respond to them. As Linus's law of software development holds, "With enough eyeballs, all bugs are shallow."

The IMP Trend Radar Process

With the limitations of conventional, "closed" forecasting in mind, let's take a closer look at the IMP Trend Radar tool that Gallus applied to such great effect. How might you implement this at your company? The process has six basic steps.

Step 1: Designate a Core Project Team

Your first move is to convene a team within your firm and assign it to drive the project and interact with outsider experts. Choose the members of this team carefully, as the project's success hinges on the knowledge they bring, their ability to think creatively, and the influence they wield within the organization. In selecting team members, pose the following questions:

- Who in my company might possess critical knowledge about one or more of the likely search fields?
- Who are the lateral thinkers in our company (those capable of thinking across disciplinary boundaries)?
- Who are the key opinion leaders in our company?
- Whom must we involve to get buy-in later from employees during the execution phase?

Although you might be tempted to draw team members from key areas of your business only, make it broader and more cross-functional. Drawing on the writings of the philosopher Isaiah Berlin, the political scientist Philip Tetlock distinguishes between two kinds of experts: those who view the world through the lens of a single grand idea (hedgehogs) and more practical-minded thinkers, who draw on a wider variety of experiences and modes of analysis in coming to conclusions (foxes). In Tetlock's view, experts of the former persuasion "[seek] to squeeze complex problems into the preferred cause-effect templates" and treat anything that doesn't fit as an "irrelevant distraction."[21] Foxes, by contrast, seek out a wealth of information about the question at hand, embracing complexity, nuance, and uncertainty.

Tetlock found in a study of political forecasts that the foxes produced more accurate predictions than the hedgehogs. And yet the hedgehogs were more confident. "They kept pushing their analyses to the limit," Tetlock said, "and as a result they were unusually confident and likelier to declare things 'impossible' or 'certain.'"[22] The foxes were tentative, using words like "maybe," "on the other hand," and "however." Make sure you have hedgehogs *and* foxes on your core team. The hedgehogs will produce cutting-edge, out-of-the-box ideas while the foxes will ensure that conclusions are still grounded in reality.

Step 2: Define the Scope

You can't track trends about everything. You need to pick and choose. The core team's first critical task is to define the search fields for the IMP Trend Radar exercise. Begin by determining the depth of your analysis, as well as the breadth and range of your search strategy. With respect to analysis, ask yourself: Do you want to study trends in a specific market segment, business unit, or at the corporate level? A IMP Trend Radar exercise at the corporate level in a diversified company is useful only if the trends are the same or very similar for all business units. Since this is rarely the case, we recommend a business-unit scope of analysis.

If significant differences exist among market segments, such as differences in geography, customer groups, technologies, or even business models, you may narrow the focus of your analysis even further. When considering range, ask yourself: What search fields will yield trends that seem most likely to have an impact on your business model? Some companies adopt one or two search fields, for example digitalization and technologies. This makes sense only if your open strategy project is also narrowly focused on these topics. But since many technological trends cannot be analyzed apart from the regulatory environment, consumer trends, and larger societal trends, a broader search is often needed to arrive at a holistic understanding. A broad roster of search fields includes market and competition, technology, consumers and society, macroeconomics and environment, political and regulatory trends, and so on.

Step 3: Pin Down the Key Dynamics

Once your team has identified key search areas to pursue during the IMP Trend Radar exercise, it must next conduct interviews with internal and external experts to understand the underlying dynamics and likely changes in each search field. To ensure that you collect as many different and competing hypotheses about the future as possible, interview a diverse group of people, posing the same questions to yourself as you did when appointing the core team. Look for experts among your stakeholders (including customers, suppliers, and even competitors), and seek them out as well in adjacent fields or in industries facing similar challenges or problems. You might also consider professional trend researchers or experts in research institutions. Some companies we've worked with have even invited science fiction writers to participate.

Bear in mind, an expert in this context isn't necessarily a narrow specialist. In their Good Judgment Project, a large-scale, multiyear prediction tournament funded by the US Intelligence Advance Research Projects Activity (IARPA), Philip Tetlock and Dan Gardner studied how proficient thousands of amateurs were in predicting future events. They compared their judgments with those of seasoned intelligence analysts, soliciting a million predictions from 25,000 forecasters answering geopolitical and economic questions such as "Will Russia officially annex additional Ukrainian territory in the next three months?," "In the next year, will any country withdraw from the euro zone?," and "How many additional countries will report cases of the Ebola virus in the next eight months?"[23] The two found that talented generalists often outperformed specialists in their predictions.[24]

In other research, Mellers and her colleagues found an association between certain character or personality traits and accuracy in prediction. The researchers identified a group of "superforecasters," individuals who "maintained high accuracy across hundreds of questions and a wide array of topics."[25] Comparing these elite analysts with others whose predictions were less consistent and reliable, the researchers found that superforecasters differed in their specific skills, cognitive attributes, and levels of motivation and commitment. Superforecasters tended to be cautious, humble, and nondeterministic (in other words, they regarded events in the world as fluid or contingent rather than preordained). They were also open-minded, intellectually curious, reflective, comfortable with numbers, pragmatic, willing to consider other views and change their minds when confronted with new facts, and aware of their biases. Finally, superforecasters had a growth mindset and were tenacious.[26] When composing the list of interviewees for your forecasts, stay alert to these traits, and take as your goal consulting as many superforecasters as possible.

You might wonder how many experts to involve. Here a bit of experimentation becomes necessary. As you interview experts, you'll reach a saturation point: you've consulted so many people that new interviews don't yield additional insights of any significance. At that point, you can comfortably stop.[27] You won't know in advance how many interviews you must conduct to reach saturation, but at least you'll recognize that point when it comes and end this part of the process. Based on our experience, we expect you will typically conduct around ten interviews per search field, split between internal and external participants (with a higher number of external participants). For example, if you have five search fields, you'll conduct fifty interviews.

Step 4: Formulate Your Hypotheses

After analyzing the interviews, your team should go on to formulate specific hypotheses about future trends. This part of the process occurs in three phases.[28] First, during what we call the "diverging" phase, team members examine each topic area from different angles. Working in smaller groups, they first review the expert interviews, then, based on these conclusions and recommendations, formulate hypotheses for the different search fields, arriving at a large number of divergent hypotheses. The groups then workshop their hypotheses with the entire team, considering any valuable feedback and incorporating it. Team members then fine-tune these hypotheses during the "evaluating" phase, deeply probing the relevant ideas and registering any new insights that emerge. They continue fine-tuning until no new hypotheses emerge. Finally, during the "converging phase" the team winnows down the initial list, arriving at an average of forty to sixty key hypotheses.

These hypotheses should be as concrete as possible and formulated to be both testable and falsifiable. Steve Ballmer's prediction that "there's no chance that the iPhone is going to get any significant market share"[29] would not qualify as a hypothesis here as it's neither specific nor falsifiable. What qualifies as a "significant market share"? Is it 10 percent of the market? 20 percent? 50 percent? And of what market? The US cell phone market? The global cell phone market? And by which date? A credible hypothesis is: "Within the next two years, fewer than ten million iPhones will be sold in the United States." At the time this would have appeared like a very ambitious projection—after all, consumers purchased fewer than 300,000 in the third quarter of 2007.[30]

Step 5: Identify Core Trends and Evaluate Preparedness

With a large set of diverse and sometimes conflicting or competing hypotheses in place, the team should then invite internal and external experts to evaluate them. You can do this in person, but it might be more convenient to use an online survey. Each expert should evaluate the hypotheses and assess how likely each is to occur and the likely extent of its impact on the industry or company, using a scale of 1 to 100. In soliciting these evaluations, the team is aiming to "cluster" or categorize the hypotheses by discerning a small group of topical trends into which they might fit.

If you study the future of mobility, for example, you could test the following hypotheses: "By 2035, mobility will fulfill completely different use cases and therefore provide new experiences, such as communication, entertainment, work, and recreation"; "By 2035, user interfaces inside vehicles will match those of personal devices"; "By 2035, the biggest margin in the automotive value chain will belong to software providers." If you scrutinize these hypotheses you might discern the overarching pattern: a shift from the driving experience to experiences while driving.

With the evaluations complete, determine how prepared you are to address each trend. Ask company leaders to rate preparedness on a simple scale of 1 to 100, with 1 equaling very low preparedness and 100 very high preparedness. With levels of preparedness attached to each trend, you can now more easily determine your vulnerabilities and how to avoid harm. It helps to respond to questions such as the following: Do we understand the future challenges to our current businesses? Where should we focus our efforts to protecting the existing businesses? Do our current strategies help us avoid future threats? At this stage, don't broach opportunities that disruption might create. This step comes further along the open strategy journey when you develop new business models.

Step 6: Construct the IMP Trend Radar Visualization

Your team is now ready to construct the IMP Trend Radar visual. Figure 6.2 represents each trend, its likelihood of occurring, the extent of its impact on the industry, and how prepared your firm is to address it. Trends that appear closest to the center are more likely to occur than those on the periphery. The size of the bubbles represents the impact on the industry (high, medium, low), while their shade of gray indicates your firm's level of preparedness. The figure shows two trends that are highly relevant and for which the company is not well prepared (big white bubbles), but only one of them has a relatively high likelihood of occurring. In developing a strategy, you will want to prioritize these trends.

Once created, the IMP Trend Radar visual should become a standard tool in your annual strategy process. It helps you generate a holistic depiction of all relevant trends, study how such trends influence your

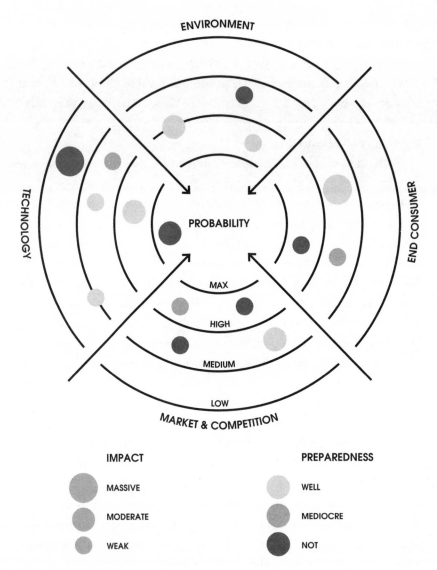

Figure 6.2
A generic IMP Trend Radar visualization.

business, and determine how, over time, they might change. Visualization of these trends in the radar also facilitates communication, helping with strategy discussions and setting priorities. As a general rule, first focus on the IMP Trend Radar visual's inner circles. Your company should be well prepared for all trends located in this range. Large (high relevance) and white (low preparedness) bubbles indicate immediate and serious threats. The outer circles of the IMP Trend Radar work like an airborne early warning and control system, helping you to detect hostile aircraft or unidentified objects when you still have time to react. If you update the trends and the evaluations on a regular basis, you will be able to see how they change and decide whether they require your attention. An expanding bubble signals the increasing relevance of a trend. Movement of a trend toward the center likewise means that the chances of it occurring have increased.

To understand these steps a bit better, let's review how one large industrial firm—we'll call it Fogland Industries—conducted its IMP Trend Radar exercise (we've changed certain identifying details to preserve anonymity). The company generated about €50 billion in revenues annually across seven business units. Of these seven, one of them, called High Technology Materials, contributed about 15 percent of Fogland's overall sales revenues, targeting such markets as automotive manufacturing, electrical engineering, packing, and sports and leisure. In 2019, High Technology Materials launched an open IMP Trend Radar exercise to understand how digitalization and market dynamics might impact the company's business going forward.

As leaders understood, the business was operating in an environment rife with challenges as well as potential opportunities. The Chinese market was expanding, poised by 2030 to account for about 50 percent of Fogland's global market. The rise in popularity of electric cars was creating a major market for both batteries and the high-tech materials that that went into making them—Fogland anticipated double-digit growth rates. In addition, governments in key geographic regions were imposing ambitious climate targets, and some of Fogland's major markets were undergoing disruptive changes. Declines in prices of commodities created enormous pressures on the company's pricing, while digitalization affected products, processes, and business models.[31] Leaders conducted an IMP Trend Radar exercise to develop a shared and holistic understanding of the possible impact of digitalization and market dynamics on High Technology Materials' business.

Fogland's core team, comprising representatives from technical development, marketing, new market development, R&D, and strategy, identified four topic areas on which to focus: the end consumer, market and competition, technology, and the environment. For each area the team formulated several core questions. For the end consumer field area, they asked: "Which (new) forms of mobility will establish themselves in the future?" and "How will end consumers act in the future?" For the environment search field, they asked: "What regulatory interventions are to be expected in the coming years?" and "What effects will political changes have on mobility worldwide?"

The team then convened a heterogeneous group of forty-nine Fogland experts and ninety-five external experts, including senior executives, scientists, and experts from twelve companies and institutions such as Siemens, Nokia, Bosch, BMW, Yale University, the Center for Cultural Studies and Technology in China, and the Agency for Science Technology and Research in Singapore. IMP interviewed all these experts to identify trends in four key markets: transportation, construction, consumer electronics, and industrial. From these interviews, the team distilled 159 hypotheses about the future. Making use of online surveys, the team then asked 332 global experts (152 Fogland personnel and 180 external experts) to evaluate hypotheses in their relevant fields. At the end of this process, the team arrived at trends grouped into different categories and an IMP Trend Radar visualization.

In the environment search field, for instance, the core team arrived at the following hypotheses:

• "Material Regulations: in 2035, plastic material suppliers will be required to salvage and reuse materials from the automotive industries."

- "End-of-Life Recyclability: by 2035, end-of-life recyclability will open the door for new material innovations (e.g., composites, carbon fiber, etc.)."
- "Shift to New CO_2 Emission Regulations: by 2035, the carbon footprint regulation will be a cradle-to-grave calculation, including manufacturing and recycling."

A group of forty-six Fogland experts and forty-seven outside experts evaluated these hypotheses, deeming some highly relevant and rejecting others (these experts had not been involved in developing the initial hypotheses). In a workshop, the core team winnowed down the total hypotheses to sixty-seven. They then conducted an online survey, asking ninety-three global experts (forty-six Fogland personnel and forty-seven external experts) to evaluate the sixty-seven hypotheses in their relevant fields. This yielded about thirty trends grouped into eight categories (figure 6.3) and an IMP Trend Radar visualization (figure 6.4).

With this IMP Trend Radar visualization in place, Fogland identified trends that had strategic implications for its businesses. For example, one set of hypotheses revolved around "cradle-to-cradle," referring to the objective of cyclically reusing waste in imitation of nature's regenerative cycles. Hypotheses like "By 2035, the carbon footprint regulation will be a cradle-to-grave calculation that encompasses manufacturing and recycling," "In 2035, the circular economy in mobility will lead to new business models and players who will challenge traditional thinking enterprises in the value chain," and "By 2035, we'll need plastic material suppliers to reuse materials from the automotive industries" all reflected a shift toward a circular economy. Such a shift had important implications for Fogland, as growing regulation in materials and end-of-use disposition would require rapid innovation in materials science. Subsequent holistic analyses the team conducted that considering the entire life cycles of materials only reinforced these conclusions.

These and other trends were not news to the company, but as a senior Fogland executive explained, major revelations about the future weren't the point of this particular exercise. "Of course, big companies

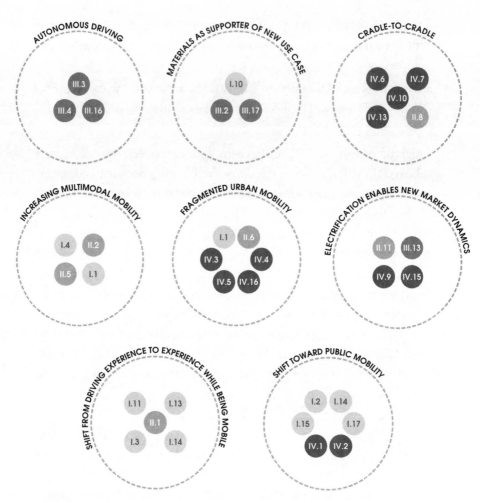

Figure 6.3
Fogland categories.

like Fogland do a lot of trend research and we know a lot about trends. You can do some Internet search and you have your trends within a few minutes. This is not the challenge. What is much more difficult for a century-old company that has done almost everything right in the past is seeing around the corner, creating a shared understanding of the challenges these trends pose to the industries, and acting on them."[32] How precisely would these known trends interact with one another?

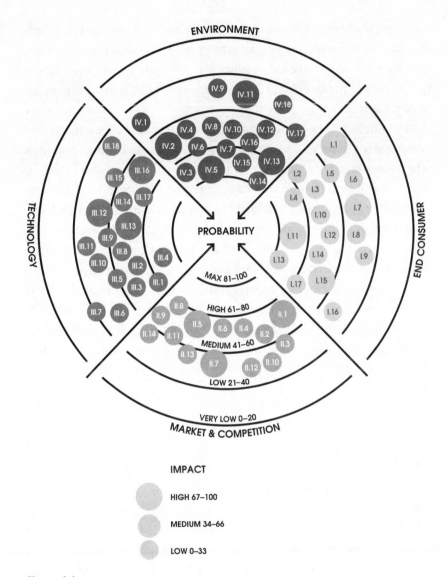

Figure 6.4
Fogland IMP Trend Radar visualization.

What precisely were the business implications? And what trends should the firm prioritize in defining its strategies? These were the intellectual challenges Fogland needed to consider. And bringing in outsiders to participate in the IMP Trend Radar exercise could help the company see around corners.

You might wonder why a company with Fogland's resources didn't simply hire a strategy consulting firm—or three—to conduct and present its own trend research. As this executive explained, outsourcing the trend-finding function in this way might yield relevant insights, but it wouldn't allow the firm to garner the executional advantages that IMP Trend Radar brings. "Sure, you can buy sophisticated trend analyses from many sources," he said. "But jointly developing a trend analysis with your managers and external experts, and mirroring internal views with what external experts think, is fives time better than any PowerPoint presentation from the best consultancies in the world." By doing the work together, teams develop a shared understanding of the challenges and so are more inclined to coalesce behind the eventual strategic decisions. "They will be much more committed to implement the changes."[33]

In Sum

Can your firm see around corners? If you're tracking trends as part of traditional, closed deliberations, your understanding of what's coming might not be as sharp as you think. As we've seen, groups of insiders can fall prey to any number of cognitive biases that impede their ability to detect weak, early signals of emerging trends. The solution is to bring outsiders into the mix. The IMP Trend Radar exercise systematically engages a group of internal and external experts to generate numerous hypotheses about the future and hone them into a few key trends. Further, the exercise allows leaders to consider disparate trends together and in relation to one another, affording a holistic view of the future as well as a shared understanding of the underlying dynamics. By engaging in this exercise themselves on an ongoing basis, leaders not only can track emerging trends early, they can prepare for subsequent phases of strategy-making by connecting their collective view of the future with the firm's own strategic considerations.

Questions to Ponder:

- How does your firm go about projecting into the future? Are your efforts as effective as people think?

- Consider past strategic decisions at your firm that didn't go so well. How exactly did leaders fail to anticipate the future, and what cognitive biases might have been in play?

- Reflect back on your experiences thinking about the future earlier in your career. What "unknown unknowns" did you miss back then that are apparent in retrospect? Are there any you might be missing today?

- Do others in your company share your expectations for the future? If the answer is "not so much," what steps are you taking to build consensus?

7   Disrupt Yourself before Others Do

When Christians seek inspiration, they travel to Rome or Jerusalem. Muslims make pilgrimages to Mecca, Sikhs gather at the Golden Temple at the Amritsar, and Jews pray at the Wailing Wall in Jerusalem. But where do executives venture? They book a flight to Silicon Valley, or at least they did prior to the COVID-19 era.

Gispert Rühl, the CEO of Europe's largest steel distributor, Klöckner, was one such corporate pilgrim. He knew that the steel industry was hopelessly inefficient—he lived that reality every day. Klöckner made money by stockpiling steel at hundreds of sites near its customers' plants, supplying them this raw material, as needed, for production lines. But stockpiling steel was necessary only because the flow of information among customers, Klöckner, and producers was so bad. If Klöckner could understand producer and customer needs in real time, steel could arrive on a just-in-time basis, without the need to stockpile.[1]

To generate a business model based on seamless information flows, Rühl sought the kind of mind expansion that fellow German executive Christoph Keese, executive vice president of Europe's largest publishing house, Axel Springer, had achieved through spending six months in Silicon Valley. Rühl had read Keese's book detailing his experience in the heart of tech innovation and outlining the "Silicon Valley challenge" for Europe.[2] Seeking his own experience, Rühl ventured to the Valley himself, meeting with founders, high-tech companies, and venture capital firms and soliciting everyone's thoughts on how to disrupt the steel industry.

He returned to Germany with the same energy and clarity that religious devotees enjoy after their holy pilgrimages. Based on his conversations, Rühl believed Klöckner should transform itself into a digital platform for the steel industry. Instead of purchasing, storing, and reselling billions of dollars' worth of steel, the company could host a platform on which customers and producers dealt with one another directly. Digitalizing the steel supply chain would accomplish everything Rühl initially sought: increased efficiency through the real-time information flows among producers and customers. "All construction sites would be stocked with thousands of sensors," Rühl explained. "Progress at the construction site would be recorded. . . . The algorithm would calculate in advance at what point steel beams would be needed for the second floor and report it to the Klöckner-platform. . . . The platform would collate all the orders in the region so that the steel mills could make bids at auction . . . [and] steel would be ordered and sold before it is even manufactured."[3]

In 2014 Klöckner introduced kloeckner.i, an innovation platform that brought steel into the digital age. Klöckner sold its own steel and metal products on the platform, which served as an Amazon-style marketplace for the steel industry. Initially launched as a Silicon Valley-esque startup with two employees in a coworking space, the business today employs more than ninety digital experts in areas from digital marketing to analytics. As of the fourth quarter of 2019, €2 billion in steel sales were taking place on the platform, generating about 30 percent of Klöckner's revenues with only 10 percent of its workforce.[4]

In traveling to Silicon Valley, Rühl, like Keese before him, was in effect "opening up" his company's strategic deliberations so as to solve the classic challenge of corporate myopia. As these executives recognized, traditional boardroom deliberations weren't imaginative enough to allow an enterprise to anticipate its own demise and plan preemptive action. Fortunately, you don't have to board a plane to gain similar insights about your business and its future. In recent years, leading-edge companies have conducted an innovative open strategy exercise developed by IMP, the company led by Stephan Friedrich von den Eichen.

The IMP Nightmare Competitor Challenge convenes a group of insiders and outsiders to conjure a fictitious disruptor of their businesses.[5]

The IMP Nightmare Competitor Challenge exercise draws inspiration from the formal war games militaries have long conducted to anticipate surprises during active combat. In war games, participants simulate conflicts using relevant rules, data, and procedures, making decisions that in turn prompt other players to act. Today the US Department of Defense, along with a number of Fortune 500 companies, participates in such games.[6] Research has shown that these games make decision-makers more vigilant, ultimately broadening the range of alternatives they consider. War game participants also spot early signals of change more clearly and recalibrate their mental frameworks accordingly, allowing for greater adaptation and nimbleness.

The IMP Nightmare Competitor Challenge adapts a war game format for the task of anticipating disruption and generating potential business models. Participants imagine a fictional competitor who makes all the right moves and, most importantly, has the right business model for a digital future. The exercise defines disruption at the outset as a threat rather than an opportunity, in the process increasing the odds that leaders will take action. At the same time, the IMP Nightmare Competitor Challenge also allows companies to spot potential *opportunities* in otherwise undesirable circumstances. In fact, companies usually participate precisely in hopes of identifying new business models they never would have conceived otherwise. This distinguishes the IMP Nightmare Competitor Challenge from conventional war games, which participants usually run to plan for worst-case scenarios. Also, while conventional war games might involve a small group of senior leaders, the IMP Nightmare Competitor Challenge includes external participants, allowing companies to move beyond groupthink.

The exercise doesn't seek to stop disruptive shifts, as that usually won't be possible. Rather, it seeks to help leaders detect and plan for such shifts earlier so that they can act before disruption undermines their businesses. It is the next step to take after the IMP Trend Radar exercise (discussed in chapter 6), helping your company to develop detailed business models of a nightmare competitor rather than simply tracking broad trends.

Participation in the IMP Nightmare Competitor Challenge has borne fruit for dozens of companies, ranging from small firms to larger companies such as BASF, Linde, and Lufthansa. These firms are now better prepared for disruption or have adopted entirely new business models, as Klöckner did. Before we examine the IMP Nightmare Competitor Challenge in more detail and explore how your company might deploy the exercise, let's look at two key challenges posed by disruption and the inadequacy of conventional closed strategy-making responses to surmount them.

Challenge 1: Cognitive Limitations

By the early 2000s, digital cameras had flooded the market, hopelessly disrupting analog photography. But not everyone was convinced. In 2004, a reporter for the German magazine *Der Spiegel* asked Hanns-Peter Cohn, CEO of the venerable German camera brand Leica Camera AG, to comment on the digital revolution and the so-called demise of conventional photography. He was unfazed, arguing that "digital technology is just an intermezzo. At latest in 20 years we will take pictures with other technologies. But film will still exist."[7] When the journalist compared Cohn to a music fan who still clung to vinyl records, Cohn had another, equally surprising answer, predicting the end of present-day digital technology. "Music is only about the storage medium. Photography is also about creativity. Digital technology bets on the mass market and on speed and is, as the email, an expression of our time. With the cellphone camera also comes the invasion of private Paparazzi. But Photography is different, it is something contemplative—it will always exist." Cohn predicted that digital camera consumers would lose their precious photographs since evolving technology would render their digital keepsakes unreadable. By contrast, "A photo album will still exist in 50 years—albeit a bit yellowed."[8] Cohn didn't remain in leadership to see his predictions through. He resigned at the end of that year.

You might think his successor, Ralf Coenen, would have come armed with brilliant new business plans that would have allowed Leica to compete in the digital sphere. Not so. Like Cohn, he continued to focus on the shrinking market for analog cameras, ignoring the unfortunate (for Leica) dominance of digital. Speaking of digital photography, he said, "The market mechanisms in this market segment are weird to me. They neither fit us nor most of our customers."[9] At Photokina, the world's largest fair for the photographic and imaging industries, Leica managers proudly strutted about wearing stickers that read "I am a photo dinosaur."[10] Four months later, Coenen left too. Leica was poised to go the way of the dinosaurs, its sales shrinking and losses mounting.

Leica's travails reflect the potentially devastating cognitive barriers that prevent incumbent companies not just from responding to disruptions on the horizon (or, in Leica's case, directly in front of them) but also from spotting them in the first place. As Clayton Christensen observes in his book, *The Innovator's Dilemma*, established companies usually excel at so-called sustaining or incremental innovations that improve the performance of existing products, services, technologies, or business models but fail spectacularly at spotting disruptive innovations. Today, disruption is much more prevalent than it was in 1997, when Christensen's book first appeared. A 2018 study of executives at more than 3,600 companies found that over two-thirds of respondents anticipated significant industry shocks from technological innovation, while a Boston Consulting Group study found that only about one-third of companies successfully navigated disruptive change. The remaining two-thirds either filed for bankruptcy, were acquired, or stumbled through years of stagnation or decline.[11]

Disruptive innovations befuddle leaders because they render existing assets and competencies obsolete and fundamentally change the rules of business. When companies use traditional strategic planning tools such as SWOT analysis, PESTEL analysis, or the Five Forces Framework, they extrapolate future trends based on a knowledge of the past, assuming that the world will continue to operate as it always has.[12] When new technologies, business models, or competitors appear, they render these planning tools ineffective, preventing leaders from spotting and appreciating game-changing innovations.

The limitations of the human mind further hamstring leaders. Since our information-processing capabilities are relatively limited, our minds tend to organize knowledge and comprehend the world in ways that simplify reality. These mental shortcuts and strategic beliefs (about who our main competitors are, for instance, or what customers value, or which forces drive competition) influence what we perceive, how we process information, and how we solve problems.[13] Such dynamics become immediately clear when we consider politics. Ohio State University researchers Heather L. LaMarre, Kristen D. Landreville, and Michael A. Beam showed 322 people a similar short video clip of comedian and satirist Stephen Colbert interviewing Amy Goodman, a progressive talk radio host. In the video, Colbert introduces the host as a "super liberal lefty" and talks with her about the embedding of journalists during the Iraq War, a practice Goodman has sharply criticized. The researchers asked participants to complete a survey in which they self-identified as liberals or conservatives and then answered questions about their interpretation of the video. Both groups found Colbert funny, but conservatives tended to take Colbert as making serious political statements, while liberals tended to view his remarks as unserious parody.[14] For members of both groups, preexisting beliefs shaped the impressions of the present.

This experiment sheds light on what happened at Leica. Leaders at the company operated with a preexisting mindset about the nature of their business, consumer desires, and so on. According to the logic of this mindset, digital photography was a passing fad. To regard digital as a fundamental shift in their industry would have been akin to a conservative seeing the world through the eyes of a progressive, or vice versa. Such a radical shift in perspective isn't realistic for most incumbent company leaders.

Most innovations emit only weak signals and so are easy to write off as peripheral, unimportant, or indeterminate. "Just as the eye is designed for focus on a central area of vision with a blurry periphery," researchers have written, "individuals and organizations are wired to see clearly what lies within their current frames and less clearly what lies in their mental shadows."[15] Apart from our mindsets, other ingrained biases prevent us from cueing in to these weak signals.[16] Our distaste for ambiguity and our gravitation toward harmony and conformity, for example, might prompt us to ignore or discount weak signals coming from our environments. We also tend to value immediate, measurable, and tangible success over long-term, difficult-to-measure outcomes. As scholars have noted, "We are creatures of the present. We try to maintain the status quo while downplaying the importance of the future, which undermines our motivation and courage to act now to prevent some distant disaster. We'd rather avoid a little pain today than a lot of pain tomorrow."[17]

At Leica, the prospect of change at first seemed distant at best, too insignificant to challenge leaders' existing assumptions about their business. As the threat of digital disruption appeared more obvious, these initial impressions lingered, and leaders' assumptions hardened. Leaders couldn't see beyond their biases to register the reality of the marketplace. Andreas Kaufmann, a German investor and hobby photographer, acquired Leica in 2004 and replaced its top management, clearing the way for digitalization and a change in strategy. Leica began to focus on a specific niche market that fit its brand, in the process embracing disruptive technology. Over the following five years the company managed to turn itself around.[18]

Research suggests that opening up deliberations through an IMP Nightmare Competitor Challenge-style exercise might help free leaders from their unhelpful mental models, just as war games do in military settings.[19] When your opponents in a war game simulate an attack, you begin to see the terrain of engagement differently. War games deliver their most compelling results when a competitor's move shocks participants, forcing them to confront shortfalls in their existing approach. During such situations, strategists are forced to think more deeply about the dynamics of competition.[20] Their existing mental models become destabilized, opening the way for new insights and fresh thinking. In a business context, the involvement of outsiders who might not operate within the same mindsets intensifies the experience, allowing leaders to break more fully with their existing assumptions.

Challenge 2: Motivating People to Act

It's not enough for established companies to spot disruptions on the horizon. If companies are to avoid being disrupted, leaders, managers, and employees must feel empowered to take preemptive action. This is often difficult. When Gisbert Rühl devised his idea of turning Klöckner into the Amazon of the steel industry, a number of managers in his company were initially skeptical. "We struggled to change our ingrained mindsets," Rühl said. "There were several naysayers ready to immediately shoot down any new idea raised in our internal innovations group. This was particularly the case for approaches that challenged the status quo. The general attitude was that 'steel distribution does not work like that,' 'that won't work for us,' and so on."[21] Beyond the cognitive barriers, Rühl had to convince leaders operating a billion-dollar business to channel resources toward a new business model that, so far, represented only a small financial opportunity and deployed untested technology. Even if this business model made perfect sense to everyone (and it didn't), pursuing it seemed risky to leaders worried about making their short-term numbers.

Motivational issues routinely cause leaders to flounder in the face of new business models because their fear of missing out on an existing, well-performing business overshadows the risk of failing to anticipate a potential disruption. Such disruptions, after all, might never materialize. But this analysis suggests a possible solution: to spur leaders to act, arouse their fear around the threat disruption poses rather than evoking all that they have to gain by adopting an innovative but untested business model.

As the psychologist Daniel Kahneman has observed, human beings have a tendency toward loss aversion. We register the fear of losing something almost twice as strongly as we do the joy of gaining something of the same magnitude.[22] Research in the business arena bears this theory out. In his analysis of companies navigating the tides of disruption,

Clayton Christensen found that incumbent leaders who perceived disruption as an opportunity failed to allocate enough resources to combat it. Those that perceived disruption as a threat to the core business allocated the required resources—they were motivated enough to go all in.[23] Likewise, as Harvard's Clark G. Gilbert found, newspapers that perceived digitalization as an important threat to their business committed much more financial and organizational resources to innovative online ventures. Executives remarked on the fear they felt of being disrupted, with one noting that "McKinsey had come in and had done a rather startling analysis of the classified business. They predicted that 20–30 percent of our classified revenue would disappear by 1998. That raised enormous alarms bells in some people."[24]

Other research has confirmed the inadequacy of focusing unduly on the potential opportunities of disruption. In 2013, Pricewaterhouse-Coopers (PwC) released a report detailing how distributed and renewable energy would disrupt standard business models that focused on centralized utility power providers.[25] Surveying executives at fifty-three companies, PwC found that about 60 percent believed that "there is a very high or high likelihood that distributed generation will force utilities to significantly change their business models." Interestingly a large majority—over 80 percent—saw such changes in power generation as an opportunity, compared with fewer than 20 percent who saw it as a threat to their existing businesses.

Within the German power industry, positive perceptions of the opportunities that disruption suggested didn't spur incumbent companies to invest. In 2013, 23.4 percent of Germany's electric power came from renewable sources, but the utilities produced only a small portion of this renewable power (12 percent). Homeowners, farmers, funds and banks, and others accounted for the rest.[26] In 2016, renewable power energy accounted for almost 30 percent of the market, but the big energy utilities still produced roughly the same small share. The utilities might have understood renewable power as an opportunity, but one that would deliver value far in the future and wouldn't compare with their lucrative core business. The potential opportunity that disruption seemed to represent was simply too small to justify the trouble of pursuing it—a pattern we see in many incumbent companies facing disruptive innovation.[27] By contrast, one German executive who had invested significantly in renewable energy perceived it as "a severe threat to our business model."[28]

The IMP Nightmare Competitor Challenge exercise can spur leaders to act because it brings disruption alive as a powerful threat to the business. The exercise prompts leaders to think about potential disruptors in detail, understanding precisely how and why disruptors' business models could overturn existing industry assumptions and norms. Leaders discover that they have two options: Develop strategies to fight the disruptor, or develop strategies that make *them* the disruptor and become their competitor's worst nightmare (more about this below). Although the cognitive barriers we've mentioned might prevent company leaders from imagining future threats, involving outsiders can help compensate for this lacuna, as they are free of the usual biases that prevail inside organizations. And while employees inside a company might shrink from openly discussing their fears about future disruption, outsiders can discuss them more comfortably. Hearing experts and distinguished business leaders in multiple fields outline the potential of a new business model can rouse a fear of disruptive forces.

Setting Up a Nightmare Competitor Challenge

How exactly does an IMP Nightmare Competitor Challenge work? Similar to the IMP Trend Radar exercise described in chapter 6, it includes a two- to three-day, in-person workshop that features a curated team of executives as well as external participants, including industry experts, researchers, potential customers, suppliers, lateral thinkers, startups and potential disruptors. (During the COVID epidemic IMP also conducted these workshops entirely online or in a hybrid format with some participants joining remotely.) Regardless of the precise format, the IMP Nightmare Competitor Challenge exercise includes the following five key steps (see figure 7.1).

Figure 7.1
Holding an IMP Nightmare Competitor Challenge exercise.

Step 1: Select Participants

In a typical IMP Nightmare Competitor Challenge, we create three teams of six to eight people, half of whom are external participants. We carefully select participants from a database we've created over the years based on specific scenarios developed in our IMP Trend Radar exercise, identifying competencies and areas of expertise that might prove relevant to the conversation. We also give some thought to the exercise's general design (see chapter 3), particularly the specific issue we wish to tackle, and allow this to inform our choices about which participants to select. Since you probably don't have a database of participants handy, you might proceed by identifying a few people who possess some of the expertise you are looking for and ask them in turn to recommend other potential participants. Be careful to reach beyond your usual network, as you want to break out from your usual way of thinking.

In a recent IMP Nightmare Competitor Challenge we conducted for a private university group in Brazil, we sought to include participants with experience in elite European and US educational institutions, online teaching practitioners, and some individuals from the startup scene with experience building business models. In other exercises we have included technology experts and those with insight into artificial intelligence because the scenarios indicated that substantial technology shifts were coming. If our scenarios reveal disruptive forces lurking on the horizon, we seek people with experience in disruption across different industries, as well as participants with unconventional approaches. At all times, we're careful to avoid naysayers, whom we defined earlier as having "yes, but" mindsets. (You might wish to use our self-assessment tool from chapter 2 to ensure that your invitees have open minds. And if you haven't developed formal scenarios using an IMP Trend Radar exercise, don't worry. You can draft scenarios just as effectively in a more conventional fashion, especially when the challenge you face is obvious.)

When selecting internal participants, dispense with questions of hierarchy and function and focus instead on ensuring adequate representation so that you can generate fresh ideas. When we work with very hierarchical organizations, we deliberately exclude top management so that participants won't defer to their perspectives. While working with adidas, we conducted an experiment in which we asked internal applicants who sought to participate to submit their ideas for nightmare competitors. We found that this vetting process had its advantages as we were able to select the most highly motivated participants with the most creative ideas about nightmare competitors in advance. Unfortunately, participants arrived at the exercise already invested in a particular approach, making them less nimble and flexible. On balance, we would probably advise against such vetting.

Step 2: Define the Task and Its Scope

This step can play out in three different ways. In the first variation, we ask each team to consider trends that might affect the environment in which the company operates. We provide team members with a stack of newspapers and magazines and ask them to cut out pictures and headlines, which they then deliver to an illustrator, who helps them create a poster highlighting the main trends. The purpose of this exercise is to open everyone's mind to new and unconventional developments in their industries. With the poster in hand, one of the participants presents a series of scenarios. Everyone else records reflections and ideas that resonated with them as they heard these scenarios, along with items that the scenarios might have overlooked, and posts these reflections and ideas on the wall.

If the scenarios from the IMP Trend Radar exercise have already been defined in great detail, we embark on the second variation, in which we present scenarios and ask participants to "destroy" them. Working collaboratively, participants use the widely known PESTEL framework (a tool to identify the macro factors—political, economic, social, technological, environmental, and legal—affecting your company) to identify weaknesses in the scenarios. Has the group overlooked a social trend or an emerging crisis such as COVID-19 that changes the economic outlook? Although, as we've noted, tools like PESTEL are rooted in the past, the scenarios based on the IMP Trend Radar exercise are future focused and as such prevent participants from falling into the trap of extrapolating from the past.

If the trend analysis has clearly identified a potential nightmare competitor, we turn to variation three. Gallus is a great example of this path because digital print was the obvious threat facing the company. In cases like this, there is no need to question the scenario. We simply remind everyone of what's going on and address the clear and present danger facing the company.

Step 3: Destroy Your Business

It's time to name your nightmare competitor. Start with the scenarios we described in the previous step, in which each participant identifies products, products and services, or platform businesses that could potentially vanquish the current business. Aim for quantity, not quality, and allow everyone to unleash their imagination and creativity. Post each of these ideas on a wall or whiteboard and organize them according to product-based, product-and-service-based, or platform-based disruptors. Such categorization helps since people tend overwhelmingly to see platforms as disruptors, given the prominence of Uber-, Airbnb-, and Amazon-style disruptions.

Once the ideas are posted and properly categorized, participants wander around the room, selecting their favorite nightmare idea, giving it a name, and selecting other posts that dovetail with this idea. Each participant works out a pitch, an illustrator by their side to help them create a poster (you can certainly perform this step without illustrators, but having them helps crystallize participants' thinking). Each participant delivers their pitch to their small group from step 1, and the group chooses two winners to advance. Half the group then fine-tunes each idea and considers business model drivers such as positioning, products and services, value chain, marketing, and revenue logic. The groups then pitch their refined nightmare competitor ideas, usually about six in total, to all workshop participants, who then vote on a winner for each group.

Step 4: Create Business Models for Nightmare Competitors

Each team details the business model for its idea, spending roughly an hour on each element of the business model (positioning, products and services, value chain, marketing, and revenue logic). As the groups work, illustrators help them create a poster, refining their ideas as they translate them into a visual medium. IMP moderators are also on hand, and if top executives haven't participated so far, they might also wander around. They can listen to the discussions but are allowed only one question or comment. We don't want them to hijack the conversation, as executives sometimes do.

Groups then take an additional hour to rethink the business model, prior to delivering a seven- to ten-minute pitch to a top management team. A ten-minute Q&A period follows. The jury, typically consisting of the top management team, discusses the ideas and selects a winner on the basis of how interesting, likely, and dangerous each idea is. Workshop participants are also asked to vote. Outsiders' votes are always most revealing, as they tend to focus on the more disruptive and radical nightmare competitors. In certain cases, a broader group of employees listens to the pitches and votes.

Step 5: Understand Risks to Your Business

After the workshop, IMP collects additional data to enrich the nightmare competitor ideas and sometimes adds additional hypotheses for how scenarios might unfold. About a month later, the top management team gathers for a one-day workshop with IMP to discuss the implications of the exercise in more detail. To kick off the workshop, IMP presents the nightmare competitor business model that emerged from the workshop, then facilitates the following discussion. Most of the time, leaders use this information to inform their strategy process, with either an internal strategy team or an external strategy consultancy developing strategic responses to anticipated developments. Around a quarter of the time, companies decide to develop a new business that turns the nightmare competitor into reality. KEBA, one of the world's leading companies developing innovative automation processes for cash machines, and WS Audiology, a leading manufacturer of hearing aids, are currently doing this. They are on track to becoming their competitors' nightmare.

To understand how these steps unfold, consider a Nightmare Competitor Challenge run by voestalpine, an Austria-based global leader in the manufacturing, processing, and development of sophisticated steel products. A European steel powerhouse, voestalpine had operations in more than fifty countries, 2017–2018 revenues of more than €13 billion, and an EBITDA of almost €2 billion. With its unique combination of materials and processing expertise, the company enjoyed a leading position in technology-intensive industries such as automotive, railway, aerospace, and energy.[29] Like other steel producers, however, the company faced an array of challenges, including a slowdown in global steel demand growth, the material substitution of steel in some segments, a growing circular economy, massive overcapacity, competition from China, a downward value-capture spiral, the rise of digital platforms as a channel for trade, a disruption of scale economies, and so on.[30] Collectively, these trends squeezed margins and prompted leaders to rethink their business models.[31] Regulatory pressures mounted as well, with steel producers scrambling to meet the EU's 2030 climate and energy goals.

In 2016, seeking new strategies to enable its continued resilience in this shifting environment, voestalpine's head of strategy asked us to facilitate a Nightmare Competitor Challenge. As Christian Presslmayer, the head of strategy in the company's steel division, told us, the company wanted to "break out of the traditional way of strategy making with the help of outsiders. We wanted to identify and point out disruptive trends that are difficult to point out internally, in a closed room and that are easier to address with the help of external advocates."[32] The company began by selecting a mix of external and internal participants. Initially voestalpine sought to include high-profile, "stardust" candidates. IMP convinced the company to focus on competence profiles (and in particular on participants with creative thinking skills) instead of on celebrity and corporate cachet, as that would yield better results.

The participants generated many future, trend-based scenarios. One focused on changing mobility habits that threatened one of their main customer segments, resulting in reduced demand. Others concerned recycling materials options, disruptive digitalization offerings, and threats posed by new materials that could substitute for steel among additive manufacturers. One interesting scenario, titled "Climate Change Reloaded," referred to the increasing pressure to develop CO_2-free steel production. Among policymakers and environmentalists, the decarbonization of steel production is an important step toward a CO_2-free future. A company that could develop new technology and a sustainable business model for decarbonized steel could potentially disrupt the entire industry. Airlines receive substantial criticism for their emissions, but voestalpine produces roughly sixteen times as much CO_2 as Austria's main airline.[33] Could the company really change its core production process?

Next, participants imagined several potential voestalpine disruptors. The first one picked up the digitalization scenario and pitched a "steel to print" business model, according to which steel materials would be developed to enable additive manufacturing, especially in the automotive industry. This imagined nightmare competitor would replace standard steel rolling with printing. The second nightmare competitor was a firm that provided holistic mobility concepts for cities, dominating the supply chain.

The third potential disruptive idea was a CO_2-free steel production system based on hydrogen electrolysis. While the idea of using hydrogen to produce steel instead of coal and coke was not radically novel, going through the Nightmare Competitor Challenge exercise allowed voestalpine to consider an integrated, fully hydrogen-based business model and to discuss and convey it in a vivid way. As Christian Presslmayer noted, the inclusion of external participants had played a big role in pushing the conversation in that direction. "The externals were an important counterbalance," he said. "Some internals were not radical enough in their thinking. Mental barriers had been removed and new perspectives emerged that can be really intriguing." Some internal executives initially ridiculed the idea of using hydrogen. But then a renowned external expert literally banged on the table, making the point that this technology already existed and that the company's failure to develop it would render it extremely vulnerable to future attacks from competitors. That got people's attention.

Following the exercise, voestalpine did in fact pursue hydrogen electrolysis technology. It was not an obvious winner during the workshop, but some members of the board had already started thinking about the company's response to climate change. The Nightmare Competitor Challenge outlined a viable path, with external input exercising a strong and decisive influence. In April 2018 the company joined an industry consortium comprising such heavyweights as Siemens and Verbund (Austria's largest electricity company) to help create the world's largest pilot facility to produce "green" hydrogen.[34] In other words, voestalpine is now on a path toward CO_2-free steel manufacturing.

In the context of rising pressures to tackle climate change and the expectation of more stringent environmental regulations in the years to come, this is no small feat. While the move has limited impact on short-term returns, it might prove decisive in the future. The project's centerpiece was the world's largest proton exchange membrane electrolyzer with a capacity of six megawatts, developed by Siemens to buffer sudden spikes in energy input and store off-peak energy. As then CEO Wolfgang Eder said, "This hydrogen pilot plant is finally paving the way for research into true breakthrough technologies. . . . The long-term goal is to move away from coal and coke . . . to use "green" hydrogen in the production process. Realistically, it will take a couple of decades before these processes can be used on an industrial scale."[35] It's too early to tell, but what started as a nightmare competitor workshop might well radically transform one of Europe's leading steel producers.

Navigating the Complexity of Digital

Although engaging in the IMP Nightmare Competitor Challenge exercise can help any leader anticipate future disruptors, leaders today find it especially helpful when grappling with the sheer complexity of digital innovation. As the economist Martin Weitzman has theorized, growth is limited not by our facility at generating ideas but by the challenge of incorporating an infinite number of *combinations* of ideas. "Knowledge," he argues, "can build upon itself in a combinatoric feedback process."[36] The more we know, the more new combinations of ideas are possible. We see such recombinant innovation at work in digital technologies, as they evolve quickly and also give rise to virtually infinite combinations of potentially valuable solutions or business models. Quite commonly, newcomers or incumbents adapt successful business models to fit new contexts—just ask any venture capitalist how often she's been pitched with "We are the Uber of. . . ." As Weitzman writes, "The core of economic life could appear increasingly to be centered on the more and more intensive processing of ever-greater numbers of new seed ideas into workable innovations. . . . In the early stages of development, growth is constrained by the number of potential new ideas, but later on it is constrained only by the ability to process them."[37]

Formerly, business leaders only had to know about existing and emerging technologies, products, and solutions in an industry, closely monitoring competitors and their strategies. In a digital world, that's not nearly enough. Leaders must also aggressively seek out new, potentially valuable business models that recombine existing and emerging ideas. And they must also find and exploit these business models faster than the competition. Happily, the IMP Nightmare Competitor Challenge exercise, coupled with the IMP Trend Radar exercise described in chapter 6, allows companies to accomplish these tasks. With the help of outsiders, the IMP Trend Radar exercise allows you to systematically scour the future, anticipating trends that might shape future business models. Once these trends are identified, the IMP Nightmare Competitor Challenge can quickly generate the promising recombinations that companies seek.

WS Audiology, a leading, century-old producer of hearing aids, turned to open strategy to help it deal with the prospect of disruption by recombination. Amazon, Apple, and Google all were vying to create a new class of products called "hearables" that would merge the functionality of hearing aids with that of headphones. And speaking of combinations: the tech giants were exploring how to combine the technology with sensors that tracked all kinds of personal health data, such as heart rate or daily step counts. As one media report noted, none of these companies wished "to be left behind should it become possible to create a general purpose, in-ear computer that allows consumers to leave their phone in the desk drawer."[38] Such a device could have immense commercial potential in part because it would help overcome the stigma that many consumers associated with hearing aids. As the report noted, fewer than 20 percent of the tens of millions of Americans who need hearing aids actually buy them because of this unfortunate societal prejudice. That is a huge potential market that the tech giants could tap—again, by combining and recombining previous innovations in a new package.

How would WS Audiology thwart this overwhelming threat, identifying the most valuable recombinations out there when most of the technologies evolved in other fields and the company lacked a deep understanding of them? As the company's innovation and strategy manager told us, open strategy was the answer, "the only approach [that would allow us] to react to the external changes and influence factors based on new technologies."[39] Lacking experts in such areas as hardware, big data, audiology, and business model construction, the company selected a dozen external industry experts, specialists from adjacent industries, and even talent from potential competitors to help it conduct IMP Trend Radar and IMP Nightmare Competitor Challenge exercises. Participants included experts from Microsoft, IBM Watson, Intel, Sennheiser, Infineon, and leading research institutions such as MIT and the University of Nottingham, and leaders in the startup space.

The group's first move was to build a IMP Trend Radar visualization tracking industry trends, including those relating to technology, customers, marketplace, regulatory regimes, social and economic developments, and so on. Participants identified sixty-one hypothetical trends and distilled them down to three potential scenarios that might unfold in the industry. One of the scenarios assumed that hearables, like smart headphones, would dominate conventional hearing aids in the future, amounting to a whole new channel for companies to use in sales and marketing. In this scenario, hearables would offer the same functionality for mild to moderate hearing loss that hearing aids once did, allowing them to dominate the hearing-aid market. Conventional hearing aids would then become a niche product for severe hearing loss only, competing against cochlear implants as medical devices. Audiologists would offer services only for medical-grade hearing aids, while patients with mild to moderate hearing loss would buy their hearables on Amazon, Best Buy, or other purveyors of audio technology.

For each of the scenarios, teams comprised of both internal and external participants went on to develop solutions, asking themselves: "What kind of business model would a nightmare competitor deploy to totally disrupt WS Audiology?" Teams generated more than three hundred rough ideas, which in turn yielded twenty-two initial nightmare competitors. Teams further winnowed these down to six, developing a detailed business model for each. After a final round of pitches, WS Audiology's senior executives chose the winner.

The nightmare competitor turned out to be a Silicon Valley–style startup that would develop and sell super-hearing apps, coupling sound engineering capacities with digital capabilities. A headset powered by this app would allow its user to have a conversation on an airplane, masking the noise generated by the massive jet engines. When the user chose to listen to music, the device would block out all ambient noise. The vision was "augmented communication" with the goal of "getting rid of the stigma associated with hearing aids." Dare we suggest that these devices might entirely overcome the societal shame associated with hearing impairment and become fashion items one day? Imagine cool granddads making teenagers jealous of their latest version of hip hearables. It was a revolutionary business model, one that could potentially disrupt WS Audiology's industry.

As WS Audiology's innovation and strategy manager Benedikt Heuer noted, the nightmare competitor business models were extremely valuable because they helped the company clarify a technology landscape that otherwise seemed overwhelmingly complex. "First, the open approach, including [the involvement of] externals, helped to broaden our horizon and to see what will be the important topics and fields, derived from a structured analysis of the future. . . . I would absolutely say that it helped us in several topics to identify new trends and describe them in the right way respectively."[40] The combination of IMP Trend Radar and nightmare competition exercises also helped the company think through the implications that key trends might have for the business. Although some in WS Audiology had known about certain of the findings, they hadn't broached them inside the organization. The IMP Trend Radar and nightmare competitor exercises accomplished that, enabling the company to develop them further into business opportunities.

Most exciting for Heuer, the exercises positioned WS Audiology to conduct detailed scenario planning for dealing with other potential disruptors. "That's the beauty of the concept," says Heuer. "You don't get a concept for WS Audiology, but you get a concept which threatens WS Audiology. . . . Based on this we have then developed a quite elaborated concept what WS Audiology could do in such scenario. This was a very important step for us, and we are now well prepared and positioned for such a scenario." As mentioned, the company is currently developing products designed to make it a nightmare for its own competitors. The specifics at the time of this writing remain top secret, but stay tuned, and prepare yourself for some very cool granddads in the years ahead.

In Sum

When in doubt, disrupt yourself. That's what militaries have long done by holding elaborate war game exercises. And it's what leading-edge companies are now doing, redefining the approach by bringing in external participants to preempt disruption in their industries. Leaders are often blind to potential disruptions because they are locked into existing mental models—they don't know what they don't know. Even when they do appreciate that markets are changing, they find it difficult to act, since doing so can seem overly risky. The result often proves fatal for businesses that had every opportunity to preempt disruption. The IMP Nightmare Competitor Challenge is a war-game-style exercise for companies that allows them to systematically imagine a disruptor and conceive how they might neutralize the threat. By including external participants, companies can overcome cognitive barriers and foster a livelier, less restricted conversation than might normally occur inside the organization. Open strategy is not always comfortable—nobody likes to immerse themselves in a nightmare. But as companies are finding, doing so can prevent a real nightmare from materializing by keeping the company several steps ahead of destabilizing change.

Questions to Ponder:

- Would a Silicon Valley startup have any interest in disrupting your industry?
- If you started from scratch, how would you design the business model of your company differently?
- What gets you out of bed every day—the opportunity to pursue new dreams or the fear that your organization will be left behind? Are your fellow executives wired the same way? Can you leverage this energy to unite everyone behind new business ideas?
- How motivated are leaders in your organization *really* to address the threats posed by disruption?

8 Develop Killer Business Models

You're in your peppy new subcompact car, cruising along an interstate at 70 miles per hour, when an eighteen-wheeler rumbles alongside you on the left, intending to pass. The truck is massive, its driver sitting so high up you can't see their face. As you glance at the truck's spinning wheels and shiny hubcaps, you can't help but think that if its trailer with its heavy load were to topple over, it would totally crush your car. Easing up on the accelerator slightly, you let the truck pass.

Are you being overly anxious? Not really. In 2017, accidents involving trucks killed almost five thousand people in the United States, with injuries running into the tens of thousands.[1] In some cases, truck drivers are speeding, fatigued, or distracted. But there is another, less obvious cause of accidents: poorly secured freight. If heavy freight isn't tied down tightly enough, it can come loose and fall, in some cases causing the trailer to tip over. Tie the freight too tightly, however, and it can become damaged. Drivers, whose job it is to secure the freight, are in a bind (no pun intended). A majority of loads—up to 70 percent—aren't tied down as they should be, accounting for about a quarter of trucking accidents. Damage to freight in Germany runs about €1.2 billion annually (or at least that's how much truckers file in insurance claims).[2]

Now there's a solution. The German company BPW Group, a provider of technological solutions and services for the commercial vehicle industry, has created an intelligent, app-based load-securing and load-monitoring system called the i.Gurt that continuously monitors the forces on a freight-securing belt while a truck is in transit. Fasten a small i.Gurt device to the strap. If the force on the strap falls below a certain value, the driver gets pinged on a cell phone and can make adjustments before an accident happens. If an accident does occur and freight is damaged, i.Gurt can help document what happened.[3]

As of 2020, customer responses to early trials have been euphoric. The i.Gurt has won two German innovation awards, and the company is forecasting a return on its investments in fewer than three years.[4] i.Gurt promises to deliver massive savings to truck operators and logistics companies, and it will play a crucial role in autonomous driving systems.[5] But when the i.Gurt hits the market, it will represent a massive shift in BPW's business model. Since the early twentieth century, BPW has built a successful €1.5 billion business by fabricating components for the transport industry, including axle systems, bearing and suspension systems, brake technologies, and fleet-tracking solutions for trucks and trailer operators. Both a digital solution and a technological product innovation, i.Gurt significantly changes the firm's positioning and revenue models. Compared with the company's previous products, i.Gurt carries a relatively low price point and will be marketed and sold more directly and aggressively through multiple digital sales channels. To bring the offering to market, BPW is engaging a potential competitor to help sell the product, an entirely new practice for the company.

How did a traditional engineering company come up with such a killer business model? You already know: it used an open strategy process. But the company didn't simply open up to brainstorm new ideas, trends on the horizon, or potential disruptors. In partnership with IMP, it went further, generating the idea for the i.Gurt but then conducting several open ideations to flesh out potential business models for it, complete with definitions of the offering, specific marketing plans, delineations of the value chain for producing, selling, and distributing the i.Gurt, and financial plans and projections. These workshops, comprised of both internal and external participants, generated several competing business models, which were refined during several rounds of judging before senior leaders made a final selection.

You might think it odd to focus so much on constructing a business model, and to involve outsiders in the process. Although leaders have embraced the concept of the business model since the mid-1990s as a "holistic description of a firm's key business processes," they usually don't spend much time purposely innovating existing business models, nor do they involve outsiders.[6] And yet more attention to business models is desirable, as leaders often struggle to distill a broad strategic direction down into specific plans and actual, working businesses.[7] While leaders might adopt new technologies or products, they often decline to innovate the logic of their underlying business models, even though companies that do reengineer their business models achieve greater profitability.[8]

As Markus Kliffken, a member of BPW's executive board, told us, the company had developed considerable expertise in digital technologies, having long foreseen the slowing of its core business. But the company had tried previously on multiple occasions to create digital offerings in the transportation space using sensors and tracking applications, and each time the results were subpar. "We couldn't bring these solutions to market," Kliffken related. "It never worked out. Because it isn't only about the technology—you also need to be able to enter the new market."

Recognizing that they didn't understand all the nuances they would have to master to successfully bring a digital offering to market, leaders at BPW resolved to open up the process of generating a business model when pursuing the i.Gurt. "If you are operating in a known, familiar business, you just have to optimize," Kliffken said. "But if you're talking about a new field, about something completely radical and different from the past, about a 'killer business,' then you have to overcome a number of barriers, and here the open approach is essential."[9] He notes that "without opening up, we would have never been able to bring [the i.Gurt] to market and generate a new business model around it. If we had just built it, we would have made everything wrong."[10]

If you already have a promising new strategic direction, perhaps one that you arrived at through using an open strategy tool, invite outsiders to help you build it out into a full-fledged model. As we'll see, the specific open strategy methodology BPW utilized—we call it Business Logic Contest—is efficient, effective, and relatively low cost, and working with it can make implementation of your completed business model easier as well. Many companies develop great ideas, only to see them falter thanks to a flawed business model. By setting aside your egos as BPW's leaders did, admitting that you don't know everything about a new market, and inviting outsiders to help you design a model, you stand a better chance of getting the details right, and succeeding.

The Trouble with Business Models

Why precisely do leaders struggle to translate innovative strategies into working businesses? Some companies don't understand their current business models very well—what works and what doesn't—and so aren't sure how best to build a new business model that corrects for the flaws of the old one. Managers also become wedded to assumptions, norms, and practices associated with the current model, independent of their level of understanding. They struggle to venture very far from what they already know and do, and therefore can't conceive of the new supply chain arrangements, marketing tactics, sales channels, and so on that might render a new model successful.[11]

All too often, leaders arrive at seemingly incisive, innovative business models that don't work financially. The customer might receive new value, but the company can't turn a profit.[12] We've seen this problem emerge with many digital platform–based services. Skype, for instance, generated immense new value for customers after its launch, so much so that by 2010 the company had attracted 660 million customers. But Skype had a much harder time building value for itself. Only eight million of its customers had signed up to pay for its premium service, while the rest made use of Skype's free service. As of this writing, it remains unclear whether Skype has found a sustainable model for generating revenues (this is Microsoft's problem today, while Skype's founders enjoy considerable wealth).[13] Or consider the airline AirBerlin, which coupled some features of a full-service airline with low fares. In 2010 the airline was growing quickly, suggesting that it was adding value for customers. Yet offering low fares meant the airline was operating at a loss.[14] Ultimately, the hybrid business model lacked coherence when it came to generating sustainable revenues and profits.

Companies are sometimes best off *not* pursuing game-changing technologies because they can't run them as a profitable, sustainable business. As Peter Drucker has asserted, "The first step in a growth policy is not do decide where and how to grow. It is to decide what to abandon."[15] This dictum holds particular sway when it comes to innovation. In 2000 the mobile phone company Orange paid $142 million for Wildfire Communications, which had developed an early form of a technology similar to what later became Amazon's Alexa virtual assistant. Although the technology was solid, the market wasn't ready for it, and Orange couldn't realize the intended business benefits. In 2005, Orange finally discontinued Wildfire for lack of demand.[16] Similar examples are legion. Blackberry had a desirable smartphone product but failed to build a successful business model. Apple found such a model with its iPhone, combining it with iTunes, the app store, and a large network of app developers.

Leaders also have trouble understanding when they might need a new business model. Very often, they retain their established business models, along with established processes and practices, even as they endeavor to deliver breakthrough products and services based on new technologies. They presume they can simply tack the new onto the old and all will run smoothly. All too often, it doesn't. In 2011, nobody in their right mind would have asked whether Google lacked technological capabilities or the know-how required to push a new product. And yet, when the company launched Google+, it went nowhere. Google had initially seen Google+ as a mere extension of its search business—in other words, part and parcel of its existing business model.[17] Consumers wondered why they needed Google+ when they were already struggling to make time for other social media tools. From their perspective, Google had created no extra value by combining search and social networking. To create more value, Google would have had to take a novel approach to marketing, sales, and revenue rather than jamming the new offering into its existing model.[18]

When managers pursue new business ideas, they often begin by asking, "Where do I stick this in my organization?"[19] According to Clayton M. Christensen, Thomas Bartman, and Derek Van Bever, who studied failing business models, managers feel compelled to fold new business ideas into old organizational structures to increase efficiency, leveraging existing organizational capabilities and resources wherever they can.[20] They might, for instance, try to use their old sales force to sell a new and different offering, or turn to conventional vendors for new supply chain needs.[21] Leaders also downplay the need for a new model because they see it as potentially cannibalizing the old one. Ultimately, though, it's hard to create new customer value and revenue streams by sticking to old ideas past their expiration date. Businesses that attempt this often survive in name only.[22] Only if leaders take on the risks of inefficiency and cannibalization will they manage to transition their businesses to new products and services.

Many familiar cognitive biases play a role here, preventing leaders from innovating business models as they should. To succeed with innovation, leaders must find ways to break free of their habitual patterns of thought and their industry's dominant logic. They must stop reverting to their traditional positionings and offerings, their established profit formula, and their existing combination of resources and processes. Opening up the process of creating new business models can help. As research at the University of St. Gallen has shown, 90 percent of successful business models are not entirely novel but rather new combinations of elements of existing business models either in the industry or beyond it.[23] Engineering potent recombinations thus requires deep familiarity with existing business models across company and industry boundaries. By involving external participants in business model deliberations, companies can tap their familiarity, enabling them to incorporate approaches they might not have considered. By involving company insiders as well, leaders can ensure that the business model will be practical given the company's capabilities and culture. They will also preempt internal resistance to a new business model, preventing others in the company from writing it off as overly foreign.

An open approach helps leaders recombine business model elements into new syntheses in two specific ways. First, it helps them with analogical reasoning. Successful leaders often build up new business models by identifying previous settings that seem similar or analogous, and transferring solutions that worked there. They take their perception of an unknown situation, map it onto a better-known situation,[24] and then creatively recombine different business model components.[25] Analogies have spawned some of the most compelling and creative thinking in business.[26] Supermarkets, a retail format dating back to the 1930s, have served as a rich source of analogies for many business leaders. Charlie Merrill relied on them when he developed the financial supermarket of Merrill Lynch. So did Charles Lazarus when he turned Toys "R" Us into a national phenomenon in the 1950s. Then Staples founder Thomas Stemberg came along, asking: "Could we be the Toys 'R' Us of office supplies?"[27]

Openness helps leaders increase the breadth, depth, and applicability of analogical reasoning.[28] By involving other perspectives, leaders can generate multiple analogical situations from which to derive business model components, dramatically improving the final business model. Research has shown that if individuals have access to one analogy from a different domain, they become 10 to 30 percent more successful in their attempts to address a problem. However, access to two analogies each from very different fields improves the odds of success to 80 percent.[29] Involving outsiders with detailed knowledge of other domains can also enhance the depth of knowledge leaders have about particular analogies, allowing for a smarter, more informed borrowing of business model elements. How useful an analogy is to the present context also matters. Some situations don't seem similar on the surface, even if their structural similarities run deep, while others that do seem similar really aren't. Convening equal numbers of internal and external participants in an open IMP Business Logic Contest can increase analogical breadth and depth, while working systematically through the game with internal employees helps to break down complex business cases to determine how applicable an analogy *really* is to the situation at hand.

Involving external participants in business model discussions can also help companies identify analogies not just in reasonably adjacent fields but also in fields that have absolutely nothing to do with the company's business. So many leaders limit their recombinations to components that are already familiar—what the biologist Stuart Kauffman described in his theory of "the adjacent possible."[30] And yet successful business models often arise as a result of what evolutionary biologists call "exaptation," the adaptation of a competence or characteristic for an entirely different purpose from that for which it was originally conceived, sometimes with astonishing results. While dinosaurs initially developed feathers to be attractive for potential mates and to provide warmth, they eventually adapted those feathers to help them fly.[31] Likewise, companies would do well to consider how they might adapt their existing competencies to entirely new marketplaces,[32] or how they might find radically new uses for their existing, mature technology, what Nintendo's Yokoi Gunpei has termed "lateral thinking"[33] and IMP refers to as cross-fertilization. Again, bringing together external experts and internal employees enables groups to understand existing capabilities and competences (thanks to internal participants) while also identifying radical new applications for those competences across company and industry boundaries (thanks to external participants).

Working with the Business Logic Contest

Now that you understand why opening up deliberations about business models makes sense, let's explore how to do it. The IMP Business Logic Contest is an exercise that helps groups of participants take pure ideas and turn them into an executable business model. On launching the game in 2012, IMP initially intended it to tackle a problem it encountered in strategy-making, the traditional detachment of strategy-making from execution. When making strategic decisions, leaders typically focus on where to compete (in which industries and markets), pushing off to the implementation phase any consideration of the competencies, resources, and value chains they'll need. IMP devised the Business Logic Contest as a means of spurring leaders to think about the "what" and the "how" of strategy together—to explicitly integrate the customer interface related to value creation with value capture and its associated process. This ensures that a company collectively engages in developing a unique proposition that works coherently for *that company*. It seemed natural to mobilize business models as a vehicle since these capture the execution details a company will need to master to achieve its goals and do so sustainably.[34] As of this writing, IMP has conducted more than 120 open Business Model Logic Contests in seventy companies.

The structure of these contests is fairly straightforward. The company convenes a group of fifteen to twenty participants and divides them into teams of four or five, each team to include a mix of internal and external participants (external participants typically do not come from competitors, reducing the risk of a conflict of interest). These teams compete to produce the detailed elements of a business model for a company's proposed new strategy. The IMP Business Logic Contest ultimately seeks to create unique, coherent, and sustainable business models that competitors will find it difficult to replicate.[35] To pull this off, each team has a coach who prompts participants to articulate and answer questions related to the various elements of a business model: desired positioning, associated products and services, value chains, marketing and sales logics, revenue structure, and so on (figure 8.1). Leaders together with external experts vote on individual elements of the business models created by the teams and select which one they would prefer to execute. Gamifying the process by framing it as a competition between teams boosts engagement while enabling leaders to discard models they might find unrealistic.

In running a Business Model Logic Contest, IMP typically begins by considering the client company's positioning in the market, brainstorming ways to sustainably differentiate a potential offering from competitors' offerings. To help the company realize this positioning, participants then define the particular products or services a company might offer, closely analyzing the specific customer needs the company is trying to

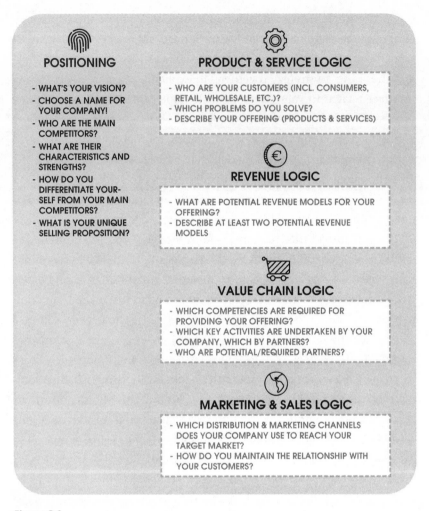

Figure 8.1
The Business Model Logic Contest.

fulfill. The goal here is to help the company stake out a "monopoly" position in customers' minds. From here, participants consider the core of the business model, the profit model, including revenues and costs, defining how the company will earn money. The final two parts of the conversation, value creation logic and sales and marketing logic, explore how the company will bring a product or service to market to acquire and retain customers. Here participants distinguish between "core" elements the company must execute itself and "noncore" elements it can execute in partnership with others, taking into account the company's core competencies and the value creation the company can achieve.[36]

As we saw earlier in the case of BPW, companies can use Business Model Logic Contests to plot out how to pursue a novel strategy based on an innovative technology. But they can also use these games to help them decide which strategies *not* to pursue. Suppose you're a firm operating in the energy and cooling industry, and your company owns a revolutionary new technology that is up to 50 percent more efficient than conventional systems. Over the years, you've invested more than €50 million in this environmentally friendly technology and you've established partnerships with universities, research labs, and suppliers. You've built a proof-of-concept prototype and your organization is enthusiastic about the prospect of introducing energy-efficient products. Customers are demanding more sustainable solutions that help them cut their carbon footprints. What should you do? Rush the product to market? Or should you slow down and take a more deliberate approach?

In 2002 the industrial conglomerate Mellsoft Systems found itself in precisely this position (The company's name and certain identifying details have been changed to support anonymity). Through an acquisition, the company had obtained licenses on the patents for magnetocaloric materials, which heat up when placed in a magnetic field and cool when removed from one. The magnetocaloric effect itself is not new: the German physicist Emil Warburg observed it as far back as 1880,[37] and the physicists Pierre Weiss and Auguste Piccard explained it in theoretical terms in 1918.[38] Previously, though, scientists could achieve it only at high temperatures. Mellsoft's technology—new magnetocaloric materials and more effective permanent magnets—achieved it at room temperature.[39] Mellsoft obtained the exclusive rights to market a new manganese-iron-phosphorus-silicon material that possessed optimum magnetocaloric properties across a whole range of temperatures.[40] With this material, even weak magnetic fields would allow large temperature differences that Mellsoft could use in refrigerators with up to half the energy of conventional cooling technology and less noise. When you consider that about a fifth of energy use was devoted to refrigeration, Mellsoft's new technology seemed highly promising indeed.[41]

Over the years, Mellsoft invested heavily to develop this technology. In 2015, Mellsoft and two global partners presented the world's first prototype of a magnetocaloric wine cooler.[42] This compressor-free cooler, developed as a pilot project, produced zero ozone-depleting gases or greenhouse gases, saved energy, cut utility bills, and reduced operating noise. Mellsoft intended to introduce the magnetocaloric technology in the household appliances markets within the next couple of years. However, in attempting to do so, Mellsoft discovered that it would be more difficult than it had expected to displace traditional, compressor-based appliances. Because compressor technology is so mature, high-end quality compressors for refrigerators are very cheap—around €18–19 per refrigerator. As good as its magnetocaloric technology was, Mellsoft struggled to make the economics appealing to customers when compared with traditional technology.

Unsure what to do, and wondering whether other potential applications existed for its technology beyond the consumer appliances market, Mellsoft engaged with IMP to undertake a series of open Business Model Logic Contests involving external participants. IMP convened a group that included scientists from the Fraunhofer Society and from several technical universities, experts from large established players within the energy sector and the commercial heating and cooling industry, and leaders from startups in the lab product cooling business and the sensor industry. Internal Mellsoft participants also joined in. Participants initially identified twenty-five potential applications of magnetocaloric technology, winnowing these to seven in the areas of process industries, transport and logistics, battery cooling/e-mobility, and waste heat utilization for energy production. Considering technical and commercial characteristics such as achievable cost relative to a given performance level, the current gap in the job to be done, and market attractiveness, participants then delved deeper into three potential opportunity areas before selecting two—anticounterfeiting protection and the cooling of rooms and buildings—for which to develop detailed business models.[43]

As it turns out, we can use the magnetocaloric effect to determine whether luxury goods or a piece of currency has been counterfeited. However, as Mellsoft found when it convened experts from Deutsche Bank, producers of luxury consumer goods, and others, the technology would not become commercially viable in this area any time soon. As for the cooling of rooms and buildings, experts suggested that it wouldn't be economically viable to develop an offering for the cooling of rooms because the technology in the field already was efficient. An opportunity did seem to exist to provide air-conditioning systems for high-end historic buildings in city centers, since in many cases architectural protection regulations prevented the installation of conventional compressors. Yet, as the group concluded, Mellsoft would need to work with engineering partners to address this market. Potential partners didn't think the economics would work to allow a viable product, and so declined to collaborate.

In the end, Mellsoft decided to postpone its attempts to commercialize magnetocaloric technology. It was a painful decision in light of all the company had invested, but a necessary one. By exposing leaders at Mellsoft to fresh, objective voices from outside the organization, the Business Model Logic Contest sessions allowed Mellsoft leaders to overcome biases that might have inclined them to continue to pursue the technology, even if doing so made little sense for the company. It gave them the reality check they needed to cut a big project with many internal stakeholders. As research has found, the management of failing investments may be at least as important to a company's fortunes as the ability to pick and manage successes, if not more so.[44] By developing detailed business plans before entering new markets, and by doing so as part of an open process, Mellsoft might have saved itself from investing millions more in other potential offerings, only to find them every bit as impractical in economic terms as its initial foray into appliances was.

The Broader Uses of Business Model Logic Contests

When companies decide to pursue a business model derived from a business logic game, they have no guarantee of success. But even if the specific business model fails to bear fruit, the benefits of the exercise remain significant. In 2017, the sportswear maker adidas conducted a four-day Business Model Logic Contest. The mission: to help the company decide how to deploy strategically the ultra-high-technology Speedfactory production plants it had piloted. These plants permitted ultra-short lead times, customization and personalization, higher product quality, cocreation, data-driven demand prediction, and positive brand awareness.[45] Since at this point it wasn't clear what the right go-to-market strategy might be, IMP was asked to help answer a slew of questions about the Speedfactories, including what business models might be possible and how they might change the industry. Adidas suggested also bringing in creatives from outside the company who weren't constrained by conventional assumptions about producing and selling sneakers.

Convening a dozen adidas employees from around the world with diverse backgrounds, along with a dozen external experts, adidas spent the first two days generating new, radical ideas for the Speedfactories and narrowing them down to a few promising concepts. During the last two days, teams worked to translate the four best ideas into full-blown business plans, covering all elements of the business model logic described above. A panel of experts voted on each of the five elements of each business model. Employees at adidas headquarters could also attend the presentations and vote remotely by scanning a QR code with their smartphones. Top management chose the winning business model, which deployed the Speedfactories to produce fully recyclable shoes. Acknowledging the important trends of sustainability and rising environmental consciousness, this business model called for a circular product that relied on the collection of old shoes, reuse of their plastic components, and sales of sneakers using a subscription model.

It turned out to become an exciting process and almost breathtakingly ambitious and creative, even though it wouldn't be easy: some of the ideas could potentially disrupt adidas's core business and existing practices. In fact, in 2019 the company announced it was closing its two pilot Speedfactories and transferring the component technologies to its established suppliers in Asia to improve their efficiency.[46] Still, the business logic sessions were not in vain. In 2019 the company introduced a first test series of its Futurecraft Loop, the first 100 percent recyclable performance running shoe and according to the company one of the first consumer products of any kind designed for a circular life cycle.[47] Adidas is considering selling this product through a subscription model, as envisioned in the winning business model.[48]

In 2020, adidas announced it would substantially reduce its plastic pollution and "end plastic waste in its products within the next decade, using recycled materials and designing fully recyclable products in the short term."[49] To make its plastic manufacturing process more sustainable and to scale up Futurecraft Loop, adidas would still rely on Speedfactory technology and associated knowledge, even if that was located at its Asian suppliers. More broadly, Speedfactory and the open strategy exercises adidas has undertaken have forced the organization to contemplate how it might innovate its production processes going forward. Whereas initially adidas had focused on customization, individualization, and the ability to adapt to customer tastes, the open strategy deliberations pointed toward utilizing Speedfactory technology to enable opportunities within recycling and sustainability.[50] Open strategy obviously had served as way to prepare the organization for likely future changes. Even if the company hadn't adopted the winning business model in the first instance, it had encouraged employees to think about doing business in new ways, which might facilitate the implementation of new business models in the future, whatever form they happen to take.

In Sum

Open strategy deliberations aren't just for idea generation. They can also help companies take the next step and formulate specific business models to deploy. Involving mixed teams of internal and external participants

Tips for Running the IMP Business Logic Contest

- *Choose the right external experts.* You want people with experience around resource allocation, business models, and implementation. Select people who seek to participate because of their desire to engage with the topic, have fun, establish relationships, and build their network.
- *Engage top leaders.* For example, you could entice participants by offering them the chance to present their ideas to members of the management board.
- *Define the parameters.* Offer clear instruction about the workshop's goal of designing a new strategic plan, highlighting what participants should and shouldn't discuss. The instructions should detail how the company will pursue a given strategic idea. Participants shouldn't question this creative idea or try to come up with a new one, as the time for that has passed.
- *Present the strategic ideas that will be used as starting points.* These ideas will come from the workshops or crowdsourcing initiatives described in previous chapters and conducted prior to the open Business Model Logic Contest. You should give participants any background information about the idea they need to elaborate a detailed business model. Don't overdo it, though, or you'll influence participants unduly and constrain the final results.
- *Don't go straight to implementation.* When the workshop is over, spend some time fine-tuning the business model, sometimes combining elements of different business models. You may wish to have some of the internal participants who created the winning plan help with this work.

can help companies draw on a wide array of elements from prior business models to recombine into a radical, new model. Doing so can also ensure that the new business model will prove realistic for the company given its competencies, norms, and culture, and make it more likely that others within the company will accept and implement the new business model.

Critically, the process of crystallizing a business model points the organization toward implementation of the strategy from the very outset. When it comes to strategy, ideas and implementation often seem to live on different planets. During the idea phase, executives typically concentrate on competitors and markets. During the implementation phase they focus on competencies, resources, and value chains. Adopting a business model forces executives to integrate both of these—the customer interface and the supply side. The result is a strategic plan that is "born ready" to implement, and, quite possibly, a new, killer business for the company.

Questions to Ponder:

- Do you and your team tend to focus more on new products or new technologies rather than on new business models?

- Is your current business model sustainable in the long run?

- Does your company really have the insights, agility, and speed it needs internally to develop new business models?

- How might you manage the turf wars that will inevitably break out when a new business model doesn't fit into the existing corporate structure?

9   Use the Crowd to Choose Better Strategies

One fall day in 1906, the eighty-five-year-old scientist Sir Francis Galton was out for a stroll when he came across a weight-judging competition. A large crowd was peering at a live ox, trying to guess how much meat it would yield after slaughter, with the most accurate guesser receiving a prize. "Many non-experts competed," Galton wrote, "like those clerks and others who have not expert knowledge of horses, but who bet on races, guided by newspapers, friends, and their own fancies."[1] The idea that such a common rabble had the intelligence and insight to come to an accurate estimation seemed laughable. As Henry David Thoreau had opined decades earlier, "The mass never comes up to the standard of its best member, but on the contrary degrades itself with the lowest."[2]

Galton saw the weight-judging competition as a perfect opportunity to prove just how dumb crowds of people really were. He obtained the competition entries (787 in all), calculated the median and the mean, and compared them to the ox's actual weight. His findings must have occasioned a double-take: the crowd's estimation was astonishingly accurate. The median guess—the one that represented the very middle of the range of guesses—came in at 1,207 pounds, just nine pounds more than the butchered ox's actual weight of 1,198 pounds. The average of the competitors' guesses was 1,197—just one pound off. Individual members of the crowd might not be as intelligent or as discerning as a studied expert, but in the aggregate, the crowd's intelligence was as competent at guessing, perhaps even more so.

In recent years, leading-edge companies have deployed Galton's discovery to help them predict future outcomes and in turn make better strategic decisions. In the equipment rental business, it's not easy to predict customer needs, behavior, and pricing across a wide network of local areas. Accuracy in these areas matters, allowing a company to respond to customers' needs efficiently and with the least amount of capital. In 2012, leaders at Zeppelin Rental, a Munich-based firm with operations in six European countries, tapped the wisdom of its employees at more than one hundred locations to improve its decision-making.

By creating a social forecasting tool and embedding it in the company's intranet, leaders identified a number of questions they needed to answer in the course of making strategic decisions: "Which new competitors will enter our markets?" "Which acquisition candidate would fit our company particularly well?" "What will rental prices be in the next months in our markets?" "Will customers accept higher prices for eco-friendly machinery?" Leaders opened the tool to the company's eight-hundred-strong workforce, posing questions in phases lasting two to five days each. In answering the questions, participants could also weight their answers depending on how confident they felt about them. Based on the weighted forecasts, the tool calculated a collective forecast and forwarded it to top management. Employees earned points depending on how accurate their forecasts turned out to be, collecting them to earn rewards.

As Christoph Afheldt, Zeppelin Rental's director of corporate development, says, this tool has proven effective, so much so that leaders use it regularly to inform their decision-making. Employees "help us analyzing customer needs, market states and trends, developments in the competitive environments and to identify potential for future developments."[3] Like members of the British public at the weight-judging competition, Zeppelin Rental's employees have proven highly accurate as a group. Comparing actual events with the forecasts, Crowdworx, the provider of the company's social forecasting software solution, found that on average more than 80 percent of the aggregated forecasts were correct, and in some cases more than 90 percent were. In light of the high levels of uncertainty that exist around the questions Zeppelin

Rental was asking and the incomplete information employees have at their disposal, these results are exceptional.

Your company can unleash the wisdom of the crowd to help with forecasting and decision-making (see figure 9.1). One option is to set up prediction markets to collect and distill information from employees or other participants. In these markets, participants buy and sell virtual shares representing future events or outcomes, with share prices reflecting the crowd's predictions of which events are more or less likely to occur. Simpler mechanisms for generating crowd predictions exist as well. Companies can set up forecasting competitions in which participants don't trade shares but rather vie to predict future outcomes. With all of these mechanisms, companies can tap the collective intelligence of employees within the firm and beyond, generating better-informed and more effective strategies than leaders could have come up with on their own.

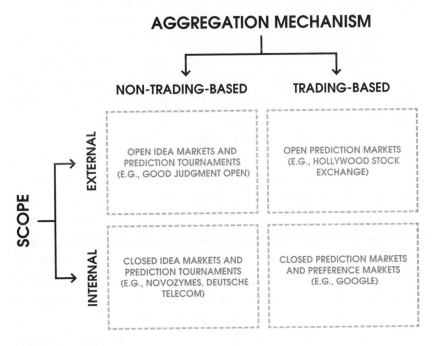

Figure 9.1
Types of crowd-based predictions.

Crowdsourcing's Untapped Potential

On the face of it, corporate strategy-making would seem especially well suited to crowdsourcing. In crafting strategies, leaders must navigate uncertainty, assessing possible scenarios and drawing information from diverse quarters. And yet, as James Surowiecki noted in 2005, "companies have remained, for the most part, indifferent to this source of potentially excellent information, and have been surprisingly unwilling to improve their decision making by tapping into the collective wisdom of their employees."[4] More companies have turned to crowd predictions for decision-making in the years since, but they still don't use them as often as they do other open source tools. According to McKinsey's Enterprise 2.0 survey of 1,700 companies from around the world, about 30 percent of companies used prediction markets to harvest collective insights in 2016, up from just 9 percent in 2009.[5] By contrast, blogs, social networks, and wikis have seen penetration rates of 50 to 70 percent.

Why are companies so timid when it comes to crowdsourcing? As the economist Donald N. Thompson has argued, the problem is an enduring belief in elite expertise, "the idea that lower-level employees might have input to management decisions. Senior managers value expertise and when in doubt hire consultants."[6] If you too harbor this belief, you should remember that expertise is hardly a guarantee of accuracy. In *The Innovator's Dilemma*, Clayton Christensen showed that market forecasts for disruptive innovations almost always are terribly wrong. Studying the disk drive industry, he compared market forecasts of several generations of technologies published by a top market research firm with actual sales. He found that *Disk/Trend Report* had a remarkable track record when forecasting sales of innovations for existing customers and existing markets, off by less than 10 percent. When it tried to predict sales for disruptive innovations, it was off by hundreds of percentage points. Forecasting methods that work well for incremental innovations, such as doing economic modeling, holding discussions with industry experts, and running focus groups with customers, don't work when market, customers, or technologies are new.[7]

On the other hand, ever since Sir Francis Galton stumbled on that weight-judging competition, crowdsourcing has distinguished itself for its accuracy. Decades of research have established what Jacob Bernoulli called "the law of large numbers," namely, that the average opinion of a large, diverse crowd usually is very close to the true value, and closer than the best estimate of any one person in the crowd. As former Wall Street strategist and adjunct Columbia Business School professor Michael J. Mauboussin explains it, "All of us walk around with a little information and [significantly inaccurate views of the world]. And when we aggregate our results, the errors tend to cancel each other out and what is distilled is pure information."[8]

If you've ever participated in a jellybean-guessing contest, you know Mauboussin speaks the truth. No individual will correctly guess the number of jellybeans in a jar, but the average guess comes very close, usually closer than the best individual guess. Serious academic research backs this up. Jack Treynor was a professor of finance at the University of Southern California and a pioneer of modern investment theory. Wondering how market prices could be so accurate, he speculated that the market reflected not the accuracy of a few experts but "the faulty opinions of a large number of investors who err independently." Treynor also posited that "the mechanism whereby a large number of error-prone judgments are pooled to achieve a more accurate 'consensus' is not confined to finance, or even economics."[9] He held up his jellybean experiments as proof. Treynor asked students in his investment classes to estimate the number of jellybeans in a jar. Treynor repeatedly showed that the mean estimate was more than 97 percent accurate, a level of accuracy confirmed by many other subsequent experiments.

Following Treynor's logic, you might suppose a large crowd would do a better job of predicting share prices than a few professional analysts at banks, brokerages, and research companies. Michael Nofer and Oliver Hinz from the Technical University in Darmstadt, Germany, collected data on more than 10,000 buy or sell recommendations from Sharewise, a large and diverse online community and Europe's largest devoted to stock prediction, over a four-year period.[10] People sign up on

Sharewise for free, choose a specific stock or index, discuss and share predictions about their favorite stocks in the forum, and communicate their opinions to others. Each community member can assign buy and sell ratings. Comparing how well the community's shared recommendations performed compared to those of professionals, Nofer and Hinz found that the internet community's recommendations yielded an average annual return 0.59 percentage points higher than that of the investment professionals. "On average," they write, "investors are better off by trusting the crowd rather than analysts."[11]

The Accuracy of Prediction Markets

Prediction markets in particular have a strong track record of accuracy. In 1988, three University of Iowa economists—George Neumann, Robert Forsythe, and Forrest Nelson—enjoyed a beer after work at a local sports bar. As they talked, they found themselves wondering why election polls proved so inaccurate time and again.[12] One of them came up with the idea of using a stock market mechanism instead of polls to predict the outcomes of elections. It was a fairly simple notion. As described by the economist and Nobel Prize winner Friedrich Hayek back in 1945, markets serve as effective mechanisms for aggregating dispersed and asymmetric information.[13] Prices, according to Eugene Fama's famous efficient market hypothesis, reflect all private and publicly available information of an underlying traded commodity on a market.[14] On a stock market, traders predict the future value of a company and trade. If they believe a share price is undervalued, they will buy; if they believe it is overvalued, they will sell.

Translate this idea to a prediction market for elections, and supply and demand would lead to a share price for the candidates. If a trader judged a stock as undervalued (that is, the candidate stands a stronger chance of winning), he would buy. If a trader believed a stock was overvalued (that is, the candidate stands a stronger chance of losing), he would sell. In this way, stock prices would aggregate all information in the market, representing the outcomes of the elections as determined by the wisdom of the crowd.

The Iowa Electronic Market, as the three economists called their market, first operated during the 1988 presidential election. Some eight hundred investors—mostly young, male, and from rural Iowa—traded contracts for the main candidates: George H. W. Bush (Republican), Michael Dukakis (Democrat), Ron Paul (Libertarian), and Lenora Fulani (New Alliance). The moment came on election night: would share prices correctly predict the winner and the vote splits between candidates? They did, and with much more accuracy than the Gallup, Harris, and CBS/*New York Times* polls. The polls carried an average margin of error of 1.9 percent, the Iowa Electronic Market's just one-tenth of a percent.

Since then, organizers have deployed the Iowa Electronic Market for a wide variety of predictions. In elections, the market has produced very accurate predictions, outperforming large-scale polling organizations most of the time.[15] Others have applied prediction markets to anticipate future outcomes in other areas, such as economic development and the success of movies.[16] Companies have successfully used prediction markets to estimate future outcomes, including those related to strategy. At Siemens, leaders used prediction markets to estimate whether teams would meet project milestones. An Austrian mobile phone provider used prediction markets to predict future market shares of all major competitors in the market.[17] Many studies in business contexts have shown that prediction markets outperform expert judgment.[18]

We ourselves have tested how well prediction markets could forecast market shares of product innovation as compared with industry experts. During the 1970s, companies sold about eight million pairs of skis annually around the world. Today they sell just 3.2 million. To survive in a declining market, companies have turned to innovation, introducing new product designs each year with great fanfare. Companies have trouble predicting demand or market share for these innovations. Forecasts can err by as much as 50 to 75 percent (although typically not quite that much). "It would be ideal," one brand manager from a leading company told us, "if the forecast error was around 3 percent. In recent years in our company, they were between 5 and 15 percent."[19] We wondered: could a prediction market yield such accuracy?

We ran a prediction market with sixty anonymous ski enthusiasts whom we recruited through Facebook. We presented these participants with innovations created by four ski producers in four product segments, letting them trade for twelve days during the autumn before ski season began. At the end of the following May, we reviewed actual sales figures and market shares. The accuracy of the market's predictions stupefied us. The mean absolute error (MAE)—our estimate for accuracy—came in at 2.74 percent in the first product segment, 3.99 percent in the second one, 4.64 percent in the third, and 9.09 percent in the fourth.[20] (The MAE is the arithmetic average of the deviations of the predictions for the products in each product segment from the true values. The lower this value, the better the prediction.) In three of the four prediction markets, the forecast beat companies' own predictions. The fourth market was somewhat less accurate than company predictions, but this market had seen small trading volumes and therefore had been less efficient in aggregating information.

Prediction markets work so well in large part because they do a better job than other forecasting tools of incentivizing people to reveal true information.[21] In an opinion survey, organizers ask a sample of people about their individual opinions on a question. Some people refuse to take part, others provide the quickest answer possible, some don't want to reveal personal information, others have no reliable information to base a decision on, and so on. Analyzing the results of their survey, organizers weight the responses of each of these participants equally. In prediction markets, by contrast, traders self-select into the market. If they possess more information or feel more confident about an issue, they put more money into the market and buy more shares."[22] As Bo Cowgill, a professor at Columbia Business School who studied Google's pioneering prediction markets extensively, noted, "If you let people bet on things anonymously, they will tell you what they really believe because they have money at stake. This is a conversation that's happening without politics. Nobody knows who each other is, and nobody has any incentive to kiss up."[23]

Running Prediction Markets

Now that we've shown that prediction markets work well as a form of trading-based crowd predictions, let's examine how to set them up:

Step 1: Formulate the Decision Problem

Prediction markets work especially well when the predictive factors that contribute to strategic decision-making hinge on knowledge scattered across different departments or locations. Such factors include prediction of market shares and technology breakthroughs, the testing of business plans, the choice of the best business model, predictions of future moves on the part of competitors, and so on. Make sure that the factors you need to pin down are concrete and specific. If, for example, you wish to determine the likelihood of success for different business models, narrow down the list of models to just a few, and let participants invest in those. When setting up a prediction market for the ski industry, we sought to know the market share of new products in four different market segments: race skis, the powder segment, technology products, and women's skis. We showed photos of the skis to prediction market participants and provided detailed technical specifications.

You must formulate the question you seek to answer very specifically so that participants can clearly answer it at a given point in time.[24] In our case, the question was: "Out of the total European quantity of sales for the following race skis in 2010/11, what percentage (market share) will be captured by each of them?" We obtained detailed information about the innovations four different ski producers planned to introduce in each of these segments. Prediction market participants could trade virtual shares of these products. If one race ski for example, traded at thirty-two, it meant that the crowd was pegging its future market share at 32 percent. If traders believed the ski held more potential, they would buy shares, seeking to benefit from the market's undervaluing of the shares. If they thought the share price was too high, they would sell.

Step 2: Recruit Participants

In general, the quality of the predictions and decisions increases with the number of participants. Hence you should try to involve as many traders as feasible. Try also to ensure sufficient diversity among your market participants. To forecast the success of a new business model, include participants who know the potential customers, competitors, technology experts, and so on. As a rule of thumb, include at least fifty participants. Any fewer, and you will very likely experience liquidity problems in the market, leading to unreliable forecasts.[25] As on any stock market, some traders will prove marginal, trading very actively and investing more capital to try to exploit all under- or overvaluations. Such traders increase liquidity and push market prices to the right value.[26] Other traders will trade less, lack information, and exert only a minor influence on prices.

If the decision problem doesn't raise confidentiality issues, you would do well to include outsiders, as they bring in new perspectives and information, increasing the accuracy of the crowd's prediction. Most participants enjoy trading, and adding traders doesn't mean taking on a great deal of marginal cost. In our ski project, the sixty Facebook users we recruited were all experienced and excited skiers, although not all were bona fide experts. We recruited them via the Facebook pages of two bigger ski producers and via an online sports platform in Austria (Laola1.at) that published an article titled "Which Technology is Convincing You?"

Step 3: Design the Market

Now you must decide how many competing ideas to include, what trading mechanism to use, and how long the market will remain open. You might wish to test many ideas, but prediction markets work best if you limit yourself to no more than four competing ideas. If you have more than that, preselect the best ones and winnow them down to between two and four.[27] As for trading mechanisms, most organizers opt for a double-auction market in which participants submit their buy and sell orders and organizers execute those immediately so long as corresponding sell or buy orders exist on the other side of the order book.[28] You can also use a call auction format, or a hybrid of a double and call auction, in which orders accumulate and organizers execute them simultaneously at a specific point in time. Double auctions usually work best, as they incorporate information into prices on a continuous basis, allowing traders to react immediately. Prediction markets can last for several months or as little as a few hours.[29] If participants need time to collect information or if additional information will become available only after some delay, keep the market open for longer. Otherwise a longer trading period offers dwindling returns, as the number of unique traders decreases over time.[30] Market research organizations such as Cultivate Labs, Crowdworx, and Prediki specialize in prediction markets and can help with the nuances of their design.

Step 4: Decide on the Incentive Mechanism
You will obtain reliable predictions only if participants actively trade. Some prediction markets use real money as incentives, linking participants' reward to their trading performance. Since certain countries (the United States included) regard this as illegal gambling, most companies use virtual money, handing out prizes or gift certificates as incentives. eBay gave $200 gift certificates to the best traders in its prediction market, while Google used its own virtual money, called Goobles (Google rubles), giving each trader 10,000 every three months. Participants could redeem their Goobles on a quarterly basis for tickets to an in-house lottery. The company picked six tickets at random, each paying $1,000. Less active traders in the prediction market received gift certificates and special t-shirts.[31]

For most strategic questions, the honor of winning and a more symbolic gift will suffice as incentives (although you might need more tangible incentives when you ask outsiders to participate).[32] In its prediction market, Google realized that intrinsic motivation, competition, and reputation served as strong incentives for participation; trading volume rose when participants made their performance "public." Encouragement from leaders also helps. Rewarding the best trader with real money can actually prove counterproductive if participants use fake money during the market exercise. Some players might place high-risk bets, perceiving no real downside (they won't lose actual money). As a workaround, pay out to the most active trader rather than the one with the most accurate predictions.

Step 5: Start Trading

If participants play for the honor of winning, as we advise, the market will run on fake money. At the start, give each player a certain amount of it. If they lack familiarity with prediction markets, participants may require some training, as well as basic information about the decision problem, the trading period, how organizers will choose the winner, and so on before they can start trading.

Step 6: Analyze the Results

In a simple, two-outcomes trading model, the share prices represent the market's collective estimation of the probability of a certain event occurring. Let's say you wish to predict whether your competitor will enter the market with a new technology by the end of this year. You would create the following contract for the prediction market: You pay $100 to the holder of a share if your competitor introduces the new technology by the end of 2021 and nothing otherwise. You set the opening price at $50 and offer the share for sale to the traders. If a participant believes that the technology stands a greater than 50 percent chance of being introduced, they would buy shares. Otherwise, they would sell. Share prices rise and fall until supply balances with demand. That balance point represents the traders' consensus about the event's probability (see figure 9.2). If at the end of the trading period the share price is $85, this means that the crowd pegs the odds of the technology's introduction at 85 percent.

HOW PREDICTION MARKETS WORK

THE PRICE OF THE SHARES REFLECTS THE PARTICIPANTS' OPINION ABOUT THE LIKELIHOOD OF AN EVENT

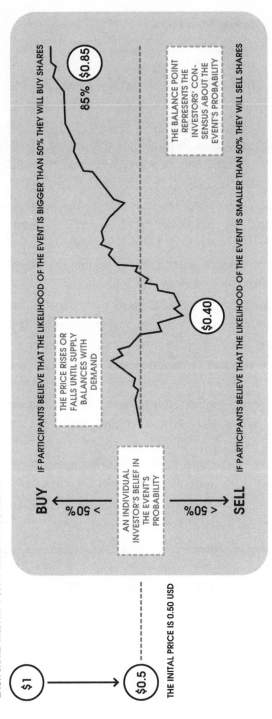

Figure 9.2

How prediction markets work.

Source: Adapted from Adam Mann, "The Power of Prediction Markets," *Nature News* 538, no. 7625 (2016): 308.

Preference or Idea Markets

Prediction markets add great value in strategy projects, but they do have their limits. Markets work well if you have an outcome in the near future you wish to anticipate in order to make strategic choices in the present. If you wish to select and evaluate potential ideas for strategies (for instance, products, technologies, or business models you might pursue), running a prediction market allows you to mobilize crowd-based insight to pick the most promising ones. You can also use prediction markets to test assumptions informing your strategy-making—about competition, say, technology breakthroughs, or societal trends. Often, though, strategy deals with long-term issues and outcomes that companies can't easily measure. For such problems, a variant of prediction markets exists: preference or idea markets.[33]

These markets are similar to prediction markets, except here participants suggest ideas that they then trade as stocks. The market mechanism allows for a collective filtering and evaluation of ideas, with the stock price attached to specific ideas representing collective thinking about their prospects of success.[34] Such an approach allows organizers to develop and evaluate multiple ideas at once. Because submitters of ideas receive real time feedback via the stock price, a learning process takes place as buying and selling proceeds. Meanwhile, constant feedback via the pricing mechanism improves submitted ideas, filters out lower rated ideas, and efficiently selects the best. Research has found that idea markets' competitive nature also spurs innovation, supporting senior executives' strategic decision-making.

A large European technology company installed an idea market that allowed employees to submit ideas for new technologies, product ideas, and business ideas the company might be pursuing ten years into the future.[35] The market unfolded in three phases: Idea sourcing, idea filtering, and idea evaluation. During the first phase, all employees could submit ideas (see figure 9.3). To encourage participation, employees who submitted the first twenty-five ideas received $30 gift certificates. During the subsequent idea-trading phase, registered participants received $10,000 each in virtual money, and the ten best traders were awarded a total of $3,000 in prizes (as suggested, you might also reward the most active traders, not necessarily the best). Although this incentive seems small, intrinsic motivations prompt most people to participate, as well as the reputational benefits and recognition that might come from winning.

At this company, 642 employees from seventeen countries registered for the idea market, submitting 252 ideas (thirty-nine ideas for new technologies, forty-nine ideas for new products, and 164 ideas for new product and business ideas) during the twenty-four-day idea submission period. Each idea judged as either "new to the company" or "new to the market" became an idea stock "candidate." During the second phase, which unfolded over the course of a week, participants collectively selected ideas for the initial public offering (IPO), buying shares of the candidate ideas for $5 each. Ideas that generated more than $40,000 qualified for the IPO. If an idea made it to the market, the submitter received a $30 gift certificate plus $1,000 in virtual money to trade.

During the third phase, trading started, with the final share prices reflecting the crowd's collective assessment of each idea's quality. For new technology ideas, the share prices reflected the "percentage of revenues that would be influenced by the technology in 10 years"; for new product ideas, they reflected the "number of units that will be sold 10 years from now"; and for new business ideas, the target was "predict the most innovative product and business ideas."[36]

In the end, senior managers embraced several of the best ideas, selecting them for further development. Three independent researchers reviewed and evaluated the market, assigning an expert committee to evaluate the ideas (the committee was comprised of senior experts at other tech, strategy, and venture capital firms). The researchers also surveyed participants' and senior management's evaluation of the market and compared the idea market outcome to the expert committee's evaluation. The researchers concluded that their study of this idea market "demonstrates the feasibility of an idea market in a real-world setting, as well as its ability to source, filter, and evaluate new product ideas and promising technologies."[37] Other large-scale research studies confirmed that idea markets conform well with assessments of expert panels and comprise valuable

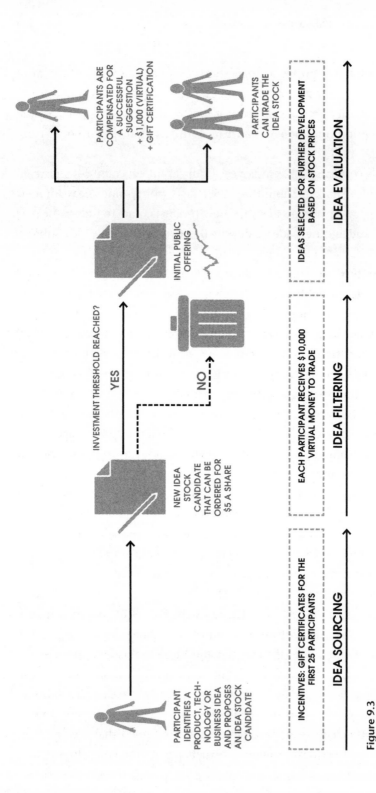

Figure 9.3
Idea market.

Source: Adapted from Arina Soukhoroukova, Martin Spann, and Bernd Skiera, "Sourcing, Filtering, and Evaluating New Product Ideas: An Empirical Exploration of the Performance of Idea Markets," *Journal of Product Innovation Management* 29, no. 1 (2012): 106.

tools to aggregate dispersed knowledge in support of senior executive's strategic decision making.[38]

Crowd Predictions and Decisions

Companies need not include a market mechanism when tapping the wisdom of the crowd. *Prediction tournaments* are competitions in which participants vie to predict future outcomes without buying or selling them on an open market. At a Fortune 100 packaged goods company, over two hundred employees from various departments and hierarchical levels participated in a tournament in which they could make forecasts on eleven strategy-related topics (for instance, unit sales across various markets), receiving points based on the accuracy of their forecasts.[39] The top two point-earners received cash prizes, while others won additional prizes through a lottery drawing. Before making their predictions, participants analyzed relevant background information related to past sales, potential marketing tactics, and so on. Organizers encouraged them to collect additional information from both inside and outside the company. Participants could view other predictions participants made in real time, revising their predictions accordingly.

Marketing professor Mark Lang and his co-authors compared the aggregated collective prediction (the mean prediction across participants) during the tournament with a company's own forecasts and actual results. They found that almost three quarters of the time, the tournament proved more accurate than the company's standard forecasting methods. The margin of error of predictions emerging from the tournament beat that produced by the company's standard methods by more than 40 percent.[40] As these researchers concluded, "crowdsourcing can yield market-oriented predictions equal to or better than those produced by the incumbent methods used by the firm. Crowdsourcing applications are also less expensive, and faster and easier to implement than many existing methods (e.g. consumer surveys)."[41]

Following repeated strategic mistakes during the 2000s, Deutsche Telekom eagerly embraced crowd prediction tournaments in 2011, piloting them to generate estimates of future market penetration, pricing, music streaming and download volumes, and so on. The results proved so impressive that the company went on to introduce prediction tournaments across the firm. Almost every week, teams test a new product idea or business model using crowd intelligence. They first define a decision problem for the crowd to address. Using a simple online tool, teams then invite employees from across the company to participate (Deutsche Telekom believes that every employee has something to add, and that combining such distributed knowledge into one system carries tremendous strategic value).

Once a team broadcasts a decision problem, employees have three or four days to enter their forecast into the online tool. They can also weight their forecast depending on how confident they feel about it. The tool aggregates these forecasts into a collective forecast. Within a week, decision-makers have their results. Employees earn points depending on how accurate their forecast turns out to be once actual outcomes become known. In addition to this incentive and the desire for recognition, employees also value receiving feedback on their ideas once the prediction project concludes. As Ulrich Meyer-Berhorn, senior manager at the Center for Strategic Projects at Deutsche Telekom, remarked, Deutsche Telekom takes crowd predictions seriously—a reality not lost on participants. The company has "invested millions of Euros on the basis of the outcomes of such projects of crowd intelligence."[42]

Although confidentiality concerns prompt most companies to restrict prediction tournaments to employees and others inside the firm, some open these tournaments to the general public. Earlier in the book, we referenced the Good Judgment Project, an initiative funded by the US Intelligence Advance Research Projects Activity (IARPA) aimed at accurately forecasting a wide array of geopolitical and economic topics.[43] As we've seen, the political scientist Philip Tetlock identified a group of "super-forecasters" in this project comprising 2 percent of all participants. Members of this group outperformed US intelligence analysts by a 30 percent margin.[44] Good Judgment Inc, a follow up to the Good Judgement Project, now offers crowdsourced forecasting services to government and corporate decision-makers on its forecasting platform. Working with clients, Good Judgment helps formulate and frame the forecasting question and recruits a group of super-forecasters. Instead of hiring one or a few expert consultants, companies can tap a network of highly diverse super-forecasters varying in age, cultural background, profession, and so on.

The forecasters then post their estimates, share their sources and rationales, discuss different interpretations of data, and update their forecasts whenever new information or analysis emerges. After just a few days, the forecasts are ready. In 2020, forecast challenges included "Crude oil price on 13 August 2020"; "When will British Airways resume commercial flights to mainland China?"; "Which party will win control of the U.S. Congress in the 2020 elections?"; and "COVID-19 cases in the US."

Prediction tournaments are hardly the only crowdsourced forecasting tool available that doesn't employ trading between participants. IMP applies a simple crowdsourcing tool in its open IMP Business Logic Contest (described in chapter 8). After groups develop competing business models, teams pitch elements of it in several rounds before finally presenting entire integrated business models. A jury comprised either of senior leaders or a mixed group of leaders and outside experts selects the winner. Digital tools support the selection and voting process. Instead of just voting for the most preferred business model with one vote per judge, jury members (and sometimes workshop participants, or even the entire workforce) can "spend" a virtual budget, investing in the various business models on a dedicated digital platform as they see fit. Participants follow these investment decisions in real time—an exciting and emotional experience for them as business models collect investment over several rounds.

In Sum

Friedrich Nietzsche once remarked, "Madness is the exception in individuals but the rule in groups."[47] As we've seen in this chapter, groups are anything but mad when it comes to predicting future outcomes.

Whom to Invite: A Closer Look

When deploying the tools discussed in this chapter, it pays to think carefully about whether you should involve only company insiders or a broader set of participants. We recommend posing the following questions:[45]

- *How dispersed is the knowledge you need in order to make a good decision?* The more diverse your sources of knowledge, the better the predictions and decision. Rely on internal crowd predictions only if enough diversity exists among participants and they either possess or can access enough knowledge.

- *Is the decision topic a wicked problem or a kind one?* Kind problems are well defined and structured, susceptible to a single best solution. To solve them, you can turn to anyone who possesses sufficient expertise. Most strategy topics, however, are wicked problems: they have countless causes, are difficult to describe, have no right answer, involve many different stakeholders, are complex and tangled at their core, and lack historical precedent.[46] A narrow group of specialists will struggle to solve wicked problems because they will lack the breadth of perspective, knowledge, and expertise. For these problems, open up the participant pool as much as you can.

- *Is legitimacy an issue?* When a strategy's success hinges on buy-in from various stakeholders, you might wish to involve external participants as their broad expertise will grant the strategy more legitimacy.

- *Is confidentiality a concern?* As we've seen, broad involvement of external participants increases the risk that sensitive information will leak, so think carefully about what information you choose to reveal.

Harnessing collective wisdom for your strategic decisions with the right tools can be a powerful way of identifying the best ideas and making wise decisions. Whether you need forecasting to make strategic or tactical decisions or you must choose between different technologies, new product ideas, strategies, or business models, prediction markets, idea markets, or prediction tournaments can deliver valuable input.

During the first two phases of strategy-making, opening up the process helps ensure that strategic ideas and the ensuing strategic plan are in sync with operational realities, and hence that execution will succeed. But companies must attend specifically to execution, especially if the organization is so large that leaders cannot personally connect with front-line employees on a regular basis. Our survey of leaders suggests that open strategy can help with implementation, with 72 percent of respondents stating that it improved the communication and understanding of strategy and 70 percent agreeing that an open approach increased organizational commitment to strategic initiatives. In the next chapter, we present tools—strategy jams and social networks—that help bridge the gap between executives and employees, dramatically improving companies' ability to execute on the strategies they adopt.

Questions to Ponder:

- Can you think of a strategic issue you face whose answer relies on highly dispersed knowledge and that you might profitably address using a crowdsourcing approach?
- Have strategic forecasts in the past failed to produce satisfying results? How did these subpar results damage the company?
- Think about your firm's use of subject matter experts to resolve critical strategic questions. Have their judgments about the future been reliably accurate in the past? What blind spots have you noticed?
- Considering that your employees collectively can outsmart the smartest consultant, how would you reward those who make many (not necessary the most accurate) predictions, knowing that your employees' ability to make predictions will depend on volume?

10 Execute Better

Environmental news can be hard to take. Every week brings another round of headlines about increasing CO_2 levels, rainforest destruction, permafrost melting, desertification, and the list goes on. But the news isn't uniformly bad. One great global environmental success story in recent years has been an initiative to save ancient rainforests on the Southeast Asian island of Borneo. Between 1980 and 2000, Borneo generated more timber than Africa and the Amazon combined, and over the last fifty years the island lost more rainforest than the combined area of England and Wales. And yet, during a five-year period between 2007 and 2012, illegal logging dropped by 68 percent in one area, Gunung Palung National Park, and has continued to decline since.[1]

This turnaround occurred thanks to a radical new strategy deployed by a group called Alam Sehat Lestari (ASRI), which means "harmoniously balanced" in Indonesian.[2] During the 1990s the group's founder, Kinari Webb, visited Borneo as a young college student. Talking to loggers, she discovered that they struggled to afford health care—that's why they cut down trees. For people living near the rainforest, one medical emergency could eat up a year's income. The locals didn't want to log illegally, but they had no choice. It was either that or suffer. As Webb recounted, "One man I know, . . . he cut down sixty trees to pay for one C-section."[3]

After going on to attend medical school, Webb cofounded ASRI as a health care system linked to conservation.[4] The system the organization established gave local villages that didn't engage in illegal logging a 70 percent discount on health care for the entire community. Residents could also pay for health care in kind, handing over readily accessible agricultural products like manure or seedlings or performing labor in exchange for services. The manure went to an organic farming project that teaches locals how to farm sustainably without expensive fertilizer, while conservationists used the seedlings to replenish the forest.

What does this ingenious solution have to do with open strategy? Quite a lot. When companies roll out new strategies as part of a traditional, closed process, they typically do it in a top-down fashion. Senior leaders craft the strategy and send it down in "finished" form through the ranks, usually by charging successive layers of management with the task of socializing the strategy and holding teams accountable. ASRI opened up its strategy, working collaboratively with villagers to fine-tune it and roll it out. "I did not know how to stop the rampant illegal logging," Webb explained, "but there was one thing I knew for certain the answer did not lie with me. . . . The people who would understand all of the interconnections and know how to solve the problems obviously were the people who were experiencing them."[5]

Engaging in what she calls "radical listening," Webb put the following question to the locals: "You are guardians of this precious rainforest that is valuable to the whole world. What would you need as a token of gratitude from the world community?"[6] Webb expected that villagers would differ in how they answered this question, but after four hundred hours of listening, a consensus position emerged. "They said in order to protect the forest and stop the logging, which they wanted to do, they would need access to high-quality, affordable health care and training in organic farming."

With access to health care, the locals would no longer feel pressured to come up with large amount of cash, which they could obtain quickly only through logging. Meanwhile, organic farming offered them an income stream that would free them from traditional slash-and-burn techniques without requiring expensive chemical fertilizers and pesticides. Working with the locals, ASRI fine-tuned a system that connected health care, farming, and conservation in a community reward system that leveraged local traditions of collective action. Not only did logging decline, a number of health indicators improved as well. Infant mortality, for instance, declined from 3.4 infant deaths per 100,000 households to 1.1 deaths over a five-year period. In 2016, ASRI received a Whitley Gold Award, one of the conservation world's most prestigious prizes, in recognition of its efforts.[7]

In business contexts, inviting front-line people to help frame or refine a strategy via an open process greatly improves an organization's ability to realize that strategy. Leaders gain better insight into the needs and concerns of front-line people and adjust the strategy accordingly, adapting to operational realities that only the front-line employees know. Even more critically, employees become more committed to the strategy and enthusiastic about realizing it. As scholars have argued, many people feel psychological ownership over ideas or solutions when they have a hand in creating them.[8] This sense of ownership prompts them to work harder to achieve specific goals.[9] One study surveyed Canadian physicians who had begun to use a new IT system to access lab tests and radiology exam results. As researchers found, the doctors' ability to help develop and fine-tune the system helped engender a feeling of psychological ownership, which in turn significantly affected how useful physicians found the system and how heavily they used it.

Companies applying traditional strategy-making methods often fail to execute them well. In our survey of senior executives, more than 40 percent faulted implementation for their strategies' failure. Other research has found that large percentages of employees don't understand the strategies they're supposed to implement, much less feel strongly about them. You might suppose that leaders aren't discussing the strategy sufficiently, but this is not so: the vast majority of middle managers feel that senior leaders do communicate frequently enough about strategy.[10] The problem is that these communications aren't sticking—precisely because employees feel left out.

Open strategy solves this problem, giving employees a voice and a role in strategy-making so that they develop a sense of psychological ownership. In our survey of more than two hundred top executives, 72 percent of respondents stated that open strategy improved the communication and understanding of strategy and 70 percent agreed that an open approach increased organizational commitment to strategic initiatives. Let's examine one especially powerful tool leading-edge companies have deployed to engage employees and embed particular strategies deeply in an organization. We'll also explore some techniques companies are using to open up ongoing discussions around strategy and sustain these conversations over time.

The Power of Strategy Jams

Remember that famous Peter Drucker slogan, "Culture eats strategy for breakfast"? Strategy only has a chance, Drucker pointedly suggests, if people actively buy in and champion it. An online event called a strategy jam helps ensure that they do, providing an opportunity for large groups of people to engage in moderated strategy discussions, usually over a two- to three-day period. Think of it as a conference-like experience in which every stakeholder can help the company land on effective strategies, and in the process, enhance their own capacity to execute.

To explore how effective strategy jams are, let's consider an extreme setting in which complexity and lack of structure render organizational alignment and execution especially challenging: NATO and EU security policy. Michael Ryan, formerly deputy assistant secretary of defense for European and NATO policy in the United States[11], is one of the world's most influential security policymakers. Explaining the task of mobilizing around a coherent strategy, he relates that leaders within NATO and the EU "have to find an intersection of our interests where we both get not everything we want but a lot of what we want. The bigger the problem, the more countries you need."[12] And let's not forget, adds Ryan, the diverse actors that operate in each country: "Political parties, different institutions in one government, different governments of relative strengths, institutions of relative strengths, a whole range of issues have to be balanced, all of that."[13]

Forging consensus in such a setting is indeed daunting, which is why Ryan sought out creative solutions. In 2008 he met IBM's Leendert van

Bochoven at a conference in Garmisch Patenkirchen, a small town in the south of Germany. As the conference drew to an end, Ryan remembers Van Bochoven asking, "How do we continue to draw from everyone's expertise and compare everyone's views and try to build it into a really synergistic way forward?" That was a great sales pitch for IBM; the obvious answer was IBM's technology, which could facilitate strategy jams.

The technology, a Yammer-like discussion platform, allows a very large group of stakeholders to engage with and ideate around discrete policy fields, building momentum behind new strategies. In the aftermath of strategy jams, a suite of analytical tools helps leaders identify the main trends and debates. For example, leaders can identify countervailing arguments around the most important issues discussed. That's fundamentally different from how policymakers typically work, considering the complexity and diversity of stakeholders involved. "We tend to work with the people we know best," Ryan explains, and "we tend to focus on our issue and we'll explain it to everyone later and they'll love it." However, he notes, "[This approach] doesn't work out."

More recently, COVID-19 posed a considerable challenge for the transatlantic security community. The issues were pressing, the way forward opaque, and in-person meetings were impossible. Having experimented with strategy jams in the past, Ryan decided that such an exercise was the best way forward. In 2020, a small team of NATO and EU policymakers, along with representatives from six trusted think tanks, initiated several work streams, began inviting stakeholders, and went live with a forty-eight-hour jam. About 2,800 participants, including 160 government ministers, military leaders, and other VIPs, posted comments and engaged in discussion. Each participant logged in an average of five times to read or comment.

A clear set of priorities emerged from the jam, including the development of a response to the "Dragonbear effect," as participants called the misinformation emanating from China and Russia. Twenty-four percent of all posts considered the increasing influence of China and Russia during the COVID-19 pandemic, and another 20 percent engaged with disinformation and fake news more generally. That might not seem extraordinary, but policymaking generally moves slowly. With the help of the jam, a consensus emerged, even though some countries shrank from cooperating on principle and just a couple of months earlier the United Kingdom had expressed little concern over the Chinese telecommunications firm Huawei's involvement in building a 5G network for the country. Participating countries all came away generally perceiving misinformation from China and Russia as a threat. "So out of the jam," Ryan explained, "what we got with 2,000 active participants and 160 very senior policymakers [was] the very rapid sharing of awareness, very rapid sharing of stories, [and] a range of ideas on how to do exactly what we wanted to do to stop the agenda of the Chinese and the Russians."

EU and NATO cooperation has indeed strengthened since the jam, and momentum is growing for the creation of an EU unit that would screen foreign direct investment from a security perspective, focusing especially on China. The bloc is also moving toward a more collaborative and comprehensive rather than narrowly national or bilateral response to misinformation threats. Again, all of this occurred in warp speed, with just four weeks elapsing from the pre-meetings to publication of the first jam results. In a policy environment, this constitutes execution on steroids. Not bad for a single strategy jam!

If a jam can help build consensus in the complex and glacially paced policy arena, thus aiding implementation, it can certainly do the same in corporate settings. The case of Barclays (described in the introduction to this book) suggests how strategy jams might aid implementation inside companies. IBM affords another example: the company has run several successful internal jams, including what was probably the world's largest to date (150,000 people from IBM and sixty-seven partner firms). Large technology companies like IBM generate many innovative ideas, but those often fizzle as leaders fail to develop them at sufficient scale. IBM's massive jam connected people across the organization who worked on similar ideas but remained unaware of how they might collaborate on more coherent strategy initiatives. Liam Cleaver, the leader who oversaw the jam,[14] related that as a result of the exercise, IBM identified ten businesses that helped comprise its "smarter planet" initiative. A few years after launching, these businesses accounted for roughly $750 million in revenue.[15] In this case, the jam's primary contribution wasn't breakthrough new ideas but the forging of connections between different ideas, and in turn, a workable strategy.

Running A Strategy Jam

To organize a strategy jam, follow the simple six-step process shown in figure 10.1.

Step 1: Clarify the Jam's Goals
Since you seek to help translate ideas into action, focus on operations and the front-line and avoid discussion of big, abstract ideas. Define a tangible set of problems employees can consider, inviting nuance and complexity in their answers. This will help leaders to refine the strategy in turn while engaging everyone to help execute it.

Step 2: Structure the Jam in an Orderly and Productive Fashion
Prior to the jam, create workgroups comprised of senior managers and line employees and task them with designing specific conversations or workstreams that dovetail with the jam's overarching theme. Think of the jam as an online conference: a thirty- to fifty-hour virtual gathering during which participants join different workstreams to share their thoughts about organizational strategy. Prepare as you would for a conference, marketing the jam internally and equipping front-line staff with a computer or tablet even if they don't ordinarily use them on their jobs (at a factory, for instance, you might create an ad hoc workstation in the break room). Identify the opinion leaders you wish to engage so that they can help generate momentum once you go live. Involve your strategy team as well, since its members possess the expertise and data required to design optimally functioning discussion streams.

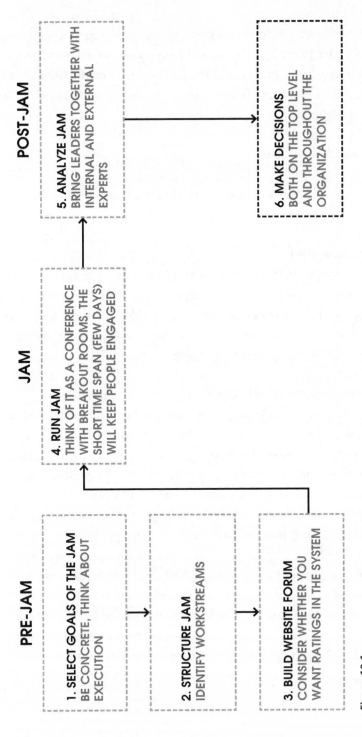

Figure 10.1
Strategy jam steps.

Step 3: Build Website Forums (Application)
for Participant Contributions

Many third-party companies can help you create online forums for a strategy jam. For large crowds of several tens of thousands of participants, IBM offers its clients a suite of analytical tools that can handle large amounts of data. Such tools help not only during the jam but afterward, when you must analyze vast troves of data to glean insights. Consider whether you wish to publicize or highlight popular contributions to the jam. Doing so can help focus the conversation, but it might also enable some topics to hijack the conversation, reducing traffic to smaller groups. To reap the benefits of spotlighting while avoiding the disadvantages, identify moderators who can direct attention to important points but also judiciously combine different streams engaging with similar issues.

Step 4: Run the Jam

Run the jam for thirty-six to forty-eight hours. Adopting such a short time horizon will lend urgency to the jam while still giving participants in different time zones a chance to post and receive reactions from peers. A short duration will also prompt everyone to set aside their daily work and arrive ready to contribute. Top leaders must participate, or employees won't take it seriously. Use these leaders strategically, engaging them progressively to maintain commitment. You can probably anticipate that some topics, coming from certain people, will generate significant interest. Capitalize on this to maintain excitement. At their core, jams are people-mobilization tools, galvanizing the organization around the strategy to an unprecedented extent. Talented moderators can prove helpful not just by connecting discussion streams but also by summarizing ongoing discussions for the benefit of new participants as they arrive. It's nearly impossible for human moderators to stay abreast of thousands of posts, so for large jams, technology providers must step in, deploying analytical tools that enable you to sort and analyze quickly.

Step 5: Analyze the Jam

After the jam concludes, convene a group of leaders and experts to analyze participant contributions and other data. Involve senior leaders, and consider engaging a panel of internal and outside experts. Analyze raw postings, as well as any content flagged as interesting or noteworthy by volunteers or moderators in small jams or by text-mining tools in large ones. In some cases, you can task managers with analyzing jam streams pertaining to their specific functional or divisional responsibilities. Try to identify popular ideas, understanding how they connect to the strategy and hence support implementation. You should also stay alert to novel ideas related to implementation that you would not have come up with otherwise.

Step 6: Make Key Investment Decisions, if Any, Based on the Jam's Findings

Based on the jam's results, finalize your strategic decision-making. Sometimes companies will make substantial investments or create entirely new businesses. After IBM's 150,000-participant strategy jam in 2008, the CEO announced an investment of $100 million and the creation of ten new businesses. At other times, the jam might allow leaders to better interpret their strategy and the contours of its implementation. Barclays' jam revealed a comprehensive picture of what the company's mobile strategy meant across the organization, creating new energy around the strategy.

A jam can infuse energy into a strategy even when its broad contours are already sufficiently clear. When Steelcase, the world's largest office furniture manufacturer, developed a new strategy in 2017, top management and the strategy group devised and executed an overall communications plan that included "traditional" elements such as cascades and town hall–style meetings. But they did not stop there. They deployed an open strategy process to further enliven that plan and galvanize the company's 13,000 employees around the strategy.

As Thomas Cook, director for strategy and corporate development, remembers, leaders "started to think about how do we implement [the strategy, knowing that it's] not what's on a piece of paper, it's like the sum total of the actions that we take. At that point we had a really nice piece of paper, but then how do you actually make that into something real? We certainly were open to the idea that there are a lot of great ideas out there, and that we haven't thought of everything, . . . so it really was a two-way dialogue."[16] Cook had read about the IBM strategy jam and wanted to hold a similar exercise by mobilizing the company's internal online communications platform. After all, people were already familiar with the platform, and using it would cost less than partnering with external vendors.

Cook and his team organized the jam around three central pillars of the company's strategy. Each pillar contained a number of key initiatives, and at the beginning of the jam the team created a specific discussion thread for each initiative. Employees spun off additional threads as the discussion developed. All along, Cook and his team harbored two equal and opposite concerns about employee participation. "We were worried, what if the platform crashes from overuse," Cook said. "We were also worried about what if nobody comments, and it's just a ghost town."[17]

To preempt the second concern, leaders identified employee influencers—some in formal leadership positions, others simply known as being influential—and engaged them in the pre-jam discussions. These individuals aggressively marketed the event through intranet sites and by hanging posters in various physical locations. Because around five thousand Steelcase employees worked on the factory floor without direct access to a computer, leaders asked shift managers to engage with staff and collect their thoughts.

When the thirty-six-hour jam kicked off, the platform did indeed crash on account of too many simultaneous logins (everyone had sought to access a video from the CEO welcoming employees to the jam). The team quickly brought the platform back online, and during the thirty-one hours that followed, lively discussions ensued. To bolster engagement, the core team and influencers posted hourly updates and created new topics on an ongoing basis. The team also mobilized senior managers at opportune times, benefiting from their natural competitive streak.

As they participated, managers vied to create the most compelling blog post titles, hoping to generate more clicks than their peers. For employees, the jam represented an opportunity to shine and thereby increase their visibility inside the organization (one employee, for example, became the go-to person for AI questions). Although leaders had already articulated the major strategy headlines, new ideas emerged during the jam, as well as new details that leaders would have to consider in implementing the strategy. As Christian Wiese, a member of the jam team, explained, the jam enabled employees across the company to explore the strategy simultaneously—a stark contrast to a phased roll-out during which leaders cascade information hierarchically down the ranks.[18]

One of the jam's livelier discussion threads focused on experiences in codesign. In collaboration with one of its clients, a US university, Steelcase developed a table with a pop-out television set. The company then standardized this design and, with the consent of the university, made it available to other clients. After hearing participants describe this situation on the jam, leaders resolved to create a new business focused on delivering a codesign experience. The business is primarily a sales tool, helping Steelcase engage important clients. "We use it strategically with really big customers," Cook said, and "if we didn't have this capability, they might look at other companies. . . . It's really like this capability we needed to have, and we needed to be differentiated in order to win these big customer accounts. It was more about understanding the customer's higher-level needs, cultural needs, et cetera, and how do you work with them, deliver a great experience." The jam had made it clear to Steelcase that "this was more of a growing trend than we realized, and the experience of working shoulder-to-shoulder with the customer was really important, not just the end product. Having this capability allows us to engage more deeply with customers and create stickiness via unique solutions."

In addition to ideas like these, the jam generated unprecedented energy around the company's strategy. Around a quarter of Steelcase's total workforce and half of its office workers participated, contributing four thousand posts.[19] "After the jam," Wiese said, "people were familiar [with the strategy . . .], could see the structure of where we were headed," and felt a strong sense of "personal ownership and narrative."[20] Cook noted that the jam allowed leaders "to help employees see how their role supports this broader strategy of growth."[21] After the jam, divisional heads mobilized data and insights from the exercise to present detailed investment and strategic action plans. As a result, their plans synced up well with employee perceptions, greatly enhancing implementation. Since the jam, Steelcase revenues have increased from 3 to 3.7 billion and net income has more than doubled. In 2020, Steelcase achieved its best performance in two decades,[22] a direct outgrowth of the strategic direction and investments made in 2017 and 2018. Leaders are considering how to deploy jams going forward to improve implementation.[23]

Social Networks: Mobilizing Organizations beyond the Jam

Strategy jams are usually discrete, short-term events designed to mobilize large groups of people around a specific strategy. Companies can also improve implementation by using social networks and related digital tools to help employees participate on an *ongoing* basis in strategy-related conversations. Social networks enhance implementation in multiple ways. First, they allow managers to increase transparency about strategy, quickly spreading information about the strategy across departments and through hierarchical levels. Second, social networks allow powerful, two-way communication. Large numbers of employees continuously exchange strategy-related information with one another, building relationships, facilitating collaboration, and increasing their collective sense of ownership of the strategy. They also discuss hobbies and other matters of personal interest. Although these conversations might seem distracting, they're actually critical, as they generate curiosity and encourage individuals to participate, connect, and share knowledge. As employees become acquainted with one another personally, they feel more comfortable discussing work-related topics, processes, and practices.[24] Such employees are more likely to develop trust in their peers, psychological safety, and a better mutual understanding, enabling the collective "sense-making" processes, social support, and collective action on which successful implementation hinges.

To understand the potential that social networks hold for strategy implementation, consider the experience of the Spanish telecom giant Telefónica. In 2009 a group of employees began to use the social network Yammer to discuss questions around customer engagement. Soon this group counted thousands of participants, with more than two thousand employees registering every month—especially impressive in light of the enterprise social network's lack of management sponsorship and formal administration. Intrigued, the senior management team decided in 2013 to mobilize Yammer, the most successful enterprise social network at Telefónica at the time, prior to the company's Executive Summit, a biannual global strategy convening the company's top leaders. Traditionally, the summit was a one-and-a-half-day closed-door event whose secrecy rendered it almost mystical in the eyes of employees. Senior leaders used the event to reveal the company's future strategies to executives, who then returned to their countries and functions and cascaded down what they had learned.

Now the board opened up the summit to 1,300 leaders, initiating a virtual summit on Yammer three months before the actual live event, which remained closed to all but top leaders. "We encouraged [participants] to share their ideas and to codecide the strategy, instead of them being passive listeners of the strategy presented to them in a two-day event," recalled Luz Rodrigo Martorell, an enterprise social strategist at Telefónica.[25] "They are drafting the strategy with us, they have an influence." Top leaders synthesized the contributions from this earlier discussion, drawing directly on submitted comments; the CEO himself repeatedly referenced quotes from the social network. While leaders didn't adopt every idea, the broader corps of executives perceived that they had studied the earlier conversations and taken them seriously. As a result, they felt motivated to participate even more fully in future online events pertaining to the strategy.[26]

And such events did come to pass. In 2015, Telefónica invited all 125,000 employees worldwide to participate with executives in the online strategy debate prior to the summit. In addition, the company for the first time allowed all employees to watch part of the physical summit livestreamed on Yammer. To encourage participation, Telefónica rewarded the social network's four most active employees by inviting them to attend the summit in Madrid. "We used the enterprise social network to say we are looking for a new attitude," Aitor Goyenechea, director of global internal communications, explained. The company wanted "everyone to be proactive, engaged, and innovative around strategy discussions to help set the future for the company. And through conversations posted on our social network, we can track the level of understanding and commitment to those strategies."[27] In 2018, Telefónica switched to the social network platform Workplace, attracted by its enhanced video and live stream capabilities. For the first time ever, Telefónica broadcast live the full Executive Summit to all employees, inviting them to comment and react in real time to what they were seeing.

Since then, Telefónica's commitment to open strategy has only intensified. In July 2019, Chairman and CEO José María Álvarez-Pallete asked all employees via the enterprise social network what steps they would take to improve the company. Employees submitted almost a thousand proposals, revealing the need for a new strategy. Leaders responded, and in November 2019 the company embarked on the biggest strategic turnaround in its history.[28] The following year the enterprise social network emerged as an important tool for engaging with employees during the COVID-19 crisis. Álvarez-Pallete asked employees to contribute ideas and suggestions for how the organization could best deal with the crisis. Such engagement and the resulting two-way dialogue made a palpable difference, leading to a 25 percent increase in employees' sense of belonging.

By all accounts, Telefónica's mobilization of the enterprise social networks has paid off. As Rodrigo Martorell says, "When our employees use the enterprise social network to be part of the discussion, they internalize and adopt the strategies and work on them with real commitment. It has a very positive impact on strategy knowledge and strategy implementation because people feel part of it."[29] At Telefónica, strategy is no longer something that employees learn about passively—it's something with which they engage. And employees continue to use the enterprise social network on an ongoing basis. In 2019 there were more than 11.5 million interactions, including posts, comments, reactions, or chat messages created through the platform, averaging 42,000 interactions per day.

Social networks are just one of the digital tools leading-edge companies have used to engage employees in ongoing strategy conversations. In 2008, Red Hat, an open source software company and the leading provider of Linux software, began connecting with employees around strategy using a number of tools that allow active engagement, including online chats, blogs, and wikis.[30] As Jackie Yeaney, executive vice president of strategy and corporate marketing at the time, remarked, "The entire company needed to own the strategy if we wanted to see it implemented. Associates needed to be an integral part of developing and implementing it."[31] As employees contributed comments and suggestions, teams synthesized them into strategic priorities, developed those priorities further, and then selected some to adopt and implement. All along, leaders held teams accountable for developing and implementing strategic priorities. As one observer noted, opening up the strategy enhanced implementation, allowing for "more creativity, accountability, and . . . commitment."[32] Red Hat's CEO Jim Whitehurst repeatedly credits open strategy with helping the company grow rapidly and impress investors.[33]

As you engage large numbers of employees, you risk losing control over the conversation. Individuals might use digital tools to promote themselves and their pet ideas, diverting attention from organizational strategies and failing to recognize others' contributions.[34] Conflict can ensue, with participants engaging in negative attacks. Bystanders in turn become disillusioned, limiting their contributions or even leaving the social network entirely.

Companies can create an atmosphere of psychological safety by specifying clear rules for participation. As leaders at Telefónica confirm, deleting potentially offending posts very rarely becomes necessary and serves as an option of last resort. The very spirit of these networks is one of free discourse, and censorship can easily discourage participation. As with crowdsourcing, you must anticipate which topics participant might raise or support, recognizing that some of them won't belong on leaders' agendas. When these topics arise, you must allow the conversation to transpire and participate in it. As an executive at the UK-based business process and technology services provider Xchanging remarked, "You can't give the people a voice and then tell them 'well, actually, you can have a voice but only if you say what we want you to say.' If you are going to give them a voice, you have to listen. I think we've given them the voice and we're learning to listen."[35]

Companies can reap benefits by allowing conversations to take place that don't strictly bear on strategic matters. As IMP has found, many participants in its in-person workshops feel drawn by the desire to forge relationships with other interesting people. As we've seen, something similar holds true for internal social networks. People don't just want to learn about the strategies and voice their opinions. They also want to get to know colleagues whom they've known about or interacted with tangentially but never had an opportunity to engage in conversation.[36]

Ultimately, companies must take internal and external participants seriously and acknowledge their expenditure of time and energy. They must keep participants apprised of how leaders have assessed their contributions and what action they have taken as a result. Employees need to know that their submissions matter and that their ideas haven't simply disappeared in some bureaucratic black hole. Organizations struggle here. At a German car manufacturer, leadership change and a change in strategic priorities prevented a social network initiative from receiving the staffing it needed to process and respond to employee contributions. As a result, employees kept submitting ideas and discussing them but never received feedback from leaders, nor did they learn how leaders were screening, developing, or implementing their original ideas. Employees became frustrated, and their participation waned. Eventually, leaders shut down the entire initiative.

Perhaps the best way for leaders to register employee contributions and affirm their importance is to engage directly in the ongoing debate. Active support from senior leaders is critical to the success of any effort to engage employees around strategy. At Telefónica, Chairman and CEO José María Álvarez-Pallete made a point of actively involving himself in strategy conversations, and it left quite an impression. As Luz Rodrigo Martorell said, "It was difficult for people to believe because he's the top manager and they were asking me, 'I got a like from José María, but has it been himself or are members of his team doing that, I don't know if it's true.' But through his ongoing feedback, his comments, and his personal engagement in the debate, and through integrating and bringing together several submitted ideas from the online social network, employees at Telefónica realized that their chairman and CEO [was] seriously engaging with their contributions and that he was truly believing in their value."[37]

Tips for Building Momentum around Strategy Using Digital Tools

- *Determine how open you want to be.* Many online platform products allow you to restrict participation to individuals inside the company or to others whom you invite. For strategy-based discussions, you probably don't want to open participation much wider than this. Just look at how much trouble Elon Musk got into by tweeting about plans to take his company private.

- *Emphasize the social element.* In addition to allowing a wide breadth of conversational topics, encourage participants to post meaningful profiles so that others can get to know them personally.

- *Establish clear rules for participation.* By laying down the terms of participation at the outset, you can shape how participants engage on the platform, reducing the odds of inappropriate behavior. You might also wish to conduct ongoing training and workshops to teach participants how to use the social network productively.

- *Establish clear expectations.* Convey exactly what participants can expect from contributing and what will happen with their contributions.

- *Link the social network to an offline event.* As Telefónica discovered, social networks work well when connected to a traditional event such as a strategy-making summit. Leaders can forge new connections with the workforce and help staff feel engaged in strategy-making at the highest levels.

- *Monitor conversations closely.* To get the most out of social networking platforms, keep track of discussions and their tenor, intervening quickly if the conversation veers too far off-track.

- *Allocate the necessary resources.* Running a social network and handling the volume of contributions can prove time-consuming. Assign a team to help leaders get the network off the ground and recognize and respond to contributions as they come in.

- *Stay personally engaged.* You can outsource some of the participation and oversight to your team, but it is vital that employees perceive top leaders as active users. When leaders reference comments made on a social networking platform, employee participation, acceptance, and satisfaction rise substantially.

- *As you begin to participate, watch your own language.* A formal, wooden tone doesn't work on social media, but the tone also shouldn't be too casual. For many executives, that takes some training and deliberate effort.

In Sum

In embracing open strategy, leading-edge companies have learned not to limit the approach to generating strategic ideas or developing them into business plans but to use the approach to enhance implementation of strategies as well. Organizations execute strategies most effectively when those who actually do that hard work—employees at all levels—have at least some hand in formulating it. To improve execution in your company, expose employees to your new strategy and solicit their thinking by running an online, short-term strategy jam. The experience of engaging actively in a two-way conversation not only educates employees about the strategy, it generates executional ideas and details leaders might not have considered. Crucially, it engenders a sense of psychological ownership over the strategy on the part of the workforce. But don't stop there. Use social networks and other online tools to maintain ongoing conversations about the strategy inside the company. Managed properly, such conversations can totally transform how organizations relate to the strategies that leaders adopt, energizing employees and helping them connect the strategy directly to the work they do each day.

Questions to Ponder:

• Why have strategies failed in your company? Did these failures owe to insufficient clarity about the strategy or an inability to mobilize people to execute?

• Why is it that some ideas look great in the boardroom but somehow fizzle when your company seeks to operationalize them?

• Do employees at your firm come up with interesting strategic ideas that somehow get lost?

• If you have existing intranets, do strategic conversations sometimes pop up? How do leaders fuel participation on these forums?

• How motivated are your employees right now to execute on strategic initiatives? Are they as informed about them as they might be?

Epilogue

Disruption is scary, but it need not prove fatal. As we've seen throughout this book, leading edge companies large and small have stayed ahead of change by opening up their strategy deliberations. In our turbulent world, tapping a few leaders or high-priced consultants to craft a vision for the future no longer suffices. You need the breadth and depth of insight a larger and more diverse group of thinkers can provide. You also need the buy-in and commitment generated by inviting larger groups of people participate.

Barclays used open strategy techniques to navigate from classic branch-networks to mobile banking. Saxonia Systems used it to become a thriving provider of software services. And WS Audiology used it to anticipate new business models in a world of hearables. For these and many other companies, an open strategy-making process has led to a slew of benefits—better ideas, more realistic plans, more effective execution—without compromising sensitive information or eroding leaders' traditional authority.

As we've intimated throughout, open strategy isn't just a set of tactics—it's a fundamentally new management philosophy premised on transparency, collaboration, and diversity. Leaders are accustomed to sharing information with diverse actors beyond the borders of the enterprise. They understand the merits of open innovation, open source coding, open science, open data, open education, and open government. Yet, that transparency has tended to stop at the boardroom door. A "closed" mentality has also persisted as an unspoken norm throughout many organizations, which remain siloed and secretive. To make the most of the tactics we've presented, and to ensure that organizations continue to use them once the initial novelty and excitement has worn off, you must commit yourself to the ideals of transparency, collaboration, and diversity and all that they entail. Here are some additional steps to take as you begin to experiment with open strategy:

1. Open Up Gradually

As promising as open strategy is, traditional strategy-making processes can still serve companies well in certain situations, notably in core businesses that don't face imminent threats of disruption. Instead of immediately opening each of your business functions, think of your businesses as a portfolio. Identify which of your businesses are true disruptors, which of them face looming threats from disruption and must become more innovative, and which of them don't face looming threats. Introduce openness in your disruptive businesses and in those that face looming threats, retaining traditional strategy-making in the others. In some cases, you'll wish to jettison traditional strategy-making entirely, but more often you'll want to partially embrace openness. Experiment with the tools presented in this book, discovering which work best. Over time, transfer these tools to other businesses in your portfolio (figure 11.1).

2. Set Up New Structures and Develop Capabilities

As you experiment, adapt organizational structures such as autonomous business units, sales forces, metrics, key performance indicators, and so on. All too often, open strategy yields new initiatives that everyone loves in principle but that they come to resist on realizing how incompatible these initiatives are with existing structures. The new initiative is underfunded, leading to disappointing results. Eventually, the initiative dies a slow death—an even more likely fate if a leadership change takes place.

Radical ideas need separate structures inside an organization—a point strongly articulated by Clayton Christensen. Fail to create such structures, and you'll likely see distracting turf wars break out. Alternatively,

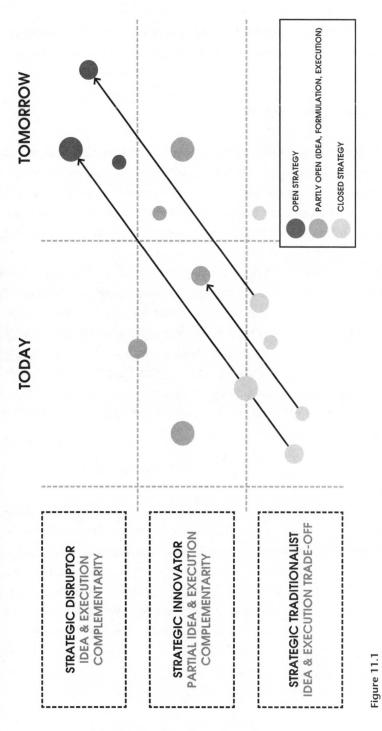

Figure 11.1

Disruptor—Innovator—Traditionalist map.

new initiatives might never see the light of day, scuttled by leaders who assume that the organization lacks the competencies required to pull it off.

3. Amplify External Voices

Throughout the book, we've pointed to the importance of external voices in the open strategy process. We'll say it once more: game-changing ideas almost always come from other industries. When new startups pitch themselves as the "Uber of industry x," they do so as a way of enticing investors, but they also highlight the reality that smart entrepreneurs tend to arrive at their ideas by studying business models in very different settings. As obvious as that might sound, most leaders still need to work quite hard to convince others to take seriously ideas from other industries. Although industry boundaries are fast disappearing (who would have expected Google to become a player in the car industry?), most executives still intuitively think in industry terms, talking over or dismissing external experts. Don't let this happen in your organization. In pursuing open strategy, involve external participants who are "loud enough," plentiful enough, and backed up by a strong facilitator or sponsor.

4. Don't Treat Open Strategy as a "Fair Weather" Approach

Embracing openness is a long, arduous journey, and it's tempting to revert to old habits, especially during tough times. When the economy is in recession, when you're acquiring a new company, when an unexpected shock like the COVID-19 pandemic hits, leaders all too often put open strategy on hold until the storm clouds clear. This is a mistake: open strategy contributes the most when disruption seems imminent and you're straining to see around the corner. Trust the power of the crowd. As we revealed in chapter 9, crowds always beat individuals when it comes to forecasting.

5. Clarify Decision Rights

As we noted early in the book, many executives feel skeptical that employees can make insightful predictions, and they feel more inclined to entrust the task to management consultants.[1] To succeed with open strategy, you must recognize at a deep level that your leadership team and consultants aren't the only geniuses in the company. Relatedly, you must part with the hierarchical command structures common in traditional organizations, as these thrive on secrecy. If you and your team feel reluctant to limit your own decision-making rights and fully commit yourselves to outputs from open-strategy deliberations, then at least frame these outputs as helpful contributions that might inform but not determine final decisions. Let the organization know that decision rights have not transferred to open-strategy participants.

6. Deepen Your Understanding of Open Strategy

Open strategy rests on the premise that we achieve more when we involve more people. As you start to consider how open strategy can function in your organization, spend time reading the supplementary materials listed in appendix A. Have your colleagues read them as well, and conduct ongoing conversations about your strategy-making process and how you might do it better. As you and your colleagues immerse yourself intellectually in open strategy, you'll start to feel more confident about how openness can help you to generate, fine-tune, and implement great ideas. And if you still have questions, contact us and we'll set you straight.

A final word of advice: expect the unexpected. As Ernesto Maurer, CEO of the centuries-old textile machine manufacturer SSM, told us, open strategy exercises taught his leadership team that the firm's traditional competencies weren't as valuable as they had assumed. Meanwhile, "capabilities which we had not paid much attention to in the leadership team suddenly got attention and significance."[2] We hear such feedback all the time. What leaders take to be core strengths are actually source of rigidity and stasis when the business environment changes, while the seeds of change exist in places leaders hadn't thought to look.

Plant these seeds. Grow them into disruptive new business models. It's hard work, but don't give up. Maurer and other leaders stayed true to the strategy they had developed by opening up. Drawing on the insights and perspectives of outsiders, they generated momentum and succeeded in reinventing their business. You can do something similar. Successful innovation will always be a perilous journey into the unknown. But it's a journey you and your leadership team need not and should not take alone. Your boardroom has been closed for too long. Isn't it time to open the doors, even if just a little, and invite others in to help?

Appendix A: Recommended Reading

Dalio, R. *Principles: Life and Work*. New York: Simon and Schuster, 2017.

Felin, T. "When Strategy Walks Out the Door." *MIT Sloan Management Review*, 58, no. 1 (Fall 2016): 96

Gast, A., and M. Zanini. "The Social Side of Strategy." *McKinsey Quarterly*, May 2012, 1–15.

Grant, A. *Think Again: The Power of Knowing What You Don't Know*. New York: Viking, 2021.

Hamel, G., and M. Zanini. "The End of Bureaucracy: How a Chinese Appliance Maker Is Reinventing Management for the Digital Age." *Harvard Business Review* 96, no. 6 (November–December 2018): 50–59.

Hamel, G., and M. Zanini. *Humanocracy: Creating Organizations as Amazing as the People inside Them*. Boston: Harvard Business School Publishing, 2020.

Hautz, J., D. Seidl, and R. Whittington. "Open Strategy: Dimensions, Dilemmas, Dynamics." *Long Range Planning* 50, no. 3 (2017): 298–309.

Heffernan, M. *Uncharted: How to Map the Future*. New York: Simon and Schuster, 2020.

Sull, D., D. Turconi, C. Sull, and J. Yoder. "Turning Strategy into Results." *MIT Sloan Management Review*, 59, no. 3 (2018): 1–12.

Whitehurst, J. *The Open Organization: Igniting Passion and Performance*. Brighton, MA: Harvard Business Review Press, 2015.

Whittington, R. *Opening Strategy: Professional Strategists and Practice Change, 1960 to Today*. New York: Oxford University Press, 2019.

Whittington, R., B. Yakis-Douglas, and K. Ahn. "Wall Street Rewards CEOs Who Talk about Their Strategies." *Harvard Business Review: Digital Articles*, 2015, 2–6.

Appendix B: The IMP Story

IMP's engagement with open strategy goes back a decade, to the years just after the Great Recession. At the time, most leaders were gunning for breakthrough innovations that would disrupt their industries. Strangely, though, these leaders conducted strategy-making in the same old ways, without giving much thought to how they might improve and adapt strategic deliberations for a new era. Open innovation offered some hope, but since such initiatives usually didn't touch the domain of strategy directly, they couldn't influence the organization's core positioning, resource allocation, and business models.

One of us (Stephan) realized that companies needed to develop truly novel strategy-making approaches if they were to generate and execute on novel technologies and business models. Drawing on his years of experience as a management consultant, Stephan perceived open strategy's potential not merely as a new methodology for leaders to follow but a new philosophy and state of mind, one that could unleash the power of outside knowledge to help companies master disruption. Stephan searched for ways that his consulting firm, IMP, could help companies rethink strategy-making and improve innovation management, bringing together internal and expertise in a way that was at once methodical, effective, and safe.

IMP had long maintained important links with academia, particularly through its IMP Network of Excellence, which convened practitioners, technology experts, entrepreneurs, and academics (Julia and Christian are part of this network). Drawing on IMP's academic relationships,

Kurt (who, like Stephan, was a professor as well as an IMP partner) initiated a research project that explored open strategy's potential and practicability for working businesses. As this research grew and matured, the ongoing interaction among firms, IMP, and academia led us to develop open strategy's methodologies and philosophical elements. In retrospect, it hardly seems surprising that open strategy would come to life in this way, as collaborations between business, consulting, and academia have often led to business and management innovations. Just think of the concept of strategic business units, developed by McKinsey and General Electric, or the experience curve and the portfolio matrix, developed by Boston Consulting Group and the aviation industry, or the balanced scorecard, developed by Robert S. Norton and David P. Kaplan along with twelve leading-edge companies.

For such collaborations to work, a few bold companies must take the lead, running experiments to help determine what works and what doesn't. IMP is greatly indebted to the early adopters of open strategy, many of whom appear in this book. Thanks to them, we've been able to improve our tools and exercises, developing open strategy into a truly revolutionary, award-winning approach. As we've discovered together, companies win when they convene internal and external participants to puzzle over problems and work passionately on new strategic solutions. Not only are the strategies that result stronger, fresher, and more powerful; the process of creating and executing on strategy also feels more empowering and fulfilling to everyone involved. In sum, the open approach helps firms enhance their ability to mobilize forcefully behind strategies, thus markedly increasing their chances of success. We invite you to join us by using the techniques in this book to transform your own strategic deliberations. It won't always be easy, but as our clients and collaborators can attest, the effort is well worth it.

Notes

Introduction

1. Interview with Ashok Vaswani, February 22, 2021.

2. The description of Barclays' open strategy process is based on authors' interviews with Ashok Vaswani, Barclays, February 22, 2021, Julian Davies, Barclays, February 2, 2017, and Liam Cleaver, IBM, August 24, 2018.

3. Interview with Vaswani, February 22, 2021.

4. Richard Whittington, *Opening Strategy: Professional Strategists and Practice Change, 1960 to Today* (Oxford: Oxford University Press, 2019).

5. Telstra, "Exponential Performance: In a Millennial, Mobile and Programmatic World," Telstra, 2017, https://www.readkong.com/page/exponential-performance -in-a-millennial-mobile-and-9704875.

6. Telstra, "Exponential Performance."

7. Barclays Bank, *Building the "Go-To" Bank,* Annual Report 2012 (London: Barclays Bank, 2012); Barclays Bank, *Delivering for Our Stakeholders*, Annual Report 2019 (London: Barclays Bank, 2019).

8. Interview with Davies, February 2, 2017.

9. See E. Mazareanu, "Size of Global Consulting Market from 2011 to 2020, by Segment," Statista, December 10, 2019, https://www.statista.com/statistics /624426/global-consulting-market-size-by-sector/, and Carlos J. F. Cândido and Sérgio P. Santos, "Strategy Implementation: What Is the Failure Rate?," *Journal of Management & Organization* 21, no. 2 (2015): 237–262.

10. Daniel Stieger, Kurt Matzler, Sayan Chatterjee, and Florian Ladstätter-Fussenegger, "Democratizing Strategy: How Crowdsourcing Can Be Used for

Strategy Dialogues," *California Management Review* 54, no. 4 (Summer 2012): 44–68.

11. Besides our practical work, we've taken the lead in elaborating the concept of open strategy among business academics. Having edited the first issue of an academic journal devoted to open strategy, one of us (Julia Hautz) defined open strategy as a bundle of strategizing practices aimed at increased transparency and inclusion regarding strategic issues, involving both internal and external stakeholders. Companies deploying open strategy make more strategic information available and enable more actors to engage in the strategic conversation. See Julia Hautz, David Seidl, and Richard Whittington, "Open Strategy: Dimensions, Dilemmas, Dynamics," *Long Range Planning* 50, no. 3 (2017): 298–309.

12. Warren Bennis and Burt Nanus, *Leaders: The Strategies for Taking Charge* (New York: Harper, 1985).

13. Chris Zook and James Allen, *The Founder's Mentality: How to Overcome the Predictable Crises of Growth* (Brighton, MA: Harvard Business Review Press, 2016).

14. Global Agenda Council on the Future of Software and Society, *Deep Shift: Technology Tipping Points and Societal Impact,* report prepared for the World Economic Forum, September 2015, http://www3.weforum.org/docs/WEF_GAC15_ Technological_Tipping_Points_report_2015.pdf.

15. Gary Hamel, "Strategy as Revolution," *Harvard Business Review* 7 (July–August 1996): 69–82, at 70.

16. Hautz, Seidl, and Whittington, "Open Strategy."

17. Gary Hamel and Michele Zanini, *Humanocracy: Creating Organizations as Amazing as the People inside Them* (Brighton, MA: Harvard Business Review Press, 2020).

18. Julia Hautz, "Opening Up the Strategy Process—a Network Perspective," *Management Decision* 55, no. 9 (2017): 1956–83; Hautz, Seidl, and Whittington, "Open Strategy."

19. João Baptista, Alex Wilson, Robert D. Galliers, and Steve Bynghall, "Social Media and the Emergence of Reflexiveness as a New Capability for Open Strategy," *Long Range Planning* 50, no. 3 (2017): 322–36.

20. Hamel and Zanini, *Humanocracy*: 190.

21. These insights are based on a survey of 347 managers and executives.

22. These insights are based on a survey of more than two hundred top executives.

Chapter 1

1. General Electric, *Annual Report 2001* and *Annual Report 2007* (Boston: General Electric, 2001, 2007). For share price information, see Yahoo Finance historical quotes (https://finance.yahoo.com/quote/GE/history?period1=1262304000&per iod2=1483228800&interval=1mo&filter=history&frequency=1mo and https:// finance.yahoo.com/quote/%5EGSPC/history?period1=1262304000&period2 =1483228800&interval=1mo&filter=history&frequency=1mo).

2. For a detailed analysis of GE's downfall, see Geoff Colvin, "What the Hell Happened at GE?," *Fortune*, May 24, 2018, https://fortune.com/longform/ge -decline-what-the-hell-happened/, and Thomas Gryta and Ted Mann, "GE Pow-ered the American Century—Then It Burned Out," *Wall Street Journal*, December 14, 2018, https://www.wsj.com/articles/ge-powered-the-american-centurythen -it-burned-out-11544796010.

3. Colvin, "What the Hell Happened at GE?"

4. Ben Lane, "GE Books $1.5 Billion for Potential Settlement with DOJ over WMC Subprime Loans," HousingWire, May 7, 2018, https://www.housingwire .com/articles/43300-ge-books-15-billion-for-potential-settlement-with-doj-over -wmc-subprime-loans/.

5. Matt Egan, "Inside the Dismantle of GE," *CNN Money*, October 1, 2018, https://money.cnn.com/interactive/news/GE-dismantling-interactive/index .html.

6. For example, the sale of GE's plastics business to Saudi Basic Industries for $11.6 billion was more than analysts expected and is widely regarded as excellent. Likewise, the business built on the back of Enron's bankruptcy auction of wind turbine manufacturing assets for $358 million was a big winner, bringing in $10.3 billion in revenue in 2017. See Colvin, "What the Hell Happened at GE?"

7. Colvin, "What the Hell Happened at GE?"

8. Interview with Jim Ezahays, GE, January 9, 2019.

9. Joe Panettieri, "GE Sell Servicemax to Silver Lake," Channele2e, Decem-ber 13, 2018, https://www.channele2e.com/investors/private-equity/ge-sells -servicemax-to-silver-lake/.

10. Darrell Rigby and Barbara Bilodeau, *Management Tools & Trends* (London: Bain & Co., 2018).

11. Carlos J. F. Cândido and Sérgio P. Santos, "Strategy Implementation: What Is the Failure Rate?," *Journal of Management & Organization* 21, no. 2 (2015): 237–262.

12. Jens Bergmann, "Beate Uhse—Es Sind die Frauen, Dummkopf," Brand Eins, 2014, https://www.brandeins.de/magazine/brand-eins-wirtschaftsmagazin/2014/beobachten/es-sind-die-frauen-dummkopf.

13. Horizont Online, "Beate Uhse—Warum der Erotik-Pionier Insolvenzantrag Stellt," *Horizont*, December 15, 2017, https://www.horizont.net/marketing/nachrichten/Beate-Uhse-Warum-der-Erotik-Pionier-Insolvenzantrag-stellt-163502.

14. Lawrence G. Hrebiniak, "Obstacles to Effective Strategy Implementation," *Organizational Dynamics* 35, no. 1 (2006): 12–31.

15. Hrebiniak, "Obstacles to Effective Strategy Implementation."

16. Lawrence G. Hrebiniak, *Making Strategy Work: Leading Effective Execution and Change* (Upper Saddle River, NJ: FT Press, 2013).

17. Anton Troianovski and Sven Grundberg, "Nokia's Bad Call on Smartphones," *Wall Street Journal*, July 18, 2013, https://www.wsj.com/articles/SB10001424052702304388004577531002591315494.

18. Timo O. Vuori and Quy N. Huy, "Distributed Attention and Shared Emotions in the Innovation Process: How Nokia Lost the Smartphone Battle," *Administrative Science Quarterly* 61, no. 1 (2016): 9–51.

19. Thea O'Connor, "Was Collective Fear the Reason for Nokia's Downfall?," *IntheBlack*, March 1, 2017, https://www.intheblack.com/articles/2017/03/01/nokia-outsmarted-collective-fear.

20. See a detailed account of NCR's problems in Alva Taylor and Constance Helfat, "Organizational Linkages for Surviving Technological Change: Complementary Assets, Middle Management, and Ambidexterity," *Organization Science* 20 (2009): 718–739, and Richard Rosenbloom, "Leadership, Capabilities, and Technological Change: The Transformation of NCR in the Electronic Era," *Strategic Management Journal* 21 (October 2000): 1083–1103.

21. E. Mazareanu, "Size of Global Consulting Market from 2011 to 2020, by Segment," Statista, Decemeber 10, 2019, https://www.statista.com/statistics/624426/global-consulting-market-size-by-sector.

22. Michael E. Porter and Nitin Nohria, "How CEOs Manage Time," *Harvard Business Review* 96, no. 4 (2018): 42–51.

23. Paul DiMaggio and Walter W. Powell, "The Iron Cage Revisited: Collective Rationality and Institutional Isomorphism in Organizational Fields," *American Sociological Review* 48, no. 2 (1983): 147–160.

24. Brian Wansink, *Mindless Eating: Why We Eat More Than We Think* (New York: Bantam, 2006).

25. Richard H. Thaler and Cass R. Sunstein, *Nudge: Improving Decisions about Health, Wealth and Happiness* (New Haven, CT: Yale University Press, 2008).

26. Thaler and Sunstein, *Nudge*, 53.

27. Thaler and Sunstein, *Nudge*, 54.

28. Eva Boxenbaum and Stefan Jonsson, "Isomorphism, Diffusion and Decoupling: Concept Evolution and Theoretical Challenges," in *The Sage Handbook of Organizational Institutionalism,* 2nd ed., ed. Royston Greenwood et al. (Thousand Oaks, CA: Sage, 2017), pt. 2, 79–104.

29. Boxenbaum and Jonsson, "Isomorphism, Diffusion and Decoupling."

30. DiMaggio and Powell, "The Iron Cage Revisited."

31. Ariel Shapiro, "Bleeding DirecTV Subscribers, AT&T Throws Five Streaming Services at the Wall," *Forbes,* April 25, 2019, https://www.forbes.com/sites /arielshapiro/2019/04/25/bleeding-directv-subscribers-att-attempts-to-lure -streamers/?sh=2f73d7862a9b.

32. Kira R. Fabrizio and L. G. Thomas, "The Impact of Local Demand on Innovation in a Global Industry," *Strategic Management Journal* 33, no. 1 (2012): 42–64.

33. Michael E. Porter, "What Is Strategy?," *Harvard Business Review* 74, no. 6 (1996): 61–78.

34. Kevin J. Boudreau and Karim R. Lakhani, "Using the Crowd as an Innovation Partner," *Harvard Business Review* 91, no. 4 (2013): 60–69.

35. Andy Murdock, "How Basic Research on Jellyfish Led to an Unexpected Scientific Revolution," UC Newsroom, University of California, November 13, 2017, https://www.universityofcalifornia.edu/news/how-basic-research-jellyfish -led-unexpected-scientific-revolution.

36. Larry Greenemeier, "Breaking Down Barriers in Science with Help from a Jellyfish: A Q&A with Martin Chalfie," *Scientific American*, October 18, 2008,

https://www.scientificamerican.com/article/breaking-down-barriers-martin
-chalfie.

37. Greenemeier, "Breaking Down Barriers in Science with Help from a Jellyfish."

38. Murdock, "How Basic Research on Jellyfish Led to an Unexpected Scientific Revolution."

39. Gary Klein, *Seeing What Others Don't: The Remarkable Ways We Gain Insights* (New York: PublicAffairs, 2013).

40. Klein, *Seeing What Others Don't.*

41. For a detailed account of this story, see Gillian Tett, *The Silo Effect: The Peril of Expertise and the Promise of Breaking Down Barriers* (New York: Simon and Schuster, 2015)

42. Quy N. Huy, "Five Reasons Most Companies Fail at Strategy Executiom," *Forbes*, June 8, 2016, https://www.forbes.com/sites/insead/2016/01/08/five-reasons -most-companies-fail-at-strategy-execution/#3beb95ad3348.

43. https://www.epa.gov/enforcement/deepwater-horizon-bp-gulf-mexico-oil -spill.

44. Augustino Fontevecchia, "BP Fighting a Two Front War as Macondo Contin-ues to Bite and Production Drops," *Forbes*, February 5, 2013, https://www.forbes .com/sites/afontevecchia/2013/02/05/bp-fighting-a-two-front-war-as-macondo -continues-to-bite-and-production-drops/#18ddd02d458c.

45. Tett, *The Silo Effect.*

46. Lars Bo Jeppesen and Karim R. Lakhani, "Marginality and Problem-Solving Effectiveness in Broadcast Search," *Organization Science* 21, no. 5 (2010): 1016–33.

47. See the Topcoder website at https://www.topcoder.com/about-topcoder/cus tomer-stories/nasa-iss-longeron.

48. Sunil Gupta, *Driving Digital Strategy: A Guide to Reimagining Your Business* (Bos-ton: Harvard Business Press, 2018).

49. Gary Hamel, "Strategy as Revolution," *Harvard Business Review* 7 (July–August 1996): 69–82.

50. For a more detailed analysis of Polaroid's failure to transition into the digi-tal age, see Mary Tripsas and Giovanni Gavetti, "Capabilities, Cognition, and

Inertia: Evidence from Digital Imaging," *Strategic Management Journal* 21, no. 10–11 (2000): 1147–1161.

51. Irving L. Janis, *Victims of Groupthink: A Psychological Study of Foreign-Policy Decisions and Fiascoes* (Boston: Houghton Mifflin, 1972).

52. Jack Eaton, "Management Communication: The Threat of Groupthink," *Corporate Communications: An International Journal* 6, no. 4 (2001): 183–192.

53. Eaton, "Management Communication."

54. Portions of text in this section were originally published in Christian Stadler, "Opening Up to Transform," in *The Transformation Playbook: Insights, Wisdom and Best Practices to Make Transformation Reality* (Brightline Project Management Institute, November 2019).

55. For more on Edzard Reuter as a leader during this period, see Christian Stadler, *Enduring Success: What We Can Learn from the History of Outstanding Corporations* (Stanford, CA: Stanford University Press, 2011), Wilfried Feldenkirchen, *"Vom Guten das Beste": Von Daimler und Benz zur Daimlerchrysler AG*, vol. 1 (Munich: Herbig Verlag, 2003), and Edzard Reuter, *Schein und Wirklichkeit: Erinnerungen* (Berlin: Siedler Verlag, 1998).

56. Jon L. Pierce, Tatiana Kostova, and Kurt T. Dirks, "Toward a Theory of Psychological Ownership in Organizations," *Academy of Management Review* 26, no. 2 (2001): 298–310.

57. Interview with Christian Kluge, board member, Daimler, December 12, 2006.

58. Stadler, *Enduring Success*.

59. Clayton Christensen, *The Innovator's Dilemma: When New Technologies Cause Great Firms to Fail* (Brighton, MA: Harvard Business Review Press, 1997).

60. Geoffrey Smith, "Can George Fisher Fix Kodak?," *Business Week*, October 20, 1997.

61. Greg Satell, "A Look Back at Why Blockbuster Really Failed and Why It Didn't Have To," *Forbes*, September 5, 2014, https://www.forbes.com/sites/gregsatell/2014/09/05/a-look-back-at-why-blockbuster-really-failed-and-why-it-didnt-have-to/; Sunil Chopra and Murali J Veeraiyan, "Movie Rental Business: Blockbuster, Netflix, and Redbox," *Kellogg School of Management Cases* 1, no. 1 (January 2017): 1–21.

62. Scott E. Page, *The Difference: How the Power of Diversity Creates Better Groups, Firms, Schools, and Societies* (Princeton, NJ: Princeton University Press, 2008).

Chapter 2

1. Jesus Diaz, "Everything You Always Wanted to Know about Lego," Gizmodo, June 26, 2008, https://gizmodo.com/everything-you-always-wanted-to-know -about-lego-5019797.

2. Jim Whitehurst, *The Open Organization: Igniting Passion and Performance* (Brighton, MA: Harvard Business Review Press, 2015).

3. Juan Miguel Campanario, "Using Citation Classics to Study the Incidence of Serendipity in Scientific Discovery," *Scientometrics* 37, no. 1 (1996): 3–24.

4. Steven Johnson, *Where Good Ideas Come From: The Seven Patterns of Innovation* (Penguin UK, 2011).

5. Miguel Pina e Cunha, Stewart R. Clegg, and Sandro Mendonça, "On Serendipity and Organizing," *European Management Journal* 28, no. 5 (2010): 319–330.

6. Paul D. Kretkowski, "The 15 Percent Solution.," *Wired*, January 23, 1998, https://www.wired.com/1998/01/the-15-percent-solution/.

7. Interview with Jackie Yeaney, Chief Marketing Officer at Tableau Software, former Executive Vice President of Corporate Strategy and Marketing at Red Hat, September 11, 2017.

8. Adam Kleinbaum, "Organizational Misfits and the Origins of Brokerage in Intrafirm Networks," *Administrative Science Quarterly* 57, no. 3 (2012): 407–452.

9. Paul Gompers and Silpa Kovvali, "The Other Diversity Dividend," *Harvard Business Review,* July–August 96, no. 4 (2018): 72–77.

10. Vivian Hunt, Dennis Layton, and Sara Prince, "Why Diversity Matters," *McKinsey Insights*, January 2015, https://www.mckinsey.com/business-functions /organization/our-insights/why-diversity-matters.

11. Margaret Heffernan, *A Bigger Prize: How We Can Do Better Than the Competition* (Upper Saddle River, NJ: PublicAffairs, 2014).

12. Herminia Ibarra and Morten T. Hansen, "Are You a Collaborative Leader?," *Harvard Business Review* 89, no. 7–8 (2011): 68–74; Dick Brass, "Microsoft's Creative Destruction," *New York Times,* February 4, 2010, https://www.nytimes.com /2010/02/04/opinion/04brass.html.

13. Mary Tripsas and Giovanni Gavetti, "Capabilities, Cognition, and Inertia: Evidence from Digital Imaging," *Strategic Management Journal* 21, no. 10–11 (2000): 1147–61.

14. Joseph Bradley et al., "Digital Vortex: How Digital Disruption Is Redefining Industries," Global Center for Digital Business Transformation, June 2015, https://www.cisco.com/c/dam/en/us/solutions/collateral/industry-solutions/digital-vortex-report.pdf.

15. Bradley et al., "Digital Vortex."

16. Harry McCracken, "Satya Nadella Rewrites Microsoft's Code," *Fast Company*, September 18, 2017, https://www.fastcompany.com/40457458/satya-nadella-rewrites-microsofts-code.

17. Herminia Ibarra and Aneeta Rattan, "Microsoft: Instilling a Growth Mindset," *London Business School Review* 29, no. 3 (2018): 50–53.

18. Carol Dweck, *Mindset: Changing the Way You Think to Fulfil Your Potential,* updated edition (London: Hachette UK, 2017).

19. Heather Landy, "All the Books Microsoft CEO Satya Nadella Talked about at Davos," *Quartz at Work* (blog), Quartz, January 24, 2020, https://qz.com/work/1790800/books-microsoft-ceo-satya-nadella-talked-about-at-davos.

20. Herminia Ibarra and Anne Scoular, "The Leader as Coach," *Harvard Business Review* 97, no. 6 (2019): 110–119.

21. Simone Stolzhoff, "How Do You Turn Around the Culture of a 130,000-Person Company? Ask Satya Nadella," Quartz, February 1, 2019, https://qz.com/work/1539071/how-microsoft-ceo-satya-nadella-rebuilt-the-company-culture.

22. Rasmus Hougaard, Jacqueline Carter, and Kathleen Hogan, "How Microsoft Builds a Sense of Community among 144,000 Employees," *Harvard Business Review: Digital Articles,* August 28, 2019https://hbr.org/2019/08/how-microsoft-builds-a-sense-of-community-among-144000-employees.

23. Hougaard, Carter, and Hogan, "How Microsoft Builds a Sense of Community among 144,000 Employees."

24. Microsoft, "Satya Nadella Email to Employees on First Day as CEO," *News,* February 4, 2014, https://News.Microsoft.Com/2014/02/04/Satya-Nadella-Email-to-Employees-on-First-Day-as-Ceo.

25. Hermann Simon, *Hidden Champions of the Twenty-First Century: The Success Strategies of Unknown World Market Leaders* (Dordrecht: Springer, 2009); Hermann Kronseder,*Mein Leben* (Regensburg: Verlag Mittelbayerische Zeitung, 1993).

26. Chris Zook and James Allen, *The Founder's Mentality: How to Overcome the Predictable Crises of Growth* (Brighton, MA: Harvard Business Review Press, 2016).

27. Johnson, *Where Good Ideas Come From.*

28. Karl Sigmund, *Exact Thinking in Demented Times: The Vienna Circle and the Epic Quest for the Foundations of Science* (New York: Basic Books, 2017). For information on the cultural ambience of Freud's salons, see the book review of *Exact Thinking in Demented Times* in the *Economist,* January 13, 2018, https://www.economist.com/books-and-arts/2018/01/13/the-scientific-debates-of-the-vienna-circle.

29. Katherine W. Phillips, Robert B. Lount Jr., Oliver Sheldon, and Floor Rink, "The Biases That Punish Racially Diverse Teams," *Harvard Business Review: Digital Articles,* February 22, 2016, https://hbr.org/2016/02/the-biases-that-punish-racially-diverse-teams.

30. Gompers and Kovvali, "The Other Diversity Dividend."

31. Erik Samdahl, "Top Employers Are 5.5x More Likely to Reward Collaboration," i4cp.com, June 22, 2017, https://www.i4cp.com/productivity-blog/top-employers-are-5-5x-more-likely-to-reward-collaboration.

32. Richard Whittington, Basak Yakis-Douglas, and Kwangwon Ahn, "Wall Street Rewards CEOs Who Talk about Their Strategies," *Harvard Business Review: Digital Articles,* December 28, 2015, https://hbr.org/2015/12/wall-street-rewards-ceos-who-talk-about-their-strategies.

33. For more on the five-hour rule—that is, setting aside five hours a week to read or learn something new—see Michael Simmons, "Why Constant Learners All Embrace the 5-Hour Rule," Accelerated Intelligence, June 20, 2016, https://medium.com/accelerated-intelligence/why-constant-learners-all-embrace-the-5-hour-rule-8836f554da1#.99stfzkbb.

34. Michael Simmons, "Bill Gates, Warren Buffett, and Oprah All Use the 5-Hour Rule. Here's How This Powerful Habit Works," *Business Insider,* February 25, 2020, https://www.businessinsider.com/bill-gates-warren-buffet-and-oprah-all-use-the-5-hour-rule-2017-7?r=US&IR=T.

35. Zameena Mejia and Marguerite Ward, "Billionaire Elon Musk Says He Was 'Raised by Books' and Credits His Success to These 8," CNBC, November 16, 2017, https://www.cnbc.com/2017/11/16/tesla-ceo-elon-musk-says-he-was-raised-by-books.html.

Chapter 3

1. Interview with Sylvie Löffler, Saxonia, October 5, 2018.

2. Quote from Marius K. Luedicke, Katharina C. Husemann, Santi Furnari, and Florian Ladstaetter, "Radically Open Strategizing: How the Premium Cola Collective Takes Open Strategy to the Extreme," *Long Range Planning* 50, no. 3 (2017): 371–384.

3. In 2012, Premium Cola sold one million units. To put this in perspective, Coke serves 1.9 billion drinks a day. For more information on Premium Cola, see www .premium-cola.de and https://www.coca-cola.co.uk/our-business/faqs/how-many -cans-of-coca-cola-are-sold-worldwide-in-a-day.

4. Gary Hamel, "Strategy as Revolution," *Harvard Business Review* 7 (July–August 1996): 69–82.

5. Julia Hautz, David Seidl, and Richard Whittington, "Open Strategy: Dimensions, Dilemmas, Dynamics," *Long Range Planning* 50, no. 3 (2017): 298–309.

6. Lars Bo Jeppesen and Karim R. Lakhani, "Marginality and Problem-Solving Effectiveness in Broadcast Search," *Organization Science* 21, no. 5 (2010): 1016–1033; Richard W. Woodman, John E. Sawyer, and Ricky W. Griffin, "Toward a Theory of Organizational Creativity," *Academy of Management Review* 18, no. 2 (1993): 293–321; Jill E. Perry-Smith and Christina E. Shalley, "The Social Side of Creativity: A Static and Dynamic Social Network Perspective," *Academy of Management Review* 28, no. 1 (2003): 89–106.

7. Interview with Heraldo Sales-Cavalcante, Ericsson, September 23, 2018.

8. Interview with Klaus Bachstein, CEO, Gallus, August 11, 2017.

9. Hautz, Seidl, and Whittington, "Open Strategy."

10. Julia Hautz, "Opening Up the Strategy Process—a Network Perspective," *Management Decision* 55, no. 9 (2017): 1956–1983.

11. Teppo Felin and Todd R. Zenger, "Closed or Open Innovation? Problem Solving and the Governance Choice," *Research Policy* 43, no. 5 (June 2014): 914–925.

12. Felin and Zenger, "Closed or Open Innovation?"

13. Stefan Haefliger, S. Monteiro, and G. V. Krogh, "Social Software and Strategy," *Long Range Planning* 44, no. 5/6 (2011): 297–316.

14. Daniel Stieger, Kurt Matzler, Sayan Chatterjee, and Florian Ladstätter-Fussenegger, "Democratizing Strategy: How Crowdsourcing Can Be Used for Strategy Dialogues," *California Management Review* 54, no. 4 (Summer 2012): 44–68.

15. Julia Hautz, Kurt Matzler, Jonas Sutter, et al., "Practices of Inclusion in Open Strategy," in *Cambridge Handbook of Open Strategy*, ed. David Seidl, Richard Whittington, and Georg Von Krogh (Cambridge: Cambridge University Press, 2019), 87–105.

16. Read more about the story in Gloria Lombardi, "Unilever Leaders Chat Strategy with Employees," The Future of Earth, March 7, 2014, https://futureofearth.online /unilever-leaders-chat-strategy-with-employees, and Christian Stadler, Julia Hautz, and Stephan Friedrich von den Eichen, "Open Strategy: The Inclusion of Crowds in Making Strategies," *NIM Marketing Intelligence Review* 12, no. 1 (2020): 36–41.

17. Lombardi, "Unilever Leaders Chat Strategy with Employees."

18. Lombardi, "Unilever Leaders Chat Strategy with Employees."

19. Lombardi, "Unilever Leaders Chat Strategy with Employees."

20. Markus Reitzig and Olav Sorenson, "Biases in the Selection Stage of Bottom-up Strategy Formulation," *Strategic Management Journal* 34, no. 7 (2013): 782–99; Markus Reitzig, "Is Your Company Choosing the Best Innovation Ideas?," *MIT Sloan Management Review* 52, no. 4 (Summer 2011): 47–52.

21. Christian Stadler, *Enduring Success: What We Can Learn from the History of Outstanding Corporations* (Stanford, CA: Stanford University Press, 2011),

22. Interview with Löffler, Saxonia, October 5, 2018.

23. Richard Whittington, Ludovic Cailluet, and Basak Yakis-Douglas, "Opening Strategy: Evolution of a Precarious Profession," *British Journal of Management* 22, no. 3 (2011): 531–544; Hautz, Seidl, and Whittington, "Open Strategy."

Chapter 4

1. See the website at https://www.topcoder.com/challenges/30041395/?type =develop&tab=details.

2. Interview with Peter Van Vories, April 2020.

3. Ryon Stewart, challenge coordinator at NASA's Center of Excellence for Collaborative Innovation, shared this story with us during an interview on November 8, 2019.

4. *Sun Tzŭ on the Art of War: The Oldest Military Treatise in the World*, translated and with an introduction by Lionel Giles (London: Luzac & Co., 1910)

5. Joel Brenner, *The Chocolate Wars: Inside the Secret Worlds of Mars and Hershey* (New York: HarperCollins Business, 2000).

6. Oliver Staley, "To Fill 70,000 Jobs, Chocolate Giant Mars Will Have to Overcome Its Deeply Secretive Past," Quartz, August 14, 2017, https://qz.com /1047136/mars-recruiting.

7. Quoted in Christoph Keese, *The Silicon Valley Challenge: A Wake-up Call for Europe* (Munich: Random House/Penguin, 2016).

8. Keese, *The Silicon Valley Challenge*.

9. Keese, *The Silicon Valley Challenge*, 51.

10. Richard Whittington, *Opening Strategy: Professional Strategists and Practice Change, 1960 to Today* (Oxford: Oxford University Press, 2019).

11. Don Tapscott and Anthony D. Williams, *Radical Openness: Four Unexpected Principles for Success* (TED Books, 2013).

12. NASA, "Citizen Scientists Find New World with NASA Telescope," January 7, 2019, https://www.jpl.nasa.gov/news/news.php?feature=7313.

13. Ray Dalio, *Principles: Life and Work* (New York: Simon and Schuster, 2017), 331–332.

14. Dalio, *Principles*, 325.

15. Duncan Neil Angwin, *Mergers and Acquisitions* (Chichester: Wiley-Blackwell, 2007).

16. Ian Harwood, "Confidentiality Constraints within Mergers and Acquisitions: Gaining Insights through a Bubble Metaphor," *British Journal of Management* 17, no 4 (2006): 347–359.

17. Tapscott and Williams, *Radical Openness*.

18. Basak Yakis-Douglas, Duncan Angwin, Kwangwon Ahn, and Maureen Meadows, "Opening M&A Strategy to Investors: Predictors and Outcomes of Transparency During Organisational Transition," *Long Range Planning* 50, no. 3 (2017): 411–422.

19. See substantial media coverage, such as that provided by *Fast Company*: Neal Ungerleider, "Wannabe SEALs Help U.S. Navy Hunt Pirates In Massively

Multiplayer Game," *Fast Company*, May 10, 2011, https://www.fastcompany.com /1752574/wannabe-seals-help-us-navy-hunt-pirates-massively-multiplayer-game; or *Wired*: Spencer Ackerman, "Navy Crowdsources Pirate Fight to Online Gamers, *Wired*, May 11, 2011, https://www.wired.com/2011/05/navy-crowdsources-pirate -fight-to-online-gamers/).

20. Ackerman, "Navy Crowdsources Pirate Fight to Online Gamers."

21. Analytic Services, Inc., "Massive Multiplayer Online Wargame Leveraging the Internet," https://web.archive.org/web/20140221213723/https://www .anser.org/mmowgli; for more information about the portal itself visit https:// web.archive.org/web/20140222220000/http://portal.mmowgli.nps.edu/game -wiki/-/wiki/PlayerResources/About+MMOWGLI.

22. See detailed account of this initiative in Kathryn Aten and Gail Fann Thomas, "Crowdsourcing Strategizing: Communication Technology Affordances and the Communicative Constitution of Organizational Strategy," *International Journal of Business Communication* 53, no. 2 (2016): 148–180.

23. Interview with Dale Moore, US Navy, November 26, 2018.

24. Aten and Thomas, "Crowdsourcing Strategizing."

25. Interview with Moore, November 26, 2018.

26. Interview with Mark Darrah, US Navy, December 13, 2018.

27. Daniel Stieger, Kurt Matzler, Sayan Chatterjee, and Florian Ladstätter-Fussenegger, "Democratizing Strategy: How Crowdsourcing Can Be Used for Strategy Dialogues," *California Management Review* 54, no. 4 (Summer 2012): 44–68; Julia Hautz, "Opening Up the Strategy Process—a Network Perspective," *Management Decision* 55, no. 9 (2017): 1956–1983.

28. Elizabeth E. Richard and Jeffrey R. Davis, "NASA Human Health and Performance Center: Open Innovation Successes and Collaborative Projects," *Acta Astronautica* 104, no. 1 (2014): 383–387.

29. Kurt Matzler and Ryon Stewart, "Crowdsourcing at NASA: About the Work behind Having Others Do the Work: An Interview with Ryon Stewart, Challenge Coordinator at NASA's Center of Excellence for Collaborative Innovation (CoECI)," *Marketing Intelligence Review* 12, no. 1 (2020): 48–54.

30. For more information, see NASA's web page on CoECI at https://www.nasa .gov/coeci/nasa-at-work.

31. Matzler and Stewart, "Crowdsourcing at NASA."

32. Interview with Stewart, November 8, 2019.

33. Interview with Stewart, November 8, 2019.

34. Interview with Stewart, November 8, 2019.

Chapter 5

1. Brandon Huebner, "The Scilly Naval Disaster—22 October 1707 (O.S.)," *On This Day* (blog), Maritime History Podcast, October 22, 2014, http://maritimehis torypodcast.com/scilly-naval-disaster-22-october-1707-o-s.

2. William E. Carter and Merri Sue Carter, "The British Longitude Act Reconsidered," *American Scientist* 100, no. 2 (2012): 102–106.

3. See the website of the Royal Museum Greenwich at https://www.rmg.co.uk /discover/behind-the-scenes/blog/why-longitude-mattered.

4. Dava Sobel, *Longitude: The True Story of a Lone Genius Who Solved the Greatest Scientific Problem of His Time* (New York: Macmillan, 2005).

5. William J. H. Andrewes, "Even Newton Could Be Wrong: The Story of Harrison's First Three Sea Clocks," in *The Quest for Longitude: The Proceedings of the Longitude Symposium Harvard University, Cambridge, Massachusetts November 4–6, 1993*, ed. William J. H. Andrews (Cambridge, MA: Harvard University Press, 1996), 190–234.

6. Anthony G. Randall, "The Timekeeper That Won the Longitude Prize," in Andrewes, ed., *The Quest for Longitude,* 236–254.

7. For further information see the website of the Royal Museum of Greenwich at: https://www.rmg.co.uk/discover/explore/longitude-found-john-harrison.

8. A. N. Thomas Varzeliotis, *Time under Sail: The Very Human Story of the Marine Chronometer* (Victoria, B.C.: Alcyone Books, 1998).

9. For further information, see the relevant web page of the Royal Museum Greenwich at https://www.rmg.co.uk/discover/explore/longitude-found-john -harrison.

10. Charles Waltner, "I-Prize Contest Proving a Winning Approach to Discovering Billion-Dollar Business Ideas," Cisco Systems, July 14, 2008, https:// newsroom.cisco.com/feature-content?type=webcontent&articleId=4429590.

11. Quoted in Ben Paynter, "The Power of Competition in Creativity: Cisco's 'Big' Jolt for Startups," *Fast Company*, May 4, 2013, https://www.fastcompany .com/3002680/power-competition-creativity-ciscos-big-jolt-startups.

12. Guido Jouret, "Inside Cisco's Search for the Next Big Idea," *Harvard Business Review* 87, no. 9 (2009): 43–45.

13. Guido Jouret, Cisco's chief technology officer, explaining the I-Prize project in Charles Waltner, "Cisco I-Prize Successfully Taps Ideas from People Outside of Silicon Valley's Mainstream," *Cisco, The Network, Cisco's Technology News Site*, July 14, 2018, https://newsroom.cisco.com/feature-content?type=webcontent &articleId=4429680.

14. Jouret, "Inside Cisco's Search for the Next Big Idea."

15. Jouret, "Inside Cisco's Search for the Next Big Idea."

16. Quoted in "Cisco Announces Winner of Global I-Prize Innovation Competition," Cisco Systems, June 30, 2010, https://newsroom.cisco.com/press-release -content?type=webcontent&articleId=5593364.

17. Kurt Matzler, "Crowd Innovation: The Philosopher's Stone, a Silver Bullet, or Pandora's Box?," *NIM Marketing Intelligence Review* 12, no. 1 (2020): 10–17.

18. For more information, see the website at https://www.innocentive.com.

19. For more information, see the website at https://www.kaggle.com.

20. Allan Afuah and Christopher L. Tucci, "Crowdsourcing as a Solution to Distant Search," *Academy of Management Review* 37, no. 3 (2012): 355–375.

21. Alan MacCormack, Fiona Murray, and Erika Wagner, "Spurring Innovation through Competitions," *MIT Sloan Management Review* 55, no. 1 (2013): 25–32.

22. Jeppesen and Lakhani, "Marginality and Problem-Solving Effectiveness in Broadcast Search," 1016.

23. Kevin J. Boudreau, Nicola Lacetera, and Karim R. Lakhani, "Incentives and Problem Uncertainty in Innovation Contests: An Empirical Analysis," *Management Science* 57, no. 5 (2011): 843–863.

24. Gary Hamel and Michele Zanini, *Humanocracy: Creating Organizations as Amazing as the People inside Them* (Brighton, MA: Harvard Business Review Press, 2020), 189–190.

25. Teppo Felin, Karim R. Lakhani, and Michael L. Tushman, "Firms, Crowds, and Innovation," *Strategic Organization* 15, no. 2 (2017): 119–140; Andrew King

and Karim R. Lakhani, "Using Open Innovation to Identify the Best Ideas," *MIT Sloan Management Review* 55, no. 1 (2013): 41–48.

26. MacCormack, Murray, and Wagner, "Spurring Innovation through Competitions," 27.

27. Kevin J. Boudreau and Karim R. Lakhani, "Using the Crowd as an Innovation Partner," *Harvard Business Review* 91, no. 4 (2013): 60–69.

28. Kevin Boudreau and Karim Lakhani, "How to Manage Outside Innovation," *MIT Sloan Management Review* 50, no. 4 (2009): 69–76.

29. See, for example, MacCormack, Murray, and Wagner, "Spurring Innovation through Competitions."

30. See A. Majchrzak and A. Malhotra, "Towards an Information Systems Perspective and Research Agenda on Crowdsourcing for Innovation," *Journal of Strategic Information Systems* 22, no. 4 (2013): 257–68, and the literature cited therein.

31. Karl Duncker and Lynne S. Lees, "On Problem-Solving," *Psychological Monographs* 58, no. 5 (1945): i–113.

32. Duncker and Lees, "On Problem-Solving."

33. MacCormack, Murray, and Wagner, "Spurring Innovation through Competitions."

34. Cisco Systems, "Cisco Announces the Cisco I-Prize to Identify New Business Ideas," press release, October 31, 2007, https://newsroom.cisco.com/press -release-content?type=webcontent&articleId=4030414.

35. Don Tapscott and Anthony D. Williams, *Wikinomics: How Mass Collaboration Changes Everything* (New York: Penguin, 2008).

36. Linda Tischler, "He Struck Gold on the Net (Really)," *Fast Company*, May 31, 2002, https://www.fastcompany.com/44917/he-struck-gold-net-really.

37. Paynter, "The Power of Competition in Creativity."

38. Katja Hutter, Julia Hautz, Johann Füller, et al., "Communitition: The Tension between Competition and Collaboration in Community-Based Design Contests," *Creativity & Innovation Management* 20, no. 1 (2011): 3–21.

39. Jouret, "Inside Cisco's Search for the Next Big Idea."

40. Anne Lange, Doug Handler, and James Vila, "Next-Generation Clusters Creating Innovation Hubs to Boost Economic Growth," Cisco Internet

Business Solutions Group, 2010, http://www.clustermapping.us/resource/next
-generation-clusters-creating-innovation-hubs-boost-economic-growth.

41. Lange, Handler, and Vila, "Next-Generation Clusters Creating Innovation Hubs to Boost Economic Growth."

42. Jouret, "Inside Cisco's Search for the Next Big Idea."

43. MacCormack, Murray, and Wagner, "Spurring Innovation through Competitions."

44. See Jouret, "Inside Cisco's Search for the Next Big Idea."

45. See Jouret, "Inside Cisco's Search for the Next Big Idea."

46. Toastiemaker, "Wakes Up Every Hour Every Fucking Night," thread initiated April 1, 2020, https://www.mumsnet.com/Talk/sleep/3867735-Wakes-up-Every -hour-every-fucking-night.

47. See the website at https://www.mumsnet.com/info/about-us.

48. Mikal E. Belicove, "8 Do's and Don'ts for Marketing on Online Forums and Message Boards," June 28, 2012, https://www.entrepreneur.com/article/223900.

49. Jenny Preece, Blair Nonnecke, and Dorine Andrews, "The Top Five Reasons for Lurking: Improving Community Experiences for Everyone," *Computers in Human Behavior* 20, no. 2 (2004): 201–223.

50. Kent D. Miller, Frances Fabian, and Shu-Jou Lin, "Strategies for Online Communities," *Strategic Management Journal* 30, no. 3 (2009): 305–322; Constance Elise Porter et al., "How to Foster and Sustain Engagement in Virtual Communities," *California Management Review* 53, no. 4 (2011): 80–110; Florian Hauser et al., "Firestorms: Modeling Conflict Diffusion and Management Strategies in Online Communities," *Journal of Strategic Information Systems* 26, no. 4 (2017): 285–321.

51. Molly McLure Wasko and Samer Faraj, "Why Should I Share? Examining Social Capital and Knowledge Contribution in Electronic Networks of Practice," *MIS Quarterly* 29, no. 1 (2005): 35–57; Jenny Preece, "Supporting Commmunity and Building Social Capital," *Communications of the ACM* 45, no. 4 (2002): 36–40.

52. Katja Hutter, Bright Adu Nketia, and Johann Füller, "Falling Short with Participation: Different Effects of Ideation, Commenting, and Evaluating Behavior on Open Strategizing," *Long Range Planning* 50, no. 3 (2017): 355–370.

53. Stieger et al., "Democratizing Strategy."

54. Boudreau and Lakhani, "Using the Crowd as an Innovation Partner."

55. Boudreau and Lakhani, "How to Manage Outside Innovation."

56. Stieger et al., "Democratizing Strategy"; Josh Bernoff and Charlene Li, "Harnessing the Power of the Oh-So-Social Web," *MIT Sloan Management Review* 49, no. 3 (2008): 36–42.

57. Gary Hamel, *The Future of Management* (Boston: Harvard Business School Publishing, 2007).

58. Ericsson, "Ericsson Reports Fourth Quarter and Full Year Results 2017," press releases, January 31, 2018, https://www.ericsson.com/en/press-releases /2018/1/ericsson-reports-fourth-quarter-and-full-year-results-2017.

59. See Anna Plotnikova, Krsto Pandza, and Hernando Sales-Cavalcante, "How Strategy Professionals Develop and Sustain an Online Strategy Community— The Lessons from Ericsson," *Long Range Planning* (in press), https://doi.org/10.1016 /j.lrp.2020.102015.

60. Interview with Sales-Cavalcante, Ericsson, September 23, 2018.

61. Rob Marvin, "Ericsson Is Building AI Networks for Our 5G Future," PCMag UK, February 26, 2018, https://uk.pcmag.com/news-analysis/93530/ericsson-is -building-ai-networks-for-our-5g-future.

62. "Ericsson to Buy CENX for Boosting Network Automation Ability," Zacks, September 5, 2018, https://www.nasdaq.com/article/ericsson-to-buy-cenx-for -boosting-network-automation-ability-cm1017894.

63. Interview with Sales-Cavalcante, Ericsson, September 23, 2018.

64. Reto Hofstetter, Suleiman Aryobsei, and Andreas Herrmann, "Should You Really Produce What Consumers Like Online? Empirical Evidence for Reciprocal Voting in Open Innovation Contests," *Journal of Product Innovation Management* 35, no. 2 (2017): 209–229.

65. Matzler, "Crowd Innovation."

66. Marion Poetz and Martin Schreier, "The Value of Crowdsourcing: Can Users Really Compete with Professionals in Generating New Product Ideas?," *Journal of Product Innovation Management* 29, no. 2 (2012): 245–256.

67. Hofstetter, Aryobsei, and Herrmann, "Should You Really Produce What Consumers Like Online?"

68. To get more insights about the Dialogue Days, see Stieger et al., "Democratizing Strategy."

69. Stieger et al., "Democratizing Strategy," 55

70. Stieger et al., "Democratizing Strategy," 55

71. Haefliger, Monteiro, and Krogh, "Social Software and Strategy."

72. Hutter, Hautz, and Füller, "Communitition."

73. Johann Füller, Katja Hutter, Julia Hautz, and Kurt Matzler, "User Roles and Contributions in Innovation-Contest Communities," *Journal of Management Information Systems* 31, no. 1 (2014): 273–308.

74. Hutter, Nketia, and Füller, "Falling Short with Participation."

75. Hutter, Nketia, and Füller, "Falling Short with Participation."

Chapter 6

1. Karl E. Weick, *Sensemaking in Organizations* (Thousand Oaks, CA: Sage, 1995).

2. Herbert Alexander Simon, *The Shape of Automation for Men and Management* (New York: Harper and Row, 1965).

3. Brad Darrach, "Meet Shaky: The First Electronic Person," *Life Magazine* 69, no. 21 (1970): 58B–68B.

4. Nick Bostrom, *Superintelligence: Paths, Dangers, Strategies* (Oxford: Oxford University Press, 2014): 4.

5. Bostrom, *Superintelligence*.

6. "Thomas Edison's Predictions: Spot On," *CBS News*, January 28, 2011, https://www.cbsnews.com/news/thomas-edisons-predictions-spot-on/.

7. "Microsoft's Ballmer Not Impressed with Apple Iphone," CNBC, January 17, 2010, https://www.cnbc.com/id/16671712.

8. Adam Shaw, "Why Economic Forecasting Has Always Been a Flawed Science," *The Guardian*, September 2, 2017, https://www.theguardian.com/money/2017/sep/02/economic-forecasting-flawed-science-data. On inaccuracy in economic forecasting, also see: Masayuki Morikawa, "The Accuracy of Long-term Growth Forecasts by Economics Researchers," *VOX EU*, February 10, 2020, https://voxeu.org/article/accuracy-long-term-growth-forecasts-economics-researchers.

9. Philip E. Tetlock, *Expert Political Judgment: How Good Is It? How Can We Know?*, new ed. (Princeton, NJ: Princeton University Press, 2017).

10. Louis Menand, "Everybody's an Expert," *New Yorker,* December 5, 2005, 98–101.

11. Bent Flyvbjerg, "Over Budget, Over Time, Over and Over Again: Managing Major Projects," in *The Oxford Handbook of Project Management,* ed. Peter W. G. Morris, Jeffrey K. Pinto, and J. Söderlund (Oxford: Oxford University Press, 2011), 321–344.

12. Emily Schultheis, "Whatever Happened to Berlin's Deserted 'Ghost' Airport?," *BBC Worklife,* November 5, 2018, https://www.bbc.com/worklife/article /20181030-what-happened-to-berlins-ghost-airport.

13. Bent Flyvbjerg, Massimo Garbuio, and Dan Lovallo, "Delusion and Deception in Large Infrastructure Projects: Two Models for Explaining and Preventing Executive Disaster," *California Management Review* 51, no. 2 (2009): 170–194.

14. Flyvbjerg, Garbuio, and Lovallo, "Delusion and Deception in Large Infrastructure Projects," 172.

15. Daniel Kahneman, *Thinking, Fast and Slow* (London: Penguin, 2012).

16. George S. Day and Paul J. H. Schoemaker, *Peripheral Vision: Detecting the Weak Signals That Will Make or Break Your Company* (Brighton, MA: Harvard Business Review Press, 2006).

17. Quoted in Kahneman, *Thinking, Fast and Slow.*

18. Flyvbjerg, "Over Budget, Over Time, Over and Over Again."

19. Rita McGrath, *Seeing around Corners: How to Spot Inflection Points in Business before They Happen* (New York: Houghton Mifflin, 2019).

20. Paul J. H. Schoemaker and George S. Day, "How to Make Sense of Weak Signals," *MIT Sloan Management Review* 50, no. 3 (2009): 89–98.

21. Philip E. Tetlock and Dan Gardner, *Superforecasting: The Art and Science of Prediction* (New York: Random House, 2016).

22. Philip E. Tetlock, "Why an Open Mind Is Key to Making Better Predictions" (video), Wharton School, University of Pennsylvania, October 2, 2015, https:// knowledge.wharton.upenn.edu/article/why-an-open-mind-is-key-to-making -better-predictions.

23. Tetlock and Gardner, *Superforecasting.*

24. Paul J. H. Schoemaker and Philip E. Tetlock, "Superforecasting: How to Upgrade Your Company's Judgment," *Harvard Business Review* 94 (2016): 72–78.

25. Barbara Mellers, Eric Stone, Terry Murray, et al., "Identifying and Cultivating Superforecasters as a Method of Improving Probabilistic Predictions," *Perspectives on Psychological Science* 10, no. 3 (2015): 267–281.

26. Tetlock and Gardner, *Superforecasting*.

27. Michael P. Grady, *Qualitative and Action Research: A Practitioner Handbook* (Bloomington, IN: Phi Delta Kappa International, 1998).

28. Schoemaker and Tetlock, *Superforecasting*.

29. Quoted in David Lieberman, "CEO Forum: Microsoft's Ballmer Having a 'Great Time'," *US Today 30*, April 29, 2007, https://usatoday30.usatoday.com/money/companies/management/2007-04-29-ballmer-ceo-forum-usat_N.htm.

30. Paul Miller, "Apple Sold 270,000 Iphones in the First 30 Hours," engadget, July 25, 2007, https://www.engadget.com/2007-07-25-apple-sold-270-000-iphones-in-the-first-30-hours.html.

31. Fogland annual report, 2019. (The actual company's name has been changed, so we do not provide a link to the report.)

32. Interview with executive, Fogland.

33. Interview with executive, Fogland.

Chapter 7

1. Gisbert Rühl at the Peter Drucker Forum 2016 in Vienna.

2. Christoph Keese, *The Silicon Valley Challenge: A Wake-up Call for Europe* (Munich: Random House/Penguin, 2016).

3. Shay Hershkovitz, "Wargame Business," *Naval War College Review* 72, no. 2 (2019): 67–82.

4. For the company's strategy, see the webpage at https://www.kloeckner.com/en/group/strategy.html.

5. Kurt Matzler, Franz Beilom, Stephan Friedrich von den Eichen, and Markus Anschober, *Digital Disruption: Wie Sie Ihr Unternehmen auf das Digitale Zeitalter Vorbereiten* (Munich: Franz Vahlen Verlag, 2016).

6. James Cares and Jim Miskel, "Take Your Third Move First," *Harvard Business Review* 85, no. 3 (2007): 20–21.

7. Quoted in an interview with Hans-Peter Cohn, CEO Leica, in "Nur ein Intermezzo," *Der Spiegel,* September 20, 2004, https://www.spiegel.de/spiegel/print/d -32205196.html.

8. Quoted in "Nur ein Intermezzo."

9. Olaf Storbeck, "Geniale Ingenieure, Miese Manager," *Handelsblatt,* March 28, 2008, https://www.handelsblatt.com/unternehmen/industrie/teures-spielzeug-fuer -puristen-geniale-ingenieure-miese-manager-seite-3/2939400-3.html.

10. Norbert Rief, "Andreas Kaufmann: Ein "Edelknipser" als Leica-Retter," *Die Presse,* July 17, 2010, https://www.diepresse.com/581895/andreas-kaufmann-ein -edelknipser-als-leica-retter.

11. Eric Wick, Jody Foldesy, and Sam Farley, "Creating Value from Disruption (While Others Disappear)" (Boston: Boston Consulting Group, 2017), https://www .bcg.com/en-us/publications/2017/value-creation-strategy-transformation-creating -value-disruption-others-disappear; O. Abbosh, M. Moore, B. Moussavi, et al., "Disruption Need Not Be an Enigma," *Accenture Digital Reports,* February 26, 2018, https://www.accenture.com/us-en/insight-leading-new-disruptability-index.

12. These tools are widely used in strategy projects. A SWOT analysis is used to analyze a company's strengths and weaknesses and opportunities and threats to formulated according strategies, in a PESTEL analysis trends in the company environment (political, economic, societal, technological, environmental, and legal factors) are identified, and the Five Forces Framework analyzes industry dynamics by focusing on customers, suppliers, substitutes, new entrants, and rivalry among existing competitors.

13. Michael Shayne Gary and Robert E. Wood, "Mental Models, Decision Rules, and Performance Heterogeneity," *Strategic Management Journal* 32, no. 6 (2011): 569–594.

14. Heather L. LaMarre, Kristen D. Landreville, and Michael A. Beam, "The Irony of Satire: Political Ideology and the Motivation to See What You Want to See in the Colbert Report," *International Journal of Press/Politics* 14, no. 2 (2009): 212–231.

15. George S. Day and Paul J. H. Schoemaker, "Driving Through the Fog: Managing at the Edge," *Long Range Planning* 37, no. 2 (2004): 127–142.

16. Day and Schoemaker, "Driving through the Fog."

17. Michael D. Watkins and Max H. Bazerman, "Predictable Surprises: The Disasters You Should Have Seen Coming," *Harvard Business Review* 81, no. 3 (2003): 72–85.

18. Clayton Christensen, Kurt Matzler, and Stephan Friedrich von den Eichen, *The Innovator's Dilemma: Warum Etablierte Unternehmen den Wettbewerb um Bahnbrechende Innovationen Verlieren* (Munich: Franz Vahlen Verlag, 2011); Liz Bolshaw, "Kaufmann Provides New Focus at Leica," *Financial Times,* June 5, 2014, https://www.ft.com/content/bc23b48a-eb0b-11e3-bab6-00144feabdc0.

19. Jan Oliver Schwarz, "Ex Ante Strategy Evaluation: The Case for Business Wargaming," *Business Strategy Series* (Åarhus University School of Business and Social Sciences) 12, no. 3 (2011): 122–135.

20. Cares and Miskel, "Take Your Third Move First."

21. Hansjörg Honegger, "'We Want to Revolutionise the Industry,' Interview with Gisbert Rühl, the CEO of Klöckner & Co.," Swisscom, October 16, 2017, https://www.swisscom.ch/en/business/enterprise/themen/iot/digitalisierung-im-stahlhandel.html.

22. Daniel Kahneman, *Thinking, Fast and Slow* (New York: Farrar, Straus and Giroux, 2011).

23. Clayton Christensen, *The Innovator's Dilemma: When New Technologies Cause Great Firms to Fail* (Brighton, MA: Harvard Business Review Press, 1997); Clayton M. Christensen, Elizabeth Altman, Rory McDonald, and Jonathan Palmer, "Disruptive Innovation: Intellectual History and Future Paths," HBS Working Paper 17-057 (Cambridge, MA: Harvard Business School, 2016), http://www.accioneduca.org/admin/archivos/clases/material/disruptive-innovation_1564407854.pdf.

24. Quoted in Clark G. Gilbert, "Unbundling the Structure of Inertia: Resource versus Routine Rigidity," *Academy of Management Journal* 48, no. 5 (2005): 741–763. As Gilbert also found, framing disruptions as a threat can backfire if you don't separate the online venture from the parent organization. Otherwise, managers in the established business rigidly focus on the existing business, seeking to protect it from cannibalization.

25. PricewaterhouseCoopers, "Energy Transformation the Impact on the Power Sector Business Model," 13th PwC Annual Global Power & Utilities Survey, 2013, https://www.pwc.com/ua/en/industry/energy-and-utilities/assets/pwc-global-survey-new.pdf.

26. TrendResearch, *Kurzstudie Eigentümerstruktur: Erneuerbare Energien* (Bremen: Institut für Trend- und Marktforschung, 2012), www.trendresearch.de.

27. Christensen, *The Innovator's Dilemma*; Mario Richter, "Business Model Innovation for Sustainable Energy: German Utilities and Renewable Energy," *Energy Policy* 62 (2013): 1226–1237.

28. Richter, "Business Model Innovation for Sustainable Energy."

29. voestalpine, *Annual Report,* 2016/2017. https://www.voestalpine.com/group
/static/sites/group/.downloads/en/publications-2016-17/2016-17-annual-report
.pdf.

30. John E. Lichtenstein and Richard Oppelt, "Five Inconvenient Truths for the
Global Steel Industry," *Natural Resources Blog,* Accenture, July 31, 2017, https://
www.accenture.com/us-en/blogs/blogs-five-global-steel-industry.

31. Lichtenstein and Oppelt, "Five Inconvenient Truths for the Global Steel
Industry."

32. Interview with Christian Presslmayer, voestalpine, May 7, 2018.

33. Johanna Ruzicka, "Voest Bleibt Größter Heimischer Co2-Emittent," *Der Standard,* 2015.

34. voestalpine, "H2Future on Track: Baustart der Weltgrößten Wasserstoffpilotan-
lage," press release, April 16, 2018, https://www.voestalpine.com/group/de/media
/presseaussendungen/2018-04-16-H2FUTURE-on-track-baustart-der-weltgroessten
-wasserstoffpilotanlage.

35. Industry Europe, "Voestalpine Gets the Green Light to Build the World's Largest
Industrial Hydrogen Pilot Plant in Linz," January 23, 2018, https://industryeurope
.com/voestalpine-and-its-partners-get-the-green-light-to-build-th.

36. Martin L Weitzman, "Recombinant Growth," *Quarterly Journal of Economics*
113, no. 2 (1998): 331–360, 331.

37. Weitzman, "Recombinant Growth," 356, 357.

38. Peter Burrows, "The Future Is Ear: Why 'Hearables' Are Finally Tech's Next
Big Thing," *Fast Company,* August 2, 2018, https://www.fastcompany.com
/90212065/the-future-is-ear-why-hearables-are-finally-techs-next-big-thing.

39. Interview with Benedikt Heuer, WS Audiology, February 18, 2020.

40. Interview with Heuer, February 18, 2020.

Chapter 8

1. Amy Keller, "Truck Accidents," *ConsumerNotice.org,* July 28, 2020, https://
www.consumernotice.org/personal-injury/traffic-safety/trucks.

2. "BPW: Make Load Securing Intelligent," *Bausicherheit* magazine, October 17,
2018, https://www.bausicherheit-online.de/d/bpw-die-ladungssicherung-intelli
gent-machen.

3. "BPW iGurt / Intelligent Cargo Securing," *iF World Design Guide*, 2019, https://ifworlddesignguide.com/entry/259574-bpw-igurt.

4. "iGurt," *German Innovation Award, Germany Design Council*, 2019, https://www.german-innovation-award.de/en/winners/preis/gewinner/igurt.

5. Staff writer, "BPW receives German Innovation Awards," *Global trailer*, May 30, 2019, http://www.globaltrailermag.com/news/article/bpw-receives-german -innovation-awards.

6. Nicolai Foss and Tina Saebi, "Fifteen Years of Research on Business Model Innovation: How Far Have We Come, and Where Should We Go?," *Journal of Management*. 43, no 1 (2017) 200–227, at 202

7. Kurt Matzler, Franz Bailom, Stephan Friedrich von den Eichen, and Thomas Kohler, "Business Model Innovation: Coffee Triumphs for Nespresso," *Journal of Business Strategy* 34, no. 2 (2013); Clayton M. Christensen, Thomas Bartman, and Derek Van Bever, "The Hard Truth about Business Model Innovation," *MIT Sloan Management Review* 58, no. 1 (2016): 31–40.

8. Zhenya Lindgardt, Martin Reeves, George Stalk, and Michael S. Deimler, "Business Model Innovation: When the Game Gets Tough, Change the Game," The Boston Consulting Group, December 2009, https://image-src.bcg.com/Images /BCG_Business_Model_Innovation_Dec_09_tcm81-121706.pdf.

9. Interview with Markus Kliffken, BPW Group, April 8, 2020.

10. Interview with Kliffken, April 8, 2020.

11. Mark W. Johnson, "Overcoming Incumbent Challenges to Business Model Innovation," *Leader to Leader* 91 (2019): 7–12.

12. Matzler et al., "Business Model Innovation."

13. See Zaw Thiha Tun, "How Skype Makes Money," company profile, Investopedia, update of June 10, 2020, https://www.investopedia.com/articles/investing /070915/how-skype-makes-money.asp; and Tom Warren, "Microsoft's Skype Struggles Have Created a Zoom Moment," *The Verge*, Microsoft, March 31, 2020, https://www.theverge.com/2020/3/31/21200844/microsoft-skype-zoom-houseparty -coronavirus-pandemic-usage-growth-competition.

14. "Rote Zahlen bei Air Berlin," *Handelsblatt*, March 17, 2011, https://www .handelsblatt.com/unternehmen/handel-konsumgueter/fluggesellschaft-rote -zahlen-bei-air-berlin/3962784.html?ticket=ST-1301463-Peig665PrpfD6CVlQYDk -ap2.

15. Jeffrey A. Krames, *Inside Drucker's Brain* (New York: Penguin, 2008), 101.

16. Bill Schweber, "Wildfire Ignites, Then Extinguishes," EDN, November 10, 2005, https://www.edn.com/wildfire-ignites-then-extinguishes.

17. Christensen, Bartman, and Van Bever, "The Hard Truth about Business Model Innovation."

18. Christensen, Bartman, and Van Bever, "The Hard Truth about Business Model Innovation."

19. Christensen, Bartman, and Van Bever, "The Hard Truth about Business Model Innovation."

20. Christensen, Bartman, and Van Bever, "The Hard Truth about Business Model Innovation."

21. Johnson, "Overcoming Incumbent Challenges to Business Model Innovation."

22. Christensen, Bartman, and Van Bever, "The Hard Truth about Business Model Innovation."

23. Oliver Gassmann, Karolin Frankenberger, and Michaela Csik, *The Business Model Navigator: 55 Models That Will Revolutionise Your Business* (Pearson UK, 2014).

24. Giovanni Gavetti and Jan W. J. Rivkin, "How Strategists Really Think," *Harvard Business Review* 83, no. 4 (2005): 54–63.

25. Gassmann, Frankenberger, and Csik, *The Business Model Navigator;* Ellen Enkel and Florian Mezger, "Imitation Processes and Their Application for Business Model Innovation: An Explorative Study," *International Journal of Innovation Management* 17, no. 1 (2013): art. 1340005.

26. Giovanni Gavetti, Daniel A. Levinthal, and Jan W. Rivkin, "Strategy Making in Novel and Complex Worlds: The Power of Analogy," *Strategic Management Journal* 26, no. 8 (2005): 691–712.

27. Gavetti and Rivkin, "How Strategists Really Think."

28. Gavetti and Rivkin, "How Strategists Really Think."

29. Steven Johnson, *Where Good Ideas Come From: The Natural History of Innovation* (Penguin, 2011).

30. Stuart A. Kauffman, *Investigations* (New York: Oxford University Press, 2000).

31. Stephen Jay Gould and Elisabeth S. Vrba, "Exaptation—a Missing Term in the Science of Form," *Paleobiology* 8, no. 1 (1982): 4–15.

32. Kauffman, *Investigations*.

33. Scott J. Warren and Greg Jones, "Yokoi's Theory of Lateral Innovation: Applications for Learning Game Design," *Journal of Educational Technology* 5, no. 2 (2008): 32–43.

34. Charles Baden-Fuller and Stefan Haefliger, "Business Models and Technological Innovation," *Long Range Planning* 46, no. 6 (2013): 419–426.

35. Matzler et al., "Business Model Innovation."

36. Matzler et al., "Business Model Innovation."

37. Emil Warburg, "Magnetische Untersuchungen," *Annalen der Physik* 249, no. 5 (1881): 141–64.

38. Pierre Weiss and Auguste Piccard, "Le Phénomène Magnétocalorique," *Journal of Physics*, no. 7 (1917): 103–109.

39. Ekkes Brück, "Developments in Magnetocaloric Refrigeration," *Journal of Physics D: Applied Physics* 38, no. 23 (2005): R381.

40. Mellsoft press release, 2013.

41. Mellsoft press release, 2009.

42. Mellsoft press release, 2015.

43. For more on the concept of "the job to be done," see Clayton M. Christensen, Taddy Hall, Karen Dillon and David S. Duncan, "Know Your customers' Jobs to be Done," *Harvard Business Review* 94, no 9 (2016): 54–62.

44. Isin Guler, "Pulling the Plug: The Capability to Terminate Unsuccessful Projects and Firm Performance," *Strategy Science* 3, no. 3 (2018): 481–97.

45. Stephanie Pandolph, "adidas Uses Speedfactory to Localize Shoe Designs," *Business Insider,* October 9, 2017, https://www.businessinsider.com/adidas-uses -speedfactory-to-localize-shoe-designs-2017-10?r=DE&IR=T.

46. Read more at the following press releases of adidas, "adidas Deploys Speedfactory Technology at Asian Suppliers by End of 2019," adidas news archive, November 11, 2019, https://www.adidas-group.com/en/media/news-archive/press -releases/2019/adidas-deploys-speedfactory-technology-at-asian-suppliers-by-end -2019.

47. "Adidas Unlocks a Circular Future for Sports with Futurecraft Loop," adidas news archive, April 17, 2019, https://www.adidas-group.com/de/medien

/newsarchiv/pressemitteilungen/2019/adidas-schliesst-den-produktlebenszyklus
-mit-futurecraftloop.

48. Mark Wilson, "Exclusive: adidas's Radical New Shoe could Change How the
World Buys Sneakers," *Fastcompany,* April 17, 2019, https://www.fastcompany
.com/90335038/exclusive-adidass-radical-new-shoe-could-change-how-the
-world-buys-sneakers.

49. Elizabeth Sergan, "Inside adidas's Ambitious Plan to End Plastic Waste by
2030," *Fastcompany,* January 28, 2020, https://www.fastcompany.com/90456454
/inside-adidas-ambitious-plan-to-end-plastic-waste-in-a-decade.

50. "Coming Full Circle: adidas Futurecraft.Loop Gen 2," *Sneakers Magazine,*
November 14, 2019, https://sneakers-magazine.com/adidas-futurecraft-loop-gen-2.

Chapter 9

1. Francis Galton, "Vox Populi," *Nature* 75 (1907): 450–51.

2. James Surowiecki, *The Wisdom of Crowds: Why the Many Are Smarter Than the
Few and How Collective Wisdom Shapes Business, Economics, Society and Nations*
(New York: Doubleday, 2004).

3. CrowdWorx has supported Zeppelin Rental and has provided the software
platform for its prediction market. Quoted in *CrowdWorx,* press release, "Neue
Fallstudie Beweist: Mitarbeitermotivation 2.0 auf dem Vormarsch," February 12,
2013.   https://www.pressebox.de/inaktiv/crowdworx/Neue-Fallstudie-beweist
-Mitarbeitermotivation-2-0-auf-dem-Vormarsch/boxid/573611.

4. Surowiecki, *The Wisdom of Crowds.*

5. McKinsey, "How Companies are Benefiting from Web 2.0," Global Survey
Results, September 1, 2009, https://www.mckinsey.com/business-functions/mckin
sey-digital/our-insights/how-companies-are-benefiting-from-web-20-mckinsey
-global-survey-results#:~:text=Their%20responses%20suggest%20why%20
Web,doing%20business%2C%20and%20higher%20revenues; Jacques Bughin,
"Taking the Measure of the Networked Enterprise," *McKinsey Quarterly* 51, no. 10
(2015): 1–4.

6. Donald N. Thompson, *Oracles: How Prediction Markets Turn Employees into
Visionaries* (Brighton, MA: Harvard Business Review Press, 2012).

7. Clayton Christensen, *The Innovator's Dilemma: When New Technologies Cause
Great Firms to Fail* (Brighton, MA: Harvard Business Review Press, 1997).

8. Quoted in Joe Nocera, "The Future Divined by the Crowd," *New York Times*, March 11, 2006, https://www.nytimes.com/2006/03/11/business/the-future-divi ned-by-the-crowd.html.

9. Jack L. Treynor, "Market Efficiency and the Bean Jar Experiment," *Financial Analysts Journal* 43, no. 3 (1987): 50–53.

10. Michael Nofer and Oliver Hinz, "Are Crowds on the Internet Wiser Than Experts? The Case of a Stock Prediction Community," *Journal of Business Economics* 84, no. 3 (2014): 303–338.

11. Nofer and Hinz, "Are Crowds on the Internet Wiser Than Experts?," 303.

12. Thompson, *Oracles*.

13. Friedrich August Hayek, "The Use of Knowledge in Society," *American Economic Review* 35, no. 4 (1945): 519–530.

14. Eugene F. Fama, "Efficient Capital Markets: A Review of Theory and Empirical Work," *Journal of Finance* 25, no. 2 (1970): 383–417.

15. Joyce E. Berg, Forrest D. Nelson, and Thomas A. Rietz, "Prediction Market Accuracy in the Long Run," *International Journal of Forecasting* 24, no. 2 (2008): 285–300.

16. Justin Wolfers and Eric Zitzewitz, "Prediction Markets," *Journal of Economic Perspectives* 18, no. 2 (2004): 107–26; Philip M. Polgreen et al., "Use of Prediction Markets to Forecast Infectious Disease Activity," *Clinical Infectious Diseases* 44, no. 2 (2007): 272–279.

17. Patrick Buckley, "Harnessing the Wisdom of Crowds: Decision Spaces for Prediction Markets," *Business Horizons* 59, no. 1 (2016): 85–94.

18. Bo Cowgill and Eric Zitzewitz, "Corporate Prediction Markets: Evidence from Google, Ford, and Firm X," *Review of Economic Studies* 82, no. 4 (2015): 1309–41; Thompson, *Oracles*.

19. Kurt Matzler, Christopher Grabher, Jürgen Huber, and Johann Füller, "Predicting New Product Success with Prediction Markets in Online Communities," *R&D Management* 43, no. 5 (2013): 420–432.

20. Matzler et al., "Predicting New Product Success with Prediction Markets in Online Communities."

21. Buckley, "Harnessing the Wisdom of Crowds."

22. Thompson, *Oracles*.

23. Quoted in Jon Brodkin, "Google Bets on Value of Prediction Markets," *Network World,* March 5, 2008, https://www.networkworld.com/article/2284098/google-bets-on-value-of-prediction-markets.html.

24. Buckley, "Harnessing the Wisdom of Crowds."

25. Ho Teck-Hua and Chen Kay-Yut, "New Product Blockbusters: The Magic and Science of Prediction Markets," *California Management Review* 50, no. 1 (2007): 144–158.

26. Christian Franz Horn and Björn Sven Ivens, "Corporate Prediction Markets for Innovation Management," in *Adoption of Innovation* (Springer, 2015), 11–23.

27. Ho and Chen, "New Product Blockbusters."

28. Matzler et al., "Predicting New Product Success with Prediction Markets in Online Communities."

29. Martin Spann and Bernd Skiera, "Internet-Based Virtual Stock Markets for Business Forecasting," *Management Science* 49, no. 10 (2003): 1310–1326.

30. Daniel E. O'Leary, "User Participation in a Corporate Prediction Market," *Decision Support Systems* 78 (2015): 28–38.

31. Thompson, *Oracles*.

32. When involving external participants, you might need more tangible incentives. The rewards should be sufficiently high that participants feel encouraged to search and reveal knowledge, but not so high that you trigger maladaptive behavior such as manipulation. Caitlin Hall, "Prediction Markets: Issues and Applications," *Journal of Prediction Markets* 4, no. 1 (2010).

33. Li Chen, Paulo Goes, James R. Marsden, and Zhongju Zhang, "Design and Use of Preference Markets for Evaluation of Early Stage Technologies," *Journal of Management Information Systems* 26, no. 3 (Winter 2009/2010): 45–70.

34. Arina Soukhoroukova, Martin Spann, and Bernd Skiera, "Sourcing, Filtering, and Evaluating New Product Ideas: An Empirical Exploration of the Performance of Idea Markets," *Journal of Product Innovation Management* 29, no. 1 (2012): 100–12.

35. Soukhoroukova, Spann, and Skiera, "Sourcing, Filtering, and Evaluating New Product Ideas."

36. Soukhoroukova, Spann, and Skiera, "Sourcing, Filtering, and Evaluating New Product Ideas."

37. Soukhoroukova, Spann, and Skiera, "Sourcing, Filtering, and Evaluating New Product Ideas."

38. Chen et al., "Design and Use of Preference Markets for Evaluation of Early Stage Technologies."

39. Mark Lang, Neeraj Bharadwaj, and C. Anthony Di Benedetto, "How Crowd-sourcing Improves Prediction of Market-Oriented Outcomes," *Journal of Business Research* 69, no. 10 (2016): 4168–4176.

40. Lang, Bharadwaj, and Di Benedetto, "How Crowdsourcing Improves Prediction of Market-Oriented Outcomes."

41. Lang, Bharadwaj, and Di Benedetto, "How Crowdsourcing Improves Prediction of Market-Oriented Outcomes," 4174.

42. Ulrich Meyer-Berhorn, Deutsche Telekom, email, April 4, 2020.

43. Philip E. Tetlock, Barbara A. Mellers, and J. Peter Scoblic, "Bringing Probability Judgments into Policy Debates via Forecasting Tournaments," *Science* 355, no. 6324 (2017): 481–483.

44. See the website at https://www.gjopen.com.

45. Buckley, "Harnessing the Wisdom of Crowds."

46. John C. Camillus, "Strategy as a Wicked Problem," *Harvard Business Review* 86, no. 5 (2008): 98.

47. Surowiecki, *The Wisdom of Crowds.*

Chapter 10

1. We picked up this story from BBC Radio Four, "Check Out Costing the Earth: Heroines of the Rainforest," March 14, 2017, https://www.bbc.co.uk/programmes /b08hnly0.

2. See the company's website at https://healthinharmony.org.

3. Kinari Webb, "Saving Lives by Saving Trees," TEDxRainier, YouTube video, February 19, 2016, https://www.youtube.com/watch?v=tJkeZ_4wuYg.

4. See the company's website at https://healthinharmony.org.

5. Webb, "Saving Lives by Saving Trees."

6. Yao-Hua Law, "How a Pioneering Clinic in Indonesia Is Saving Lives—and the Rainforest," *Independent,* November 29, 2017, https://www.independent.co.uk /news/long_reads/rainforest-healthcare-asri-indonesia-conservation-a8060681 .html.

7. BBC Radio Four, "Check Out Costing the Earth."

8. Jon L. Pierce, Tatiana Kostova, and Kurt T. Dirks, "Toward a Theory of Psychological Ownership in Organizations," *Academy of Management Review* 26, no. 2 (2001): 298–310; Jon L. Pierce, Michael P. O'Driscoll, and Anne Marie Coghlan, "Work Environment Structure and Psychological Ownership: The Mediating Effects of Control," *Journal of Social Psychology* 144, no. 5 (2004): 507–534; Linn-Van Dyne and Jon L. Pierce, "Psychological Ownership and Feelings of Possession: Three Field Studies Predicting Employee Attitudes and Organizational Citizenship Behavior," *Journal of Organizational Behavior* 25, no. 4 (2004): 439–459.

9. Michael P. O'Driscoll Jon L. Pierce, and Ann-Marie Coghlan, "The Psychology of Ownership: Work Environment Structure, Organizational Commitment, and Citizenship Behaviors," *Group & Organization Management* 31, no. 3, (2006): 388–416.

10. Donald Sull, Stephano Turconi, Charles Sull, and James Yoder, et al., "Turning Strategy into Results," *MIT Sloan Management Review,* September 28, 2017, https:// sloanreview.mit.edu/article/turning-strategy-into-results; HBR Staff, "When CEOs Talk Strategy, Is Anyone Listening?," *Harvard Business Review,* June 2013, https:// hbr.org/2013/06/when-ceos-talk-strategy-is-anyone-listening.

11. The views expressed by Michael Ryan are his own and do not necessarily reflect the position of the US Department of Defense.

12. Interview with Michael Ryan, NATO, June 10, 2020.

13. Interview with Ryan, June 10, 2020.

14. Liam Cleaver worked closely on this with Kristine Lawas, Jim Newswanger, and Kevin Vaughan in the IBM InnovationJam Program Office.

15. Interview with Cleaver, IBM.

16. Interview with Thomas Cook, Steelecase, June 5, 2020.

17. Interview with Cook, June 5, 2020.

18. Interview with Christian Wiese, Steelecase, June 5, 2020.

19. Interview with Cook, June 5, 2020.

20. Interview with Cook, June 5, 2020.

21. Brightline Project Management Institute, "Organizational Transformation: How Steelcase Developed a Strategy for Growth in a Changing Workplace," Case Study, May 14, 2019, https://www.brightline.org/resources/how-steelcase -developed-a-strategy-for-growth-in-a-changing-workplace.

22. Steelcase, *Annual Report 2020*, http://ir.steelcase.com/static-files/8276e01c -79b2-4b07-9261-ecdd8629703c.

23. Brightline Project Management Institute, "Organizational Transformation: How Steelcase Developed a Strategy for Growth in a Changing Workplace."

24. Tsedal B. Neeley and Paul Leonardi, "Enacting Knowledge Strategy through Social Media: Passable Trust and the Paradox of Non-Work Interactions," *Strategic Management Journal* 39, no. 3 (2018): 922–946.

25. Interview with Luz Rodrigo Martorell, Telefónica, December 20, 2017.

26. Read story also in Adam Zawel, "Strategy and the Social Enterprise," *Palladium*, 2016, https://silo.tips/download/strategy-and-the-social-enterprise.

27. Quoted in Microsoft, "Telefonica Empowers Employees, Achieves Digital Transformation with Social Communities" *Office 365*, https://customers .microsoft.com/en-us/story/telefnica-empowers-employees-achieves-digital -transformation-with-social-communities available at https://de.scribd.com /document/369798847/Telefonica-Case-Study.

28. Telefonica, "Letter from José María Álvarez-Pallete," November 27, 2019 https://www.telefonica.com/ext/the-new-telefonica.

29. Interview with Rodrigo Martorell, December 20, 2017.

30. Jim Whitehurst, *The Open Organization: Igniting Passion and Performance* (Brighton, MA: Harvard Business Review Press, 2015).

31. Jackie Yeaney, "Democratizing the Corporate Strategy Process at Red Hat," Management Innovation Exchange, November 10, 2011, https://www .managementexchange.com/story/democratizing-corporate-strategy-process-red -hat.

32. Arne Gast and Michele Zanini, "The Social Side of Strategy," *McKinsey Quarterly* May (2012): 1–15.

33. Yeaney, "Democratizing the Corporate Strategy Process at Red Hat."

34. For such dilemmas arising with open strategy, see, for example, Julia Hautz, David Seidl, and Richard Whittington, "Open Strategy: Dimensions, Dilemmas, Dynamics," *Long Range Planning* 50, no. 3 (2017): 298–309; Daniel Stieger, Kurt Matzler, Sayan Chatterjee, and Florian Ladstätter-Fussenegger, "Democratizing Strategy: How Crowdsourcing Can Be Used for Strategy Dialogues," *California Management Review* 54, no. 4 (Summer 2012): 44–68; or Arvind Malhotra, Ann Majchrzak, and Rebecca M. Niemiec, "Using Public Crowds for Open Strategy Formulation: Mitigating the Risks of Knowledge Gaps," *Long Range Planning* 50, no. 3 (2017): 397–410.

35. Described in João Baptista, Alex Wilson, Robert D. Galliers, and Steve Bynghall, "Social Media and the Emergence of Reflexiveness as a New Capability for Open Strategy," *Long Range Planning* 50, no. 3 (2017): 328.

36. Neeley and Leonardi, "Enacting Knowledge Strategy through Social Media."

37. Interview with Rodrigo Martorell, Telefónica, December 20, 2017.

Epilogue

1. Thomas Wolfram, "Have Corporate Prediction Markets Had Their Heyday?," *Foresight: The International Journal of Applied Forecasting*, no. 37 (2015): 29–36.

2. Interview with Ernesto Maurer, SSM, August 8, 2017.

Index

Abbiss, Jim, 28
Adele, 28
Adidas, 158–159
Aequorea victoria, 7
Afheldt, Christoph, 164
Afri-Cola, 43
Ahn, Kwangwon, 38
AirBerlin, 148–149
Alam Sehat Lestari (ASRI), 185–187
Alexa, 149
Allen, James, 37
Alstom, 1
Álvarez-Pallete, José María, 199, 202
Amazon, 30, 139, 149
America's Got Talent, 28
Analogical reasoning, 151–152
Anchoring bias, 13–15, 105
Antioco, John, 18
Apple, 10, 29, 64, 139, 149
Archibald, Nick, 83
Artificial intelligence (AI), 101–102
Art of War, The, 61
Atkinson, Neil, 50
Audiologists, 140–141
Authority bias, 105
Aviation strategies, 66
Axel Springer, 121

Bach, Sebastian, 24
Bachstein, Klaus, 47
Balanced scorecard, 214
Ballmer, Steve, 10, 30, 102
Barclays UK, 56, 190, 194, 205
Barth, John, 25–26
Bartman, Thomas, 150
Beam, Michael A., 126
Berlin, Isaiah, 106–107
Berlin-Brandenburg Willy Brandt airport, 103
Bernoulli, Jacob, 167
Bias
  anchoring, 13–15, 105
  authority, 105
  biased strategies, 12–15
  confirmation, 14–15, 105
  in-group, 51
Bison migration photography, 59–60, 73
Blackberry, 149
Bligh, William, 76
Blockbuster, 18
Borneo, 185
Boston Consulting Group, 214
Bostrom, Nick, 102
BP, 10–11
BPW Group, 145–146

Brehm, Paul, 7
Bridgewater Associates, 63–64
Buffett, Warren, 2
Bureaucrats, 103
Business Logic Contest. *See* IMP
   Business Logic Contest
Business models, 145–161. *See also*
   IMP Business Logic Contest
  and analogies, 151–152
  defined, 147
  discarding, 155, 157
  and disruption, 123–124, 128
  and implementation, 153, 160–161
  and innovation, 147, 150
  new contexts, 139
  and nightmare competitors, 124,
   134–135
  problems with, 148–152
  recombining, 151–152
  and revenue, 148–149
  successful, 150, 152
  and trend forecasting, 107–108
Business-unit scope of analysis, 107

Cable TV, 6
Call auction markets, 173
Cameras, 14, 18, 124–125
Candle experiment, 82
Candy companies, 61
Captain Philips, 66
Career paths, 27
Carl Zeiss, 57
Cash machines, 135
Channel Tunnel, 103
Chatter, 50
Chelfie, Martin, 7–8, 19
China, 189–190
Christensen, Clayton, 18, 125, 129,
   150, 166, 206

Chronometers, 76
Cisco Systems, 77, 82–85
Cleaver, Liam, 190–191
Clinical trials, 63
Clocks, shipboard, 76
Codesign, 196
Coenen, Ralf, 125
Cognitive diversity, 50–51
Cohn, Hanns-Peter, 124
Colbert, Stephen, 126
Collaboration, 28–29, 38, 84
Combining competencies, 10
Combining ideas, 138–139
Comdex trade show of 1999, 9
Commercial vehicle industry,
   145–146
Communication, 52
  benefits of, 63
  and social networks, 197
Communitition, 93
Competition. *See also* IMP Nightmare
   Competitor Challenge
  competitive strategies, 7, 61, 69–70
  and crowdsourcing, 84, 92–93
Compressor technology, 156
Confidentiality agreements, 61–62
Confirmation bias, 14–15, 105
Contests, online, 59–60, 70, 77–86
Cook, Captain James, 76
Cook, Thomas, 194–197
Cooling, magnetocaloric, 155–157
Corporate myopia, 122
Corporations. *See also* Organizations
  corporate culture, 37–38
  and crowdsourcing, 166–167
  and disruptive change, 125
  efficiency, 23
  and secrecy, 61–62
  and stakeholders, 62–63

COVID-19 pandemic, 189
Cowgill, Bo, 170
Crimea crowdsourcing project, 60, 73
Cross, Rob, 38
Cross-fertilization, 152
Crowd, intelligence of, 163–164, 167
Crowdsourcing, 11–12, 53, 75–95.
    See also Predictions
  accuracy of, 167–168, 179
  active moderation, 91–92
  collaboration and competition,
    70–71, 84, 92–93
  communitition, 93
  contests, 59–60, 70, 77–86
  crowd-based predictions, 164–168,
    179–181
  evaluating ideas, 85–86, 91
  feasibility, 91
  and industry experts, 78–79
  participant selection, 85, 182
  prizes, 82–83
  resistance to, 166–167
  and secrecy, 59–60
  stock predictions, 167–168
  and strategic ideas, 79
  strategy communities, 86–94
  and strategy generation, 78
  tournaments, 179–181
Crowdworx, 164
Culture, corporate, 37–38

Daimler, 15–17
Dalio, Ray, 63
Danvers, Rosie, 28
Darrah, Mark, 67
Davis, Jeff, 70
Davis, Miles, 24
Day, George, 104–106
Debates, social, 37

Decision-making, 57, 171–172,
    194–197, 209
Deepwater Horizon oil spill, 10–11
Design, open strategy, 43–57
  degree of openness, 43–45
  digital/analog format, 48–49, 53–55
  elements of, 43
  external participants, 45–47, 53,
    55–56
  goals, 51–52
  number of participants, 47–48
  participant selection, 49–51
  phases of, 52–55
Deutsche Telekom, 179–180
"Dialogue Days," 92
Digital photography, 14, 18,
    124–125
Digital platforms, 2, 46–47
  criteria, 90–91
  financial success of, 148
  using, 202–203
Digital technologies, 100, 138–142,
    147
Dirks, Kurt T., 16
Disruption, 29–30, 88, 121–143
  and business models, 123–124, 128
  and cognitive limitations, 124–128
  and implementation, 18
  innovative, 125, 166
  market forecasts, 166
  and motivation, 128–130
  opportunities of, 129–130
  recombinant, 138–142
  as threat, 129–130
  and traditional strategic planning,
    18–19, 125–126, 206
  and war games, 123, 127–128
Distributional information, 104
Diverse ideas, 26–28

Diversity
  cognitive, 50–51
  educational/socioeconomic, 45–46
  ethnic/racial, 27–28, 38
  gender, 27–28, 38
Double-auction markets, 173
Dragonbear effect, 189
Drucker, Peter, 37, 149, 188
Dweck, Carol, 31

eBay, 173
Eder, Wolfgang, 138
Edison, Thomas Alva, 102
Efficiency, corporate, 23
Einstein, Albert, 37
Election polls, 168–169
Electronic computing, 4
Employee networks, 31
Employee ranking, 29
Employees
  employee buy-in, 16–17
  empowerment of, 87–88
  engagement, 31, 43
  front-line, 36–37, 55–56, 187
  idea markets, 176–177
  and implementation, 20, 187
  leadership feedback, 201–202
  motivating, 128–130
  and predictions, 164–166
Ericsson, 46, 88–90
Etherton, Sarah, 50
EU security, 188–190
Exaptation, 152
Execution. *See* Implementation
Executives, 4, 12
  and front-line employees, 187
  goals, 52
  as strategy-makers, 22–23
Experience curve, 214

Experts
  and crowdsourcing, 78–79
  forecasting success, 108–109, 166
  interviewing, 108–109
  kinds of, 107–108
  predictions, 103
External participants, 45–47, 53,
    55–56, 130, 208

Fama, Eugene, 168
First Ion Track, 1
Fletcher, Christian, 76
Flyvbjerg, Bent, 103–105
Fogland Industries, 113–118
Forecasting trends, 104–109,
    164–165, 180–181. *See also*
    IMP Trend Radar; Predictions
Forsythe, Robert, 168
Founder's Mentality, The, 37
Fractal Graphics, 83
Framing a problem, 80–82
Franklin, Benjamin, 38–39
Freight damage, 145
Freud, Sigmund, 37
Front-line employees, 36–37, 55–56,
    187
Futurecraft Loop, 159

Gallus, 44, 46–47, 98–100
Galton, Sir Francis, 163–164, 167
Gardner, Dan, 108
Gates, Bill, 10, 39
GE Capital, 1–2
GE Homeland Security, 1
Gender diversity, 27–28, 38
General Electric (GE), 1–2, 29, 214
GE Power, 1
Gilbert, Clark G., 129
Glaxo-Smith-Kline, 63

Gödel, Kurt, 37
Goldcorp Inc., 82
Gompers, Paul, 38
Goobles, 173
Good Judgment Inc, 180–181
Good Judgment Project, 108, 180
Goodman, Amy, 126
Google, 26, 139, 149–150, 173–174
Google+, 149
Goyenechea, Aitor, 199
Green fluorescent protein (GFP), 7–8
Groupthink, 15, 19, 105
Growth mindset, 30–32
Gunpei, Yokoi, 152

H4 clock, 76
Hamel, Gary, 12, 79
Hanks, Tom, 66
Harrison, John, 76
Hayek, Friedrich, 168
Healthcare access, 185–187
Hearables, 139–141
Hearing aids, 135, 139–141
Heidelberger Druckmaschinen, 44
Heuer, Benedikt, 141–142
Hewlett-Packard (HP), 44, 98
Hinz, Oliver, 167–168
Hofstetter, Reto, 91
Hrebiniak, Lawrence G., 3
Huawei, 190
Hydrogen electrolysis, 137–138

IBM, 44–45, 56, 188–191, 193–194
Icahn, Carl, 18
Idea generation, 3, 52
  combinations of ideas, 138–139
  diversity, 26–28
  evaluating ideas, 85–86, 91
  and secrecy, 68–69, 73

Idei, Nobuyuki, 9
i.Gurt, 145–147
Illegal logging, 185–187
Immelt, Jeff, 1–2
IMP, development of, 213–214
IMP Business Logic Contest, 148,
    151–159
  analogical reasoning, 151–152
  crowdsourcing tool, 181
  guidelines, 160
  structure of, 153–155
  unexpected outcomes, 159
Implementation. *See also* Strategy
    jams
  and business models, 153, 160–161
  and disruption, 18
  and employee involvement, 20, 187
  failure, 187
  and secrecy, 69–70, 73–74
  and social networks, 197–203
  and strategic planning, 3, 52–56,
    69–70, 152–153, 182–183
  successful, 3–4
IMP Network of Excellence, 213
IMP Nightmare Competitor
    Challenge, 46, 123–124, 130–138
  business models, 124, 134–135
  combining ideas, 139
  nightmare scenarios, 134
  participant selection, 132–133
  scope of task, 133–134
  trend analysis, 133–134
Improvisation, 24
IMP Trend Radar, 98–101, 106–118,
    139
  evaluating hypotheses, 110–111
  expert interviews, 108–109
  Fogland case study, 113–118
  formulating hypotheses, 109–110

IMP Trend Radar (cont.)
preparedness, 111
scope of analysis, 107–108
team members, 106–107
visualizations, 111–113
Information flows, 121
Information processing, 126
Innocentive, 70–71, 78
Innovation, 11, 26, 125–126
business models, 147, 150
digital, 138–142
disruptive, 125, 166
and market readiness, 149
open, 213
and prediction markets,
169–170
and preexisting beliefs, 126–127
recombinant, 138–139
Innovator's Dilemma, The, 125, 166
Inside Bill's Brain, 39
Intellectual property, 71, 84
Intelligence Advance Research
Projects Activity (IARPA), 108, 180
Intelligence Community (IC), US,
60, 73
International Space Station, 11
Internet forums, 86
Interviews, expert, 108–109
Investors, 38
InVision, 1
Iowa Electronic Market, 169
iPhone, 3, 102, 149
I-Prize, 77–78, 82–84
Isomorphous strategies, 5–7, 19

Jellybean-guessing, 167
Jellyfish, 7–8
Jeppesen, Lars Bo, 11, 78
Jouret, Guido, 77–78, 85–86

Kaggle, 78
Kahneman, Daniel, 128
Kaplan, David P., 214
Kauffman, Stuart, 152
Kaufmann, Andreas, 127
KEBA, 135
Keese, Christoph, 62, 121
Keyes, James W., 18
Klein, Gary, 8
Klein, Viola, 41–42
Kleinbaum, Adam, 27
Kliffken, Markus, 147
Klöckner, 121–122, 128
kloeckner.i, 122
Kluge, Christian, 17
Kodak, 18
Kostova, Tatiana, 16
Kovvali, Silpa, 38
Krones AG, 36
Kronseder, Hermann, 36

Lakhani, Karim, 11, 78–79
LaMarre, Heather L., 126
Landreville, Kristen D., 126
Lang, Mark, 179
Laola1.at, 172
Lateral thinking, 152
Law of large numbers, 167
Lazarus, Charlie, 151
Leadership
buy-in, 22–23
feedback from, 201–202
mindset, 30–32, 205
style, 24–25
Lego Technic, 22
Leica Camera AG, 124–127
Lindemann, Christian, 3
Linus's law of software development,
106

Löffler, Sylvie, 41, 56–57
Longitude, 76
Longitude Act of 1714, 75
Longitude problem, 75
Loss aversion, 14–15, 105, 128–129
Loungani, Prakash, 102

Machine learning, 102
Madonna, 28
Magnetocaloric cooling, 155–157
Management, 23, 57
Maps, 97
Marginal problem solvers, 11
Market prices, 38, 167–169
Markets. *See also* Prediction markets
    call auction, 173
    double-auction, 173
    idea, 84, 176–179
    preference, 84, 176–179
Mark & Spencer, 14
Mars, Forrest, Sr., 61
Mars candy company, 61
Mauboussin, Michael J., 167
Maurer, Ernesto, 209–210
McEwen, Rob, 82–83
McGrath, Rita, 104
McKinsey, 214
Mean absolute error (MAE), 170
Mellers, Barbara, 109
Mellsoft Systems, 155–157
Memory-stick Walkman, 9
Menand, Louis, 103
Mergers and acquisitions, 64
Merrill, Charlie, 151
Merrill Lynch, 151
Meyer-Berhorn, Ulrich, 180
Microsoft, 10, 29–32, 148
*Mindset: Changing The Way You Think
    to Fulfil Your Potential,* 31

Minsky, Marvin, 101
Misinformation, 189–190
Misrepresentation, strategic, 104–105
MMOWGLI (Massive Multiplayer
    Online Wargame Leveraging the
    Internet), 65–67
Mönch, Andreas, 41–42
Moore, Dale, 66–67
Moore, Geoffrey, 85
Mumsnet.com, 86, 90
Munich Re, 17
Musk, Elon, 39

Nadella, Satya, 30–32
NASA, 11–12, 63, 70–71
NASA@WORK, 70–71
NATO security, 188–190
Naval Air Warfare Center Aircraft
    Division (NAWCAD), 66–67
Navigation, 75–76
Navy, US, 65–68
NCR, 4
Nelson, Forrest, 168
Nestle, 61
Netflix, 6, 30
Neumann, George, 168
Newspapers, 129
Newton, Sir Isaac, 76
Nietzsche, Friedrich, 181
Nightmare Competitor Challenge,
    IMP. *See* IMP Nightmare
    Competitor Challenge
Nintendo, 152
Nofer, Michael, 167–168
Nokia, 3, 10
Nokia 9000 Communicator, 3
Norton, Robert S., 214
Nudge, 5
Nuovo, Frank, 3

Oil industry, 10–11
Online advertising, 12
Online communities, 53, 86–94
Online contests, 59–60, 70, 77–86
Online forums, 193
Open calls, 53
Open-mindedness, 24–25
Open strategy. *See also* Design, open
    strategy; Strategic ideas; Strategic
    planning
  and execution, 20
  as fair weather approach, 208
  history of, 213–214
  as management philosophy, 205
  opposition to, 21–22
Optimism bias, 104
Orange, 149
Organizations. *See also* Corporations
  combining competencies, 10
  new structures within, 206–208
  and outside involvement, 11–12
  resemblances among, 6
  siloes within, 10–11
Outsourcing trend prediction, 118
Overconfidence trap, 14
Ownership, psychological, 16

Page, Scott E., 19
Participant selection
  crowdsourcing, 85, 182
  external, 45–47, 53, 55–56, 130, 208
  Nightmare Competitor Challenge,
    132–133
  prediction markets, 172
Partnerships, 28–29
Pasteur, Louis, 26
PESTEL framework, 133
Pharmaceutical industry, 6
Photography, digital, 14, 18, 124–125

Photokina, 125
Piccard, Auguste, 155
Pierce, Jon L., 16
Pixar, 26
Polaroid, 14, 29–30
Porter, Michael, 7
Portfolio matrix, 214
Post-It notes, 26
Power generation, 129
Precision questioning, 31
Prediction markets, 165–166, 168–175
  accuracy, 168–169
  analyzing results, 174–175
  decision problem, 171–172
  designing, 172–173
  elections, 168–169
  incentive mechanism, 173–174
  Iowa Electronic Market, 169
  liquidity problem, 172
  and opinion surveys, 170
  product innovation, 169–170
  recruiting participants, 172
  trading, 171–174
  uses of, 169, 176
Predictions, 101–109. *See also*
    Crowdsourcing; IMP Trend Radar;
    Prediction markets
  crowd-based, 164–168, 179–181
  expert, 103
  outsourcing, 118
  prediction tournaments, 179–181
  sources of bias, 105
  stock prices, 167–168
  superforecasters, 109, 180–181
Preexisting beliefs, 126–127
Preference markets, 84, 176–179
Presslmayer, Christian, 136–137
Price Is Right, The, 12
PricewaterhouseCoopers (PwC), 129

Principles: Life and Work, 63
Printing technology, 44, 46–47, 98,
   100
Problem solving, marginal, 11
Proprietary information, 63
Proton exchange membrane
   electrolyzer, 138
Psychological ownership, 16, 187
Public infrastructure, 103

Racial and ethnic diversity, 27–28
Radical transparency, 63–64
Rainforests, 185–186
Ranking, employee, 29
Reading, 38–39, 211
Recommended reading, 211
Red Hat, 25, 27, 200
Reinsurance, 17
Renewable energy, 129
Retail strategy, 73–74
Reuter, Edzard, 15–17
Roberts, Justine, 86
Rodrigo Martorell, Luz, 198–200, 202
Rühl, Gispert, 121–122, 128
Russell, Bertrand, 37
Russia, 189–190
Ryan, Michael, 188–189

Sales-Cavalcante, Heraldo, 45–46,
   88–90
Salesforce communication, 4
Saxonia Systems, 41–43, 56–57, 205
Schärer Schweiter Mettle AG (SSM),
   55
Schoemaker, Paul, 104, 106
Secrecy, 59–74
   and competitive advantage, 61,
      69–70
   and crowdsourcing, 59–60

data security, 62
disadvantages of, 62
elements of control, 67–68
and idea generation, 68–69, 73
and implementation, 69–70, 73–74
and intellectual property, 71
necessity of, 64
and online games, 65–68
and proprietary information, 63
protection strategy, 68–74
and stakeholders, 62–63
startups, 64
and strategy formation, 69, 73
and transparency, 63–64
Seeing What Others Don't, 8
Self-assessment tool, 32–35
Semiconductor industry, 41–42
Sensemaking in Organizations, 97
Serendipity, 25–26
Sex shop industry, 3
Shared information bias, 105
Sharewise, 167–168
Shimomura, Osamu, 7
Siemens, 30, 93, 138, 169
Silicon Saxony, 41
*Silicon Valley Challenge: A Wake-up
   Call for Europe, The,* 62
Silicon Valley, 25, 62, 121
Simon, Herbert A., 101
Ski sales, 169–170
Skype, 148
Small business survival, 104
Smartfire, 46–47, 98
Smartphones, 3, 10
Sobel, Dava, 76
Social forecasting tool, 164–165
Social networks, 197–203
Solar particle events, 70
Somali pirates, 65–66

Sony, 9–10
Space Poop Challenge, 70
Speedfactories, 158–159
SSM, 209
Staples, 151
Startups, 64
Status quo trap, 14
Steam locomotives, 102
Steelcase strategy jam, 194–197
Steel industry, 121–122, 135–138
Stemberg, Thomas, 151
Stewart, Ryon, 70–71
Stifter, Linda, 51
Stock prices, 38, 167–169
Strategic business units, 214
Strategic ideas. *See also* Idea
    generation
  and crowdsourcing, 79
  implementing, 3–4
Strategic misrepresentation,
    104–105
Strategic planning. *See also* Strategy
    communities; Strategy jams;
    Traditional strategic planning
  analysis and formulation, 52–55,
    69, 73
  and implementation, 3, 52–53,
    69–70, 152–153, 182–183
  and maps, 97
  success rate, 2, 4
Strategy communities, 86–94
  and accumulated knowledge, 87
  building, 90–94
  digital platforms, 90–91
Strategy jams, 188–197
  analyzing, 194
  decision-making, 194–197
  goals, 191
  as online conference, 191

running, 193
speed of, 190
structure, 192–193
technology, 189
website forums, 193
Strategy Perspective, 46
Strategy presentations, 38
Subprime mortgage crisis, 1–2
Sunk-cost trap, 14
Sunstein, Cass, 5
Sun Tzu, 61
Super-forecasters, 109, 180–181
Superintelligence, 102
Supermarkets, 151
Surowiecki, James, 166
Surveys, opinion, 170
Swiss watch industry, 12
Sydney Opera House, 103

Tableau Software, 27
Target, 30
Taylor Wall & Associates, 83
Team members, selecting, 106–107.
    See also Participant selection
Technology clusters, 41
Telefónica, 198–200, 202
Tesla, Nikola, 102
Tetlock, Philip, 107–108, 180
Thaler, Richard, 5
Thiel, Peter, 62
Thompson, Donald N., 166
Thoreau, Henry David, 163
3M, 26
"Three Princes of Serendip, The," 25
topcoder.com, 59
Tournament lab, NASA, 70
Tournaments, prediction,
    179–181
Toys "R" Us, 151

Traditional strategic planning
  biased strategies, 12–15
  and disruption, 18–19, 125–126, 206
  and execution, 20, 187
  isomorphous strategies, 5–7, 19
  and marginal problem solvers, 11–12
  and openness, 4–5
  rollout of, 186
  sequential model, 8–9
  unimaginative strategies, 7–12
  unpopular strategies, 15–17
Transparency, 38, 63–64
Trend Radar, IMP. *See* IMP Trend Radar
Treynor, Jack, 167
Truck accidents, 145
Tsien, Roger, 7

Uhse, Beate, 3
Unilever, 50
Unimaginative strategies, 7–12
Unpopular strategies, 15–17

Vai, Steve, 9
Vaio MusicClip, 9–10
Van Bever, Derek, 150
Van Bochoven, Leendert, 188–189
Van der Hooft, Serge, 3
Van Vories, Peter, 60
Video community, 84
voestalpine, 135–138

Walpole, Horace, 25
Warburg, Emil, 155
War games, 123, 127–128
Webb, Kinari, 185–186
Weick, Karl, 97–98
Weight-judging competition, 163
Weiss, Pierre, 155
Weitzman, Martin, 138–139

Welch, Jack, 29
"Which Technology is Convincing
  You?," 172
Whitehurst, Jim, 25, 200
Whitley Gold Award, 187
Whittington, Richard, 38
Wiese, Christian, 196–197
Wildfire Communications, 149
WMC, 1–2
Workplace platform, 199
Worms, 8
WS Audiology, 135, 139–142, 205

Xchanging, 200

Yakis-Douglas, Basak, 38
Yammer, 31, 198
Yeaney, Jackie, 26–27, 200

Zanini, M., 79
Zappos, 63
Zeppelin Rental, 164–165
Zook, Chris, 37